SPEAK OUT

SPEAK OUT
AGAINST THE NEW RIGHT

**Edited by
Herbert F. Vetter**

Beacon Press • Boston

Grateful acknowledgment is made to the following: Norman Lear and People for the American Way for permission to reprint Norman Lear's "America Is Strangling on Its Obsession with the Bottom Line"; Peggy Charren and Kim Hays for permission to print "Changing Television: Why the Right Does It Wrong"; Karen Rothmyer and *Columbia Journalism Review* for permission to reprint Karen Rothmyer's "Citizen Scaife," reprinted from the *Columbia Journalism Review,* July/August, 1981; John Kenneth Galbraith and *The New York Review of Books* for permission to reprint "The Conservative Onslaught," reprinted with permission from *The New York Review of Books* © 1981 N.Y. Rev., Inc.; Lester Thurow and *The New York Review of Books* for permission to reprint "How to Wreck the Economy," reprinted with permission from *The New York Review of Books* © 1981 N.Y. Rev., Inc.; Seymour Martin Lipset, Earl Raab, and *Commentary* for permission to reprint "The Election and the Evangelicals," reprinted from *Commentary,* March 1981, by permission, all rights reserved; James M. Wall and The Christian Century Foundation for permission to reprint "An Ominous Threat to Books," © 1981 Christian Century Foundation, reprinted by permission from the May 20, 1981, issue of *The Christian Century*; Leo Pfeffer for permission to print "The Separation of Church and State"; Helen Caldicott for permission to print "This Beautiful Planet"; Thomas J. Watson, Jr., for permission to print "What Future Lies Ahead?"; George Kennan for permission to print "Cease This Madness!"; Robert McAfee Brown for permission to reprint "The Need for a Moral Minority"; Jack Mendelsohn for permission to print "A Heimlich Maneuver for America"; to Gloria Steinem and *Ms.* magazine for permission to reprint "The Nazi Connection," © Ms. Foundation for Education & Communication, Inc., 1981; Charles Hartshorne and the Christian Century Foundation for permission to reprint "Concerning Abortion," © 1981 Christian Century Foundation, reprinted by permission from the January 21, 1981, issue of *The Christian Century*; Carl Sagan and Scott Meredith for permission to print "Science and Survival," published by permission of Dr. Carl Sagan and his agents, Scott Meredith Literary Agency, Inc., 845 Third Avenue, New York, New York 10020; Isaac Asimov and *The New York Times* for permission to reprint "The 'Threat' of Creationism," © 1981 by The New York Times Company, reprinted by permission; Stephen Jay Gould and *Discover* for permission to reprint "Evolution as Fact and Theory"; Victor F. Weisskopf and *Technology Review* for permission to reprint "On Avoiding Nuclear Holocaust."

Beacon Press books are published under the auspices of the Unitarian Universalist Association, 25 Beacon Street, Boston, Massachusetts 02108

Published simultaneously in Canada by Fitzhenry and Whiteside Limited, Toronto

All rights reserved

Printed in the United States of America

(hardcover) 9 8 7 6 5 4 3 2 1
(paperback) 9 8 7 6 5 4 3 2 1

Library of Congress Cataloging in Publication Data

Main entry under title:

Speak out, against the New Right.

    1. Conservatism — United States — Addresses, essays, lectures.   2. United States — Politics and government — 1981-   — Addresses, essays, lectures.   3. United States — Politics and government — 1977-1981 — Addresses, essays, lectures.
I. Vetter, Herbert F.
E876.S63   320.5'2'0973   81-68355
ISBN 0-8070-0486-3   AACR2
ISBN 0-8070-0487-1 (pbk.)

Preface

This book emerged from action to organize a live national broadcast at a continental gathering in Philadelphia. The overview in the first chapter describes that event, which touches upon a host of issues being answered by liberals and humanists now under attack by the New Right in America. The person who initially recommended that Cambridge Forum concentrate program attention on the New Right controversy is Theodore Jones, President of the Charles River Broadcasting Company.

The encouragement of MaryAnn Lash, Director of Beacon Press, was joined with that of her colleagues in leading us to supplement the broadcast with the book. Special appreciation goes to Jeff Smith, not only for overseeing the design and production of the book, but for editorial processing of the manuscript, as well as for unfailing helpfulness in seeing the project through.

This work was facilitated by the unstinting will of the authors to unite in this published *Speak Out* concerning the sudden transformation of the nation in the direction of the radical right.

A fellow member of the United Ministry at Harvard University, Thomas Ferrick, the Humanist Chaplain, substantially assisted me in bringing this material together.

Two members of my Cambridge Forum staff, Executive Secretary Carole Findley and Harvard College student Bryan Eric Simmons, also assisted in a variety of vital ways to prepare these pages for publication.

The wise counsel of my wife, Dorothy, is evident throughout this undertaking.

H.F.V.

Contents

OVERVIEW

America's New Battle of Faiths

HERBERT F. VETTER

Speak Out emerged from weekly forums in the Parish House of the Church in Harvard Square. When the founder and president of Action for Children's Television, Peggy Charren, spoke at the Forum, she told us she was even more alarmed by the censorship tactics of the New Right than she was about the critical poverty of children's TV programs. As her words were aired on the Forum's weekly national radio broadcast and on our weekly local TV show, it was evident that we needed to find a way to put these fighting words in print.

In a special Forum series, "I Call That Mind Free," recorded for national public television broadcast, our speakers defended the liberal lifestyle against the New Right. For example, not only did Representative Shirley Chisholm warn of the New Right attacks on civil liberties, but Dr. Helen Caldicott warned of the nuclear threat to our children and us. At a planning session devoted partly to this TV series, Natalie Gulbrandsen, President of the Unitarian Universalist Women's Federation, observed: "On every single issue of life, right on down the line, I find that we religious liberals emphatically oppose the New Religious Right."

In recognition of this fact, Cambridge Forum decided to hold a live national public radio broadcast from the Philadelphia Sheraton during the 1981 continental General Assembly of the Unitarian Universalist Association. We called it "SPEAKOUT: Religious Liberals Reply to the New Religious Right." Among the interfaith voices for freedom at the SPEAKOUT were Protestant Paul Washington, Rector of The Church of the Advocate, Episcopal, Philadelphia; Roman Catholic John T. Logue, Director of the Common Heritage Institute, Villanova University; American Jewish Congress attorney Leo Pfeffer; Humanist Edward L. Ericson, Leader of the New York Society for Ethical Culture; and Greg Denier, Research Director with the interfaith People for the American Way. I thank them for preparing the way for this book. Among the others who joined the SPEAKOUT, and to whom I am likewise indebted, are O. Eugene Pickett, Jack Mendelsohn, Loretta Williams, David P. Osborn, Natalie Gulbrandsen, James M.

Olson, Nancy Warshaw, Richard S. Scobie, Edwin A. Lane, Doris L. Pullen, Brooks Walker, and Dana McLean Greeley.

Following the SPEAKOUT, this book began to take form. Many people helped to shape its contents. For example, I thank Priscilla Cummings for sending me a tape of Robert McAfee Brown's address at a Town Hall Forum of the Westminster Presbyterian Church in Minneapolis. It was broadcast by Minnesota Public Radio.

The twenty-two *Speak Out* authors who wrote and released their pages for publication here did so *pro bono*, in the public interest. Without the enthusiastic cooperation of these authors, as well as their literary associates, agents, and publishers, no such book would have been possible. Thanks to their unfailing sense of our common commitment in an unprecedented struggle for freedom and survival, we now have a book which does speak out with authority.

Speak Out is the first Cambridge Forum book. In editing these essays concerning America's new battle of faiths, I selected six fields of action: media, winners/losers, politics, peace/war, religion, sex, and science. Each section is prefaced with an interpretation of the present struggle as I have experienced it during my fifteen-year ministry of social responsibility in Cambridge, Massachusetts. As Director of the Forum and Chaplain to the University, I have been engaged in a media ministry on behalf of The First Parish, the First Church in Cambridge (Unitarian Universalist), the Church in Harvard Square which has been at the center of a continuing battle of faiths since the 1630s. In serving a church, a college, and a city whose life extends for 350 years, I have become aware of how generations who have gone before have likewise fashioned working principles of socially responsible liberal religious living. As they too have daily expressed their faith in action, they have cried *Yes* to what enhances life and cried *No* to all that thwarts movement toward the fullness of life. Therefore, let us be mindful of past wisdom enabling us to yoke our Yeas and our Nays to make evident the affirmations of our own free faith. As we speak out against the New Right, we also declare:

WHAT WE STAND FOR

We stand for individual freedom of inquiry and belief as a vital center of a responsibly creative and concerned community. Therefore, we stand opposed to every idol of infallibility: Idols of the Book, the Person, the Church, the State, the Tradition — idols meant to have immunity to criticism, idols which forever retard advancing truth by rigid requirements of conformity in faith and life.

We stand for unrestricted use of reason in religion as a guiding, disciplining agent of the faith that makes men free and whole, members one of another in an emerging world community of life. Therefore, we stand opposed to every wall of antirational devotion which cripples life: Walls of nationalistic prejudice, religious exclusiveness, racial arrogance, and vindictive caste and class.

We stand for tolerance of differing religious views and practices within a context of commitment to the democratic process in church and state, school and industry and home.

We stand for religion as experience of what is real, yet waiting to be realized; what is ideal, yet the greatest of present facts; religion as adventure, a flight after the unattainable; religion as integrating encounter with life as it is and life as it can be. Therefore, we stand eternally opposed to the irreligious force of fragmentary purpose which disregards the religious vision; and, likewise, to every form of faith that surrenders creative zest to stifling uniformity.

We stand for fellowship which is truly ecumenical, embracing east and west and north and south; uniting men and women and children of diversity of faith in sacred common quest for truth for the mind, good words for the hand, love for the heart, and for the soul that aspiring after perfection, that unfaltering faith of God which, like lightning in the clouds, shines brightest when elsewhere it is most dark.

MEDIA

The American Counterrevolution is empowered not only by the electronic direct mail of Richard Viguerie's data banks in Falls Church, Virginia, but by the suave political electronic presence on stage of New Right President Ronald Reagan.

America's new battle of faiths is being waged not only in board rooms of corporations and the caucus rooms of the Congress but also in control rooms of the TV studios and in the trustees' rooms of the libraries. All media are engaged in the battle for control of the culture.

Consider the attack from the religious New Right. The new imperative is: Clean up television by threatening to boycott advertisers' products. Yes, simply stop buying anything that is promoted on "immoral" shows such as "Charlie's Angels," and let the advertisers know what you are doing and why.

Sears, Roebuck and Company withdrew advertising on "Charlie's Angels" when it was told the show contained too much sex. Merely deferring a boycott does not necessarily matter, if you get results from advertisers, anyhow.

The religious New Right's crusade against TV sex, violence, and profanity declares: Soap operas are the epitome of immorality and altogether contrary to the profamily standards of the Bible; situation comedies cause people to laugh at adultery; television pours filthy words and pictures into children's minds; illicit sex has now invaded prime time. They also exclaim: Television constantly projects not the faith in Almighty God and in Jesus Christ, whom the nation needs for redemption from decay and destruction, but TV expresses secular humanism, which has no absolutes, no standards.

What are the commands of the new crusade:

> End the $4 billion pornographic industry, the No. 1 enemy of the family.
>
> Ban godless books from our libraries.
>
> Remove immoral textbooks from our schools.

Speak Out *selections on media respond to this New Right challenge. We begin with Norman Lear's selection "America Is Strangling on Its Obsession with the Bottom Line." Boston's Ford Hall Forum presented its annual First Amendment Award to Norman Lear, the television producer noted for "All in the Family," "Maude," and "Mary Hartman, Mary Hartman."*

If readers want more information concerning the organization Norman Lear has begun to Speak Out *against the New Right's Media, they can get it from People for the American Way, 1015 19th Street, N.W., Washington, D.C. 20036.*

The second selection, "Changing Television: Why the Right Does It Wrong," grew out of Cambridge Forum radio and television broadcasts featuring Peggy Charren, the founder and President of Action for Children's Television (ACT). The high priority given by her to the need to Speak Out *against the New Right led to our request for this article by her and Kim Hays, Executive Director of ACT (which may be reached at 46 Austin Street, Newtonville, MA 02160).*

Our third selection is "Citizen Scaife," by Karen Rothmyer, a former Wall Street Journal *reporter who teaches at the Columbia University School of Journalism. Her research was funded in part by the Center for Investigative Reporting. While many people have heard of the bankrolling of the Radical Right by the mail solicitations of Richard Viguerie, here is a rare revelation of "the prime founder of the Media-Savvy New Right," Richard Mellon Scaife.*

America Is Strangling on Its Obsession with the Bottom Line

NORMAN LEAR

At an occasion such as this, it is customary to say how honored one is. Well, I had hoped to say something different to you tonight — but the fact is, I am honored to be receiving this award from the Ford Hall Forum and to follow the distinguished men and women who have been honored here.

And I am honored to be mentioned on this special occasion in the same breath as the First Amendment. I wish I could share this moment with all of the people I have loved and who loved me, and who helped me through the years to this evening. Such as my father, long gone, and my grandmother.

If my mother's mother were alive today — she died some years ago at 94 — I would rush to her linoleum-and-oilcloth kitchen in that tiny, third-floor walk-up that always smelled of freshly baked bread — and show her a copy of tonight's program and say: "Look, Baba, see? They gave me an award in the name of the First Amendment!" My grandmother would have looked hard at the program for a long moment — and then said: "The First Amendment? That's good for the Jews?"

Yes, Baba, the First Amendment is good for the Jews. And for the blacks, and the Poles, and the Irish, and the Hispanic, and the poor, and the elderly, and the infirm, the enfranchised and the disenfranchised — yes, Baba, the First Amendment is good for all people!

And here, tonight, I find myself associated with the First Amendment. Suddenly I feel stately . . . venerable . . . old! But I love being associated with the First Amendment. With the Constitution. The Declaration of Independence. As a writer, I treasure the words in these documents. (We all know them — but like the classic songs we sing throughout our lives — they can't be repeated too often.) These, from the Declaration of Independence: "We hold these truths to be self-evident, that all men are created equal; that they are endowed by their creator with certain unalienable rights; that among these are life, liberty, and the pursuit of happiness. . . ." Terrific words — precise; impeccable — I love them.

And the First Amendment itself: "Congress shall make no law respecting an establishment of religion, or prohibiting the free exercise thereof; or abridging the freedom of speech, or of the press; or the right of the people peaceably to assemble, and to petition the government for a redress of grievances."

I am a fool for those words. I am a fool for the concept. To me, the words of the First Amendment are absolute. "Congress shall make *no* law . . ." it says. It doesn't say that there will be freedom of expression provided said expressions do not run contrary to popular thought. It doesn't say that there will be freedom of expression provided said expressions have no tendency to subvert standing institutions.

In the Soviet Union, and within the governments of dozens of other totalitarian nations, there are debates concerning courses of action to follow and procedures to be used — but no one is allowed to challenge the government itself, nor any activity of the government. How different it is in America, with the blessings of the First Amendment.

Now, I am not comfortable with many of the excesses that take place in the name of the First Amendment. No need to enumerate them, we all know what they are.

Wait — I know you won't want me to get away with that. How can I tell what *you* may judge to be an excess? And isn't that just the point of the First Amendment? Even when it comes to expressing or publishing the most unpopular idea or the most admittedly offensive material — unless, perhaps, the material is designed and likely to produce imminent lawless action — excesses must be tolerated. Because the First Amendment speaks in absolute terms. It recognizes that what may be trash or trivia or indecency or obscenity to me, may be quite another matter to you. In the words of Justice Harlan, "One man's vulgarity is another's lyric."

John Stuart Mill believed that literature and morality should enjoy competitive coexistence. Literature, the vehicle of ideas, must be unrestricted by the political, religious, or moral dictates of the controlling group of the day. There can be no freedom of expression in the full sense, Mill said, unless all facets of life can be portrayed, no matter how repulsive the disclosures may be to some people.

"Those who desire to suppress an opinion deny its truth," Mill continued, "but they are not infallible. They have no authority to decide the question for all mankind and exclude every other person from the means of judging. To refuse a hearing to an opinion because they are sure that it is false, is to assume their certainty is the same thing as absolute certainty. All silencing of discussion is an assumption of infallibility. Every age has held opinions that subsequent ages have deemed not only false, but absurd. How, then, can an individual be infallible when ages are not?"

And every generation must deal with its own Infallibles. In the 1950's, Joe McCarthy considered himself an Infallible. To challenge his thinking or his methods was to be tagged immediately with being soft on Communism. Today, the self-styled Infallibles are known as the Religious New Right, or the Christian New Right. To disagree with their conclusions on numerous matters of morality and politics is to be labeled a poor Christian, or unpatriotic, or anti-family.

The National Christian Action Coalition publishes ratings of congressmen and senators — based on how they voted on what the Coalition describes as "fourteen key moral issues." During the 1980 election, on the basis of these ratings, it listed 36 members of the House and Senate whose voting records established them, in the eyes of the Coalition, as having a "poor moral voting record." In California, for example, Alan Cranston was rated a double zero on his moral voting and Senator Hayakawa a plus–90.

Christians Concerned for Responsible Citizenship circulates a booklet which lists: "Your five duties as a Christian Citizen." The main duty is to "help elect godly people" whose godliness is determined by their voting record. How arrogant the use of the word *godly* . . . with the implication that office-holders who cast differing votes are ungodly.

The Plymouth Rock Foundation, another member organization of the Religious New Right, issues a list of "Biblical Principles Concerning Issues of Importance to Godly Christians." To qualify as a godly Christian, the elected official here must agree with the Foundation on matters ranging from the Salt II agreements to nuclear superiority, capital punishment, the ERA, abortion, defense spending, the Department of Education, and more.

Similar activities are engaged in by the National Political Conservative Caucus, the Christian Roundtable, the Campus Crusade for Christ, the Christian Voice, and the Moral Majority, which, through the clever media manipulation of its founder, the Reverend Jerry Falwell, has become a kind of generic term describing the mind-set of the Religious New Right.

Currently sitting on every television talk show that will have him, Mr. Falwell appears benign, insisting he does not mix religion and politics. Yet Mr. Falwell is the author of a paper entitled "Ninety-five Theses for the 1980's," which he suggests as a litmus test to determine the Christian dedication of elected officials. Number twelve in this list states that any attempt to weaken our defense systems — which means disagreeing with the Moral Majority's version of defense — is an act of treason! (Sound like the 1950's?) Number 21 states that all elected officials found guilty of sexual promiscuity, whether heterosexual or otherwise, be promptly removed from public office. (Some claim that to accept that thesis would be to rid Washington of most of the Congress.) Number 35 says that the husband is looked upon as the divinely appointed head of the institution of marriage — and numbers 49 and 52 tell us the Equal Rights Amendment is wrong because it is anti-family and ridicules the historic role of the woman as the faithful housewife and mother.

The Christian Voice favors a constitutional amendment to balance the budget because "The Bible tells us we should not live in debt." The Christian Roundtable says: "The Constitution was designed to perpetuate a Christian order." And the Committee for a Free Congress says: "We're working to overturn the present power structure in this country . . . we are talking about the Christianizing of America."

Then there is the Reverend Jim Robison, one of the "biggies" among the electronic ministers, who has said on television, "Let me tell you something else about the character of God. If necessary, God would raise up a tyrant — a man who might not have the best ethics — to protect the freedom and the interests of the ethical and the godly."

Too kooky to be a threat? Not when you realize how far the Religious New Right has come in the six-plus years it has been active. In the 1976 and 1980 general elections they were instrumental in defeating numerous congressmen and senators — Republicans and Democrats alike. And they are targeting a new group of senators and congressmen to defeat in 1982.

According to reports, there are now more than 1,300 Christian radio stations broadcasting religious programming — with one new station being added each week; there are some 40 independent Christian television stations with a full-time diet of religious programming; and two Christian broadcasting networks — largely fundamentalist. There is Falwell, Baker, Robertson, Robison, Humbard, Roberts and others — the "superstars" among television evangelicals — many of them taking in more than $1,000,000 a week from their direct solicitations and the sale of religious merchandise. There are also scores and scores of local television and radio evangelicals — blanketing the country — espousing the same far-right, fundamentalist points of view — while attacking the integrity and the character of anyone who does not stand with them.

It is estimated that the electronic church attracts 130,000,000 viewers and listeners a week. According to the Gallup Poll, that is more people than go to church. Then there are the millions of pieces of computerized mail that are pumped, weekly, into homes across the nation by the ultra-right organizations that are their secular counterparts. In the name of these organizations — and in ad hoc organizations without names — let's look at what else is going on at the local level across the country:

• The American Library Association reports that libraries in some 30 states are being pressured to remove as many as 132 titles and authors from library shelves. They include John Steinbeck (*Grapes of Wrath*), Kurt Vonnegut (*Slaughterhouse Five*), Aldous Huxley (*Brave New World*), George Orwell (*1984*), Bernard Malamud (*The Fixer*), and J.D. Salinger, who had the temerity to write *Catcher in the Rye*. In many states, librarians are being taken to court by groups seeking the names of people who had taken certain books out on loan. On television news broadcasts we have seen the spectre of bookburning in Indiana and Louisiana. And textbooks across the country are not being bought by some school boards — under pressure from local groups — until all "liberal dogma and secular humanism" has been excised by the Gablers, a fundamentalist couple in Texas.

• After traveling long distances, speakers on such subjects as sex education and the nuclear arms race have arrived in towns to find that their speaking engagements have been canceled because the local Holiday Inn had been threatened with a boycott if the event took place as scheduled.

• In the states of Indiana, Washington, and elsewhere, suits have been filed to roll back the laws covering wife and child abuse — on the fundamentalist grounds that the state may not interfere with "the husband's divine right to discipline" his own family.

• And in California and other states we are witnessing attempts to pass laws that would require doctors to report any sexual activity by unmarried female patients under the age of 18 to law enforcement authorities.

In response to all of this, I hasten to say — and this is both the pain and the glory of the First Amendment — that these leaders and organizations have every First Amendment right to express themselves as they wish. But if we agree that the American experiment is based on the conviction that a healthy society is best maintained not by an attempt to impose uniformity, but through a free and open interchange of differing opinions, then the dogma of the Religious New Right violates the spirit of the First Amendment — and the spirit of liberty.

What is the spirit of liberty? Learned Hand once raised the question — and answered it. "I cannot define it," he said. "I can only tell you my own faith. The spirit of liberty is the spirit which seeks to understand the minds of other men and women; the spirit of liberty is a spirit which weighs their interests alongside its own without bias; the spirit of liberty remembers that not even one sparrow falls to earth unheeded; the spirit of liberty is the spirit of him, who, near two thousand years ago, taught mankind a lesson it has never learned, but has never quite forgotten."

The spirit of the New Right and the Religious New Right is antithetical to the spirit of liberty, as defined by Judge Hand.

It is not difficult to understand how the current, self-appointed Infallibles have grown so strong as to threaten the spirit of liberty for this generation. Throughout history, in times of hardship, voices of stridency and division have replaced those of reason and unity. The results are a tension among races, classes, and religions; a deterioration of free and open dialogue; and the temptation to grasp at simplistic solutions for complex problems.

In our time of hardship, it is the Moral Majority mind-set that feeds on the deep and valid concerns of Americans. There is widespread feeling today that our society is seriously flawed. With rampant inflation, the decaying of our most vaunted industries, the increase of street crime and violence, the surging growth of our drug problem, the increase in alcoholism, the splintering of family life, and the mounting concern over nuclear proliferation and the potential for nuclear holocaust — our people are more frustrated, anxious and fearful than at any other time in our history.

Responding to this time of crisis is the Religious New Right with its simplistic solutions to our most complex problems. We have lost our way, they say, because we have turned our backs on God and followed the devices and desires of our own hearts — and America's purity and strength can be restored only if the nation submits to the political and moral answers which they see as self-evident. There follow positions on the Panama Canal Treaty, Taiwan, nuclear superiority, a scuttling of the

Department of Education — and the issues they feel are destroying the American family: the ERA, abortion, sex education, prayer in school, gay rights, and others.

I have listened for years as the Moral Majority mind-set has offered these issues as an explanation for all the country's ills. I disagree, as you may know, and helped to form an organization to counter them. In so doing I have traveled the country several times forming an association with the leaders of most of America's main-line churches. As we formed People for the American Way and worked through our agenda, we came to feel that perhaps we owe a debt of gratitude to the Religious New Right. In the marketplace of ideas, our adversaries do us a very big favor. They force us to think through, to reappraise, to hone, and ultimately to strengthen our own convictions.

One of these convictions is that we must take the Religious New Right seriously. Because they are serious. They are sincere, dedicated people, consumed with the rightness of their mission. They attempt to fill a great spiritual void. Heightened by an absence of convincing leadership and the continued deterioration of our society, the spiritual need has grown greater in most of us — and the Religious New Right reaches people by tugging at those common umbilicals of the spirit: the need for faith and hope and love and warmth and assurance, and the comfort of belonging.

These are great needs — and it is no wonder that so many Americans have fallen into the embrace of Falwell and company. It's obvious that we have to do more than criticize. We have to offer our own solutions, go public with our own set of moral priorities. What do *we* believe are the reasons America is so beset with problems? It's time for each of us to make a declaration of our beliefs.

We have reached the place where we know what we think as a society only when Lou Harris or George Gallup tell us what their polls reveal. The polls say: More Americans are for ERA than not; more Americans are proabortion than not; and more Americans favor gun control than not. But the political tide on these issues is not turning in the direction that the polls would suggest. Because the 2,000 people who may participate in any given Harris poll are outnumbered by single-issue zealots, while the rest of us are failing to speak out — and we must speak out if we want to see the process working again. In that spirit, I would like to tell you where I stand.

I believe in God. And I was born a Jew. Therefore I am unable to accept Jesus Christ as my saviour. Several Sunday mornings ago, I heard Jerry Falwell, on his "Old Time Gospel Hour," tell an estimated 20,000,000 viewers that only those people who accept Jesus Christ as their saviour will go to heaven, and that all others will roast for an eternity in hell.

With all respect to Falwell and his interpretation of scripture, I don't believe that my spending eternity impaled on a spit is necessarily a *fait accompli*. Because God, whom Falwell would be the first to say is responsible for all life, obviously arranged for me to be born of Jewish parents — and I cannot believe the God of us all would follow so closely the mating habits of my parents simply to condemn me to hell the instant I was conceived!

Nor that He would play the game of putting me on this earth as a Jew just to see if one day I might renounce my faith and the faith of my father and mother to accept Christ as my saviour. I don't think He plays those games.

No, I think God placed Christians and Jews and Buddhists and Moslems and other religions on this earth (the *Encyclopedia of American Religions* lists 1,200 practicing religions in this country alone); I think God placed them here because He wanted them here. Maybe because He knew He would be bored to tears if 4,500,000,000 people worshiped Him in exactly the same way. So, I think there's a chance that maybe God favors this Jew every bit as much as He favors Jerry Falwell. And tonight maybe even more — because William O. Douglas could be putting in a good word for me up there!

Now — about abortion: I am pro-choice. I don't know when life begins from a scientific standpoint, but I *do* know that I do not resonate to the belief that life begins at conception and — this is a big confession — in a world where the suffering and starvation of 10,000,000 displaced persons goes relatively unfelt, where I admit, though it shames me, how difficult it is for me to really relate to those photographs of hungry children across the globe with bellies distended from malnutrition — photographs that represent the plight of millions of children through the years. I look at those photos, I feel sorrow, perhaps I write a check — but then I forget and go on with my life. I am touched — but how much, and at what distance?

Now, if it is true, as I suspect, that most of us react this way; if, much as it shames us, people are generally unable to relate fully to distant horror, then I do not understand those who declare themselves to be more concerned with the thought of aborting a fetus than the thought of bringing another unwanted child into the world — to a 14-year-old unmarried mother, or a pregnant rape victim, or to a family whose emotional and economic situation would make another child an impossible and tragic burden.

I think it important to mention my admittedly unfortunate lack of understanding of the right-to-life position because I respect the fact that they don't understand the right-to-choice position. My point, then, is: I can't control the way I feel — but, even as I "seek to understand the minds of other men and women," to repeat Learned Hand, I can control my behavior. So, while it is my First Amendment right to point fingers and call names, I will decline that right — even as I would like to see those who don't understand me decline the right to label me as a murderer.

As to what may be the root cause of some of our most serious concerns, my sense of things tells me that the problems America faces are not a consequence of the women's movement, or the fact the gays have come out of their closets and wish to take prideful places in American life, or that sex education is taught in some public schools, or that children may pray privately and individually in school or out of school, but not in school as a matter of law. I would submit that none of these, and no combination of these, is the reason why our automotive industry, once America's greatest non-military symbol of pride and macho, is lying limp and flaccid, a symbol of how far we have fallen. School prayer and sex education are *not* the reason why more than 7,000,000 individuals are out of work. Homosexual teachers are not the reason why Americans are losing faith in our basic institutions. And neither the ERA nor the Department of Education is responsible for what inflation is doing to our nation's poor, nor for all the wealthy Americans who are now talking privately of establishing residences in other parts of the world to which they can retreat if things should get too tough here.

To me, the most destructive societal disease of our time, and the biggest reason for the decline of public morality and ethics, is American leadership's fixation with what has come to be known as the bottom line. Whether it is in industry, government, or academia, leadership everywhere seems to be all too ready to sell the future short for a moment of success. We are observing a growing misuse of human potential for short-term gain at the expense of all of our tomorrows.

Because of its high profile, my industry — television — is a prime example of this destructive phenomenon. Fanned by the daily press — which operates on its own bottom line — the fires of competition between the networks have resulted in an unparalleled and hysterical competition for ratings — ratings which translate to profits. I've talked to many television programming executives who are trapped in this rating war, and who wish things were different.

The network programmers are trapped in the system for short-term gain, and they know they will have to pay for it in the long term.

As if all the new technology were not threatening enough, they're under daily attack by a ton of organizations for the taste and the quality and the unoriginality of their programming. Yet they go on, blithely pandering with anything they can put together for that high rating and the profit statement that follows.

"It's suicidal," says one. "If everyone at the network were to stand in a big circle and slash each other's throats, we wouldn't be expressing a death wish better than the way we're going now. You might think we would learn a lesson from the three motor companies. They saw the handwriting on the wall once, too. But what did they do about it?"

He's right. Wasn't it Detroit's fixation with the bottom line that brought it to its present state? Years ago, the big three watched the growth of Volkswagen imports and observed the Japanese tooling up to follow suit, and they had to know that eventually we might be overrun with smaller, less expensive, more fuel-efficient cars from abroad — unless Detroit directed its talents and energies and some of its profits to developing its own small cars. But to do that would have resulted in a diminished current profit statement — and the name of the game then, as now, for each chief executive officer was to show a larger profit statement for every succeeding quarter.

The New York Times recently reported that America's business leaders are so obsessed with short-term gain that, in an almost total preoccupation with quarter-to-quarter profits comparisons, more and more contracts for chief executive officers call for bonuses tied to short-term performance.

The *Times* traced the career of an executive who ran a fast-food restaurant chain for the parent company, a large conglomerate. His contract called for a substantial bonus if his second year's profits, quarter-to-quarter, were higher than his first — and initially he succeeded, but not by the margin that his company set as its goal. So the executive cut back on investment, stopped construction of new franchises, and began to show a spectacular return. He earned the bonus he set for himself all right, but the most important strategy in the fast-food restaurant business is market share and new franchises — so his short-term profit and subsequent reward came at the expense of the long-term growth of the company he ran. Eventually the company went belly-up — but not before his bonuses had provided all the money he would ever need.

There are situations when this obsession with the bottom line affects more than profits and jobs. The Food and Drug Administration, for example, has banned several pesticides because scientific research has established that they do chemical harm to the body. But the companies manufacturing the pesticides have a big investment in them, so rather than discontinue their manufacture, they have been exporting them. But the irony is that these pesticides are purchased and used overseas by large multinational corporations — most of them American corporations. The outlawed chemicals then find their way into foods prepared abroad by these American companies — foods which are shipped back home to be sold in the United States. Last year, Americans bought 600 food commodities — worth more than $13,000,000,000 — that contained the restricted pesticides.

The New York Times has written: "In contrast to Japan's long-term planning, American corporations have been unduly attentive to next quarter's profit. Such short-run, bottom line thinking may avert personal risks, but it jeopardizes the corporation's ability to survive."

I would suggest that since this is occurring everywhere; since we see the same obsession with short-term gain in government, in sports, in education, and ultimately, in our *individual* lives; that what we are really talking about is the nation's ability to survive. I believe the nation will survive. Someone once said that hope is the adrenalin of survival; so I will continue to hope. One day leadership, at the highest levels, will face the fact that America is strangling on its obsession with the bottom line. We have created a climate of opportunism in our country in which this obsession thrives, and all of us in leadership positions — as parents, teachers, employers — control our part of that climate.

But the master thermostats are in the Congress, and in the room with the greatest potential for educating us all: the Oval Office. My hope is that one day there will be sufficient members of the Congress — and perhaps an occupant of the Oval Office — who will find these thermostats and begin to adjust the climate by telling us what we need to hear: That in this country the individual still matters. That so long as we believe, we can still affect the course of our lives — and in groups, we can still affect the course of our nation. The New Right is proving that point every day. The rest of us must be encouraged to come back into the process, to take positions, to declare ourselves on every issue that faces us: for guns, against guns; pro-choice, against choice; pro-high defense spending, against high defense spending.

We can control the political, emotional, and spiritual climate in which we live. We don't have to steal from all of our tomorrows to satisfy our todays. And we don't have to continue this lunatic obsession with the bottom line — in the false and unproductive and anti-human belief that life is about winning and losing and that there is nothing in between!

There is something in between. It is succeeding at the level of doing one's best. We all ride on the same carousel in this life — and occasionally there is a brass ring. It is exciting to reach for that ring. Let's never stop reaching — but since only a few can ever possess it, the rest had best enjoy the reach and be happy with the ride.

I thank you for tonight. I like living in a country where I can speak out. I like the First Amendment. I like pluralism. I like diversity. And I like the flag; it is not the exclusive property of the far right. Call me a liberal, or a moderate, or a progressive — I think I'm a bleeding-heart conservative — but it's my flag too. It is more than a symbol of America's might. It is a symbol of America's people. Fifty stars stand for more than fifty gun boats; they stand for fifty states — and that's us.

Yes, the flag flies with "the rockets' red glare, the bombs bursting in air" — but it also flies over our libraries and our schools and our courts.

And yes, patriotism can be the last refuge of the scoundrel, but it can also be the first refuge of the individual who isn't so afraid of the cynicism of our time as to say, "I love this country."

And I do love it. We all do. Let's face it, we love the premise that we are all created equal in the eyes of the law. We love the notion that our government, including the President, works for us, on our payroll. We love the Constitution. We love the Bill of Rights. And we love the American experiment. So let's cut the lunacy with the bottom line and get on with it!

Changing Television:
Why the Right Does It Wrong

PEGGY CHARREN & KIM HAYS

The religious New Right worries a lot about television. The Reverend Jerry Falwell of Moral Majority, Inc. calls TV a "vendor of perniciousness."[1] The Reverend Donald Wildmon, founder of the National Federation for Decency and chairman of the Coalition for Better Television (CBTV), has been monitoring television programs and rating them and their sponsors for decency since 1977. His Coalition for Better Television's board of directors includes Ronald S. Godwin, vice president and chief operations officer for Moral Majority, Inc.; Phyllis Schlafly, national chairman of STOP ERA and president of the Eagle Forum; Judie Brown, director of the American Life Lobby; Lottie Beth Hobbs, head of the Pro-Family Forum; Beverly LaHaye, head of Concerned Women for America; and the Reverend John Hurt of the Joelton, Tennessee Church of Christ, founder of his own Clean Up TV Campaign. This group of ultra-conservative leaders wants to eliminate what they consider violence, vulgarity, sex, and profanity from TV.

Action for Children's Television (ACT) has been working to improve children's experiences with television since 1968, so we have seen a great many television reform movements come and go. Most of them seem to take their rhetoric from television's soap commercials; they are obsessed with cleaning up, eliminating, removing, and controlling the content of television programs. No matter how noble their intentions, no matter what their political leanings, these groups' ultimate goal is censorship, because they set up their own standards against which television programs should be judged and, ideally, eliminated. That the viewing tastes of the nation may not match the groups' standards is, to them, immaterial.

Advocates of censorship are not always citizens' groups. Sometimes the government lends a hand. In 1975, CBS's president Arthur Taylor introduced the concept of the Family Hour, and it was adopted into the *Television Code* provided by the National Association of Broadcasters (NAB). The Family Hour provision in the code requests that each broadcaster show programming that is suitable for family viewing between 7:00 P.M. and 9:00 P.M. E.S.T.; in other words, it encourages two hours

13

of "cleaner" adult television. This restriction on viewing options had the blessing of Federal Communications Commission (FCC) Chairman Richard Wiley.

ACT joined the Writers Guild of America in filing suit against the FCC, claiming that the Family Hour provision in the NAB *Television Code* was unconstitutional. In the eyes of some, the Family Hour "reformed" children's television. But not as far as ACT was concerned. The new code provision did not encourage broadcasters to produce and air a wider choice of programs designed specifically for young audiences. In fact, the Family Hour was a kind of red herring that drew attention away from broadcasters' continued failure to provide sufficient programming designed for young viewers. In addition, the new provision for "purer" adult fare created a form of censorship by restricting program choice for adult audiences every evening for two hours.

The National PTA, National Federation of Decency, Citizens for Better TV, Morality in Media, Clean Up TV Campaign, Coalition for Better Television, National Coalition on Television Violence, and National Citizen's Committee for Broadcasting are all TV reform organizations that protest specific programs. The tabloid-like headlines of the National Federation for Decency's newsletter ("Mother Watches Exorcist II on CBS; Cuts Heart From Little Daughter") are a far cry from the National Coalition on Television Violence's low-key "Research Review." But all of these organizations, despite their different concerns and political preferences, seem bent on setting themselves up as television's quality control inspectors. They talk about television reform in terms of narrowing TV choices by getting programs off the air.

Action for Children's Television does not support television reform that protests individual programs. ACT is proud of the fact that it has never once in its history told a broadcaster to "take this program off the air because we don't like it." ACT supports a broadening, not a narrowing, of television viewing options, and we believe that children and young adolescents are best served by programming designed especially for them, not by cleaned-up adult TV fare.

However, although ACT may have disagreed with the methods of a number of television reform groups in the past, we never actually protested the TV protesters until the Coalition for Better Television came along. The censorship tactics of this coalition of New Right groups are so disturbing that ACT launched a national petition campaign to provide citizens with a means of speaking out against the coalition's crusade to clean up the airwaves.

What is different about the Coalition for Better Television?

First, it is a coalition dominated by political organizations; by far the largest of these is Moral Majority, Inc. The executive director of the Coalition for Better Television is Moral Majority's vice president, and Moral Majority President Jerry Falwell has served as spokesman for the coalition several times. When an organization with the political clout of

Moral Majority seeks to determine what television programs Americans may or may not see, the threat of television censorship suddenly takes on a new meaning.

With Moral Majority behind it, the Coalition for Better Television is also richer than other television reform groups. By his own report, Falwell makes $1.25 million each week;[2] according to *The New Yorker*, his "Old-Time Gospel Hour" raised about $115 million between 1977 and 1980.[3] Whatever the actual numbers, there is no doubt that Moral Majority is rich and that it is glad to put some of its riches into the CBTV's coffers. Whether or not the coalition carries out its threatened boycott of the sponsors of "offensive" programs, Moral Majority has pledged its support of the TV clean-up effort in the form of full-page newspaper ads and direct mailings worth $2 million.[4,5]

Unlike most television reform groups, whose representatives are not welcome onto television programs to air their criticisms, the CBTV has easy access to the airwaves. Jerry Falwell's "Old-Time Gospel Hour" draws about 1½ million viewers, and television "pornography" is a subject he enjoys preaching about.[6] Even before Falwell became a spokesman for the CBTV, he was eager to make television content a Moral Majority concern. His chief fundraiser, Richard Viguerie, has explained that Moral Majority's campaign against television is designed to provide new names for the organization's political fund-raising lists. "The networks may beat us," says Viguerie. "They may after three or four years still have their sex and violence on television — but in the meantime, Jerry Falwell and others may increase their list of supporters by three- or four- or five-fold. And we can do something the networks cannot do, which is get involved in political campaigns."[7]

Perhaps the most dangerous aspect of the CBTV's program of reform is the group's focus on specific issues. Most TV reform groups are worried about the overall quality of TV programming and the quantity of sexual and violent program content. But Wildmon, Falwell, Schlafly, and the other coalition backers are quick to list controversial topics they do not want television to deal with at all — or, worse, that they want television to portray from a New Right point of view. Issues like abortion, teenage pregnancy, sex education, contraception, homosexuality, premarital sex, nontraditional families, drug use, the Equal Rights Amendment, feminism, national defense, communism, prayer in public schools, and the teaching of evolution are the focus for moral outrage and political activity from many members of the CBTV. In a recent interview, Wildmon said, "I found it interesting that ABC ran a documentary on the killing of the whales but they've been silent on the killing of babies — unborn babies."[8] CBS broadcasters say Wildmon has also objected to some segments of "CBS Reports" and "30 Minutes."[9]

Protesting some of the sleazier "sexploitation" shows on television is a small-but-sure first step toward dictating how television should cover major social and political issues. At the height of the McCarthy era in the

'50s few dared to mention Communism over the airwaves unless they railed against it in the next breath. Are we coming to a time when television will not dare to mention abortion, homosexuality, or the ERA for fear of scaring away sponsors and upsetting the New Right?

The product of these clean-up TV campaigns — the PTA's as well as the New Right's — is hit lists: hit lists of programs, commercials, advertisers, networks. Behind most of these hit lists is a veiled, and sometimes not-so-veiled, threat. "We will write down who the sponsors of that show are," said Wildmon about NBC's projected new series "Love, Sidney," which features a homosexual in the title role. "It won't be on very long."[10]

Blacklists are nothing new to the communications industry. *Red Channels: The Report of Communist Influence in Radio and Television* was published in 1950; it listed 151 well-known writers, directors, and performers. Within a very short time, many of these people had lost their jobs and were unable to get others. The fact that the accusations against them were ridiculous (actor Philip Loeb was accused of "helping communism" because he had sponsored an "End Jim Crow in Baseball Committee") or totally untrue was immaterial. The blacklist made them "controversial" and that was enough for advertisers and broadcasters, who hurried to drop them.[11]

What we seem to be threatened with by the New Right is another kind of blacklist, a blacklist of ideas. The message to broadcasters and advertisers is that a great many subjects for drama and even news had better not be dealt with . . . or else. The religious New Right's television reform groups demand that television conform to their standards of morality or else they will scare away its sponsors. Judging from the sponsors' eagerness to avert a CBTV boycott during the summer of 1981, they are not very hard to scare. In the 1950s no manufacturer of soap or cereal wanted to be labeled a sponsor of "communist" programs in the eyes of his buying public, even though the accusations were false. In the 1980s, it would seem that manufacturers are frightened of being accused by Donald Wildmon and Jerry Falwell of being a "leading sponsor . . . of violence, vulgarity, immorality, and profanity" or of "tell[ing] children to experiment with homosexuality." (These quotes are from two of Wildmon's National Federation of Decency newsletters.)[12,13] The fact that many of these offenses exist only in the eyes of the accusers does not remove the threat of the allegations. The fear of "controversy" is still a powerful force among advertisers. That is why Jerry Falwell can speak confidently about "sitting down behind closed doors" with leaders of large corporations and telling them, "Here is what the American people would prefer not to have on the air."[14]

At Action for Children's Television, we believe that controversy is one of the things television does best. It is the responsibility of the broadcasting media to provide as wide a range of opinions as possible and to keep the public informed about all sides of a controversial issue. Of course not all controversial topics are appropriate subjects for children's television. But a surprising number are, if they are handled in an age-specific manner. Television can offer children the opportunity to learn about a wide variety of places, people, occupations, ideas, lifestyles, and value systems, many of which will effect the way they live the rest of their lives. The role of the television is not to replace families and teachers as the chief influence on children in our society. But television, viewed selectively and in moderation, can encourage children to discuss, wonder about, and even read about new things. Above all, it can lead them to ask questions.

It is, perhaps, this question-inspiring tendency of television which most frightens the religious New Right. Jerry Falwell has said that "Christians, like slaves and soldiers, ask no questions."[15] He and his followers seem to believe that they know all the right answers, which are in the Bible; to question their doctrine is tantamount to apostasy. "I was studying mechanical engineering before I even became a Christian," Falwell has explained. "You come to exact simplistic answers if you follow the proper equations and the proper processes . . . Theology is an exact science. God is God. The Bible is the inspired, inherent word of God. And if everyone accepts the same theses and the same equations, they will arrive at the same answer."[16] It is no wonder, then, that Falwell and his colleagues seek to censor and suppress the content of television; they would seek to censor and suppress any form of communication that could encourage people to form their own opinions, to find their own answers.

The religious New Right's chief excuse for their assault on freedom of expression and thought is children. Donald Wildmon's crusade against television began, he has told reporters, when he tried to find something on television that he considered suitable for watching with his four young children.[17] It is in the name of children that most complaints against television program content are made, by liberal TV reform groups as well as conservative ones. Their idea seems to be that all of television must be sanitized into appropriate children's TV fare.

The great majority of these TV reform groups fail to make the distinction between the TV *seen* by children and the TV *designed* for children. Children watch a great deal of television that is not designed for them, largely because there *is* so little children's television programming provided by broadcasters, especially on weekdays. Broadcasters are to blame for this. But broadcasters don't force children to spend 30 hours a week in front of the set. The television schedule is full of adult programs that confuse, frighten, disturb, and just plain bore most children. These shows are not suitable for children, they are not intended for children, and children probably shouldn't be watching them. If children are watching them, are broadcasters to blame?

ACT is not trying to suggest that broadcasters have no responsibility toward their child and young adolescent audiences. For the past thirteen years, ACT has stressed broadcasters' legal responsibility to serve the public. Each broadcaster is licensed by the FCC to use the public airwaves for a five-year period; the license renewal process holds broadcasters accountable to the public. Under the Communications Act of 1934, broadcasters are required to operate "in the public interest." The FCC's 1974 *Children's Television Report and Policy Statement* emphasizes that broadcasters and the FCC have special obligations to serve and protect children. Children's programs are specified in the list of program categories the FCC requests broadcasters to provide in order to satisfy their public interest mandate.

Operating in the public interest means providing a wider choice of programming for preschool, school-age, and young adolescent viewers. It also means *not* airing promos for R rated movies in the middle of early morning cartoon shows. It means *not* airing deceptive advertising targeted to young children. Broadcaster responsibility means providing enough information in TV guides to help parents decide what programs their children should or shouldn't see; it may mean prefacing potentially disturbing programming with warnings. But it does not mean making every program on television fit for the eyes of a five-year-old or even a thirteen-year-old. That would not be serving the public, and it would not even be serving children, because children deserve programs especially designed for them and them alone.

ACT believes that improving children's experiences with television is the joint responsibility of television providers (broadcasters, cable operators, video disc makers, etc.), government officials, and television viewers. Unless all three of these groups exercise their rights and carry out their responsibilities, television will be no more than, at best, a moneymaking leisure machine and, at worst, a tool for propaganda. Working jointly (albeit on opposite sides of many fences), the television providers, government, and viewers can bring the medium closest to operating in the public interest.

What exactly is the public interest? ACT doesn't know. The Reverends Wildmon and Falwell don't know. Neither does the FCC. Nor do broadcasters, cablecasters, and the other providers of video services. There are approximately 226 million people in the United States, but no single one of them could define the public interest. The American public is an extraordinarily heterogeneous mass of people representing a myriad of special interests, each clammering louder than the last for attention and service. No single one of their demands represents the public interest.

ACT's conclusion is that the only service television providers can supply that is indisputably in the public interest is diversity. No one can, or should, determine exactly what each member of the American public needs from television. So only the greatest possible variety of program types offered through the greatest possible number of technological media will provide the public with sufficient choice. And only television reform groups that promote a greater diversity of viewing options are working in the public interest.

ACT's primary purpose is to increase the diversity of service television offers children. Like the members of the religious New Right, we are trying to change television, but unlike them, we work within the existing system set up by the federal government to protect the public interest. That system is not perfect and it tends to be slow, but it does attempt to maintain a balance of power among the competing television providers, the competing advertisers, the various levels of government, and the wide spectrum of public pressure groups. When this system of checks and balances is by-passed, even for the best of reasons, there is the threat of censorship.

What are ACT's strategies for broadening children's viewing options within the existing system?

First, ACT petitions the Federal Communications Commission to increase the amount of service that broadcasters are required to provide for young audiences, so children and young adolescents will have more choice.

Second, ACT works in support of Affirmative Action to bring more minorities and women into positions of power in the television industry, because this will help to eliminate racism and sexism from television programming.

Third, ACT encourages increased funding of public television, which provides a noncommercial alternative for children.

Fourth, ACT educates broadcasters and cablecasters about the diverse needs of young audiences.

Fifth, ACT encourages the development of the alternate technologies, such as cable television and video discs, which increases program choice for young people.

Sixth, ACT educates parents to take responsibility for their children's television viewing experiences by getting involved with cable television in their local communities, by carefully consulting the television schedule, and by turning the TV off more often.

Seventh, ACT helps teachers, school principals, pediatricians, dentists, and other professionals who are concerned with the welfare of children to be more aware of the influence of television on young audiences.

Eighth, ACT petitions the Federal Trade Commission to eliminate deceptive advertising targeted to children, because the First Amendment does not protect deceptive commercial speech.

These eight strategies do not encompass ACT's entire program. But they demonstrate that television reform does not have to mean censorship and repression. It does not have to mean interference with program content, which violates the public's right to know.

Both ACT and the Coalition for Better Television make use of threats to pressure broadcasters. The CBTV operates outside the federal system of checks and balances, threatening broadcasters with sponsor boycotts. ACT threatens broadcasters with the possibility of FCC rules requiring more service to children. The TV reform groups of the religious New Right seek not only to determine TV content themselves but to give control of TV content over to advertisers. ACT prefers to leave decisions about content in the hands of broadcasters, because broadcasters are licensed by a federal agency and are therefore accountable to the public. The religious New Right wants "moral" television, by their definition. ACT wants broadcasters to design and air more programs for the two- to fifteen-year-old audience, under mandate from the FCC if necessary.

Both ACT and the Wildmon-Falwell coalition work in the name of children. But our goals for America's children are in opposition. The religious New Right wants American children trained with the help of television into its own particular system of social, political, economic, and religious morality. ACT wants each American child to grow up with the ability to thoughtfully determine his or her own individual set of rights and wrongs, based on the widest possible amount of information that parents, schools, and television can provide.

The religious New Right would call ACT's goal for American children a sample of amoral secular humanism. We call it freedom. So does Pulitzer Prize–winning poet, professor, and statesman Archibald MacLeish. He has said, "What is freedom? Freedom is the right to choose: the right to create for yourself the alternative of choice. Without the possibility of choice and the exercise of choice a man is not a man but a member, an instrument, a thing."

NOTES

1. Sasthi Brata and Andrew Duncan, "Penthouse Interview: Reverend Jerry Falwell," *Penthouse* (March 1981), p. 152.

2. David Nyhan, "The Conservative Crusade," *The Boston Globe Magazine* (May 3, 1981), p. 12.

3. Frances FitzGerald, "A Reporter At Large (The Reverend Jerry Falwell)," *The New Yorker* (May 18, 1981), p. 90.

4. Tom Shales, "Television Boycott Dropped," *Washington Post* (June 6, 1981), p. C9.

5. Tony Schwartz, "400 Rightist Groups in National Coalition Start a Boycott of TV Sponsors This Week," *New York Times* (June 22, 1981), p. A12.

6. Jeffery K. Hadden and Charles E. Swann, *Prime Time Preachers: The Rising Power of Televangelism* (Reading, Mass.: Addison-Wesley, 1981), p. 52.

7. David Nyhan, "The Conservative Crusade," *The Boston Globe Magazine* (May 3, 1981), p. 36.

8. Christine Doudna, "At Issue: The Rev. Donald Wildmon," *CHANNELS of Communications* (June/July 1981), p. 21.

9. Harry F. Waters, George Hackett, *et al.*, "The New Right's TV Hit List," *Newsweek* (June 15, 1981), p. 102.

10. Ibid., p. 101.

11. Erik Barnouw, *The Golden Web, A History of Broadcasting in the United States Vol. II 1933–1953* (New York: Oxford University Press, 1968), pp. 265–73.

12. National Federation for Decency, *NFD Newsletter* (March 1980), p. 1.

13. National Federation for Decency, *NFD Newsletter* (December 1979), p. 6.

14. David Nyhan, "Those TV Ad Sinners Are Now Seeing the Light," *The Boston Globe* (December 4, 1980), p. 23.

15. Frances FitzGerald, "A Reporter At Large (The Reverend Jerry Falwell)," *The New Yorker* (May 18, 1981), p. 107.

16. Sasthi Brata and Andrew Duncan, "Penthouse Interview: Reverend Jerry Falwell," *Penthouse* (March 1981), p. 150.

17. "NFD's Donald Wildmon: The Medium Is The Mission," *Broadcasting* (February 9, 1981), p. 28.

Citizen Scaife

KAREN ROTHMYER

Five years ago, George Mair was bored with his job as editorial director of KNX, the CBS radio affiliate in Los Angeles. As Mair recalls it now, he and John E. Cox, Jr., an aide to Republican congressman Barry Goldwater, Jr., hit on the idea of starting a nonprofit organization aimed primarily at improving relations between business and the media. The one thing they didn't have was money, so when they heard that Richard Larry, an administrative agent of the Scaife Family Charitable Trusts, was coming to town, they called up to see if they could talk to him.

"The only reason he agreed to have dinner with us is that he thought Jack was another man named Cox he was supposed to be meeting," Mair, now an editorial columnist for the Los Angeles Times Syndicate, says with a laugh. "But he was very polite and listened to our ideas. He came again a few months later and we had lunch. He gave us a check. When we opened it, it was far, far beyond our wildest dreams — one hundred thousand dollars."

Thus was born the Foundation for American Communications, one of a large number of organizations that owe their existence to the generosity of one of the richest men in America, Richard Mellon Scaife. Scaife, a great-grandson of the founder of the Mellon empire, has made the formation of public opinion both his business and his avocation.

Over the past twelve years, Scaife, whose personal fortune is conservatively estimated at $150 million, has bought or started a variety of publications, mainly in the Pittsburgh area. But he has increasingly turned his attention from journalism to other, more ambitious efforts to shape public opinion, in the form of $100 million or so in grants from Scaife charities to conservative, particularly New Right, causes. These efforts have been dramatically successful. Indeed, Scaife could claim to have done more than any other individual in the past five or six years to influence the way in which Americans think about their country and the world.

Since 1973, Scaife charitable entities have given $1 million or more to each of nearly a score of organizations that are closely linked to the New Right movement. These range from the Institute for Foreign Policy Analysis, a Massachusetts think-tank that examines political and military issues, to California's Pacific Legal Foundation, the oldest and largest of a dozen

22

conservative legal groups, all Scaife beneficiaries, which function as mirror-images of the Nader-inspired public-interest law groups.

The press has generally overlooked Scaife, even when reporting on organizations that are financially dependent on him. For example, Scaife is the single largest donor to the Mountain States Legal Foundation — $200,000 toward a $1-million budget in 1980 — as acknowledged by Mountain State officials. Yet, earlier this year, when James Watt, then-president of Mountain States, was up for Senate confirmation as Interior Secretary in the Reagan cabinet, the press reported — on the basis of available information — that Mountain States was primarily funded by timber, utility, and mining interests.

Similarly, officials of The Heritage Foundation, a conservative think-tank that supplied eleven members of the Reagan transition team, acknowledged that Scaife is a far larger contributor than Joseph Coors, whose name has been the only one mentioned in most press reports on the group. Scaife, who joined with Coors to launch Heritage seven years ago, gave close to $900,000 — three times Coors's gift — to help meet the current $5.3–million Heritage budget.

A November 17, 1980, *New York Times* story on conservative think-tanks reported that "When the Heritage Foundation announced the other day that it was forwarding to Mr. Reagan a suggested 'blueprint for a conservative American government,' requests for details poured into the foundation's Capitol Hill office, and a dozen reporters from the nation's major papers and broadcasting networks showed up for the briefing." The article went on to quote Hugh Newton, a Heritage official, as saying, "We've never had this kind of attention before . . . A lot of people who used to toss our stuff into the trash can are going to have to start reading it."

There is certainly plenty to read. Heritage, with a staff of sixty and a budget this year of $5.3 million, is probably the most media-oriented of the New Right research and policy study groups, producing a steady stream of reports and publications aimed at both policymakers and the news media. Richard Scaife has given almost $4 million to Heritage — including seed money — since it began operating seven years ago. This year, Scaife grants total about $900,000, including money specifically allocated to an editorial briefing series, distribution of the *National Security Record*, and a Distinguished Journalism Fellow program.

The day-long, twice-yearly editorial briefings for journalists cost about $15,000, of which Scaife gives two-thirds. About fifty to sixty journalists attend the sessions. Recent topics have included Enterprise Zones (a Reagan-backed urban revitalization plan), the Heritage "alternative budget" prepared for Reagan, relations with China and Taiwan, and the SALT II treaty.

The *National Security Record*, aimed primarily at Congress, is a monthly report on defense and national security issues. As an illustration of the *Record*'s influence, the foundation's September/October 1980 newsletter noted that "Liberal Carl Rowan devoted two columns in a single week to an attempt to refute the assertion in the July *National Security Record* that the Soviets were manipulating events in the Caribbean through the Cubans and other surrogates. Shortly thereafter, John Chamberlain, [Joseph] Kingsbury-Smith and [Smith] Hempstone wrote columns bolstering the *National Security Record*'s argument — all citing the Heritage research." Chamberlain, a King Features syndicated columnist, was chosen by Heritage last year as its Distinguished Journalism Fellow.

Other Heritage activities include serving as a consultant to WQLN, the public television station in Erie, Pennsylvania, which espouses free-market economics.

Heritage also publishes a quarterly, *Policy Review*, and produces a twice-monthly column, *Heritage Foundation Forum*, which it says is used by more than 450 newspapers.

According to John Von Kannon, assistant to the president of Heritage, Scaife and his aides rarely participate in Heritage functions. "They look for organizations they agree with," he says, and then leave them alone.

"They're playing all sides of the street: media, politics — the soft approach and the hard," says George Mair, referring to Scaife and his advisers. Mair left the Foundation for American Communications just over a year ago, forced out, he claims, over the issue of what he regarded as the group's increasingly conservative bias. FACS president Jack Cox says, "The decision was made by the board of trustees to sever Mr. Mair's relationship with the foundation and that decision was not based on any political or ideological disputes."

Scaife himself has never publicly discussed his motivations or goals. Indeed, he has repeatedly declined requests for interviews, as he did in the case of this article.

Richard Scaife rarely speaks to the press. After several unsuccessful efforts to obtain an interview, this reporter decided to make one last attempt in Boston, where Scaife was scheduled to attend the annual meeting of the First Boston Corporation.

Scaife, a company director, did not show up while the meeting was in progress. Reached eventually by telephone as he dined with the other directors at the exclusive Union Club, he hung up the moment he heard the caller's name. A few minutes later he appeared at the top of the Club steps. At the bottom of the stairs, the following exchange occurred:

"Mr. Scaife, could you explain why you give so much money to the New Right?"

"You fucking Communist cunt, get out of here."

Well. The rest of the five-minute interview was conducted at a rapid trot down Park Street, during which Scaife tried to hail a taxi. Scaife volunteered two statements of opinion regarding his questioner's personal appearance — he said she was ugly and that her teeth were "terrible" —

and also the comment that she was engaged in "hatchet journalism." His questioner thanked Scaife for his time.

"Don't look behind you," Scaife offered by way of a goodbye.

Not quite sure what this remark meant, the reporter suggested that if someone were approaching it was probably her mother, whom she had arranged to meet nearby. "She's ugly, too," Scaife said, and strode off.

Officials of most organizations that receive money from Scaife charities say they rarely if ever see Scaife himself, but deal instead with aides like Richard Larry, who has also been unavailable for comment. Most of the more sensitive Scaife donations are made through a family trust that is not legally required to make any public accounting of its donations, and most institutions that receive money from Scaife, like their more liberal counterparts, do not volunteer information about their contributors. The story of Scaife and his activities has to be pieced together from public records, such published reports as exist, and conversations with people who for the most part decline identification — some because of business or professional reasons, others because they fear retaliation. (Shortly after "Citizen Scaife" was completed, the *Pittsburgh Post-Gazette* published a four-part series on Scaife. Written by staff writer David Warner, the late-April series detailed Scaife's publishing and some of his New Right connections, relying in part on documentation also privately made available to this reporter.)

Scaife's secretiveness is but one aspect of a complicated personality. A handsome man in the blond, beefy style one associates with southwestern ranchers or oil millionaires, the forty-eight-year-old Scaife dresses like a Wall Street executive. His astonishingly blue eyes are his most striking feature. A friend from an early age of J. Edgar Hoover and a long-time admirer of Barry Goldwater, Scaife is said by those who know him to be fascinated by military and intelligence matters. At the same time, he is so shy and so insecure about his intellectual capacities, according to one business acquaintance, that "he never speaks business without two, three, four people around him."

David Abshire, who as chairman of the Georgetown University Center for Strategic and International Studies, a major Scaife beneficiary, has known Scaife for nearly twenty years, describes him as "likable, enthusiastic, and a very fine, public-spirited individual." A Democratic officeholder in Pittsburgh, on the other hand, views Scaife as a "lone wolf" whose clout "is through his money and nothing else." Pittsburgh acquaintances add that Scaife is rarely seen on the social circuit, and suggest that Scaife's relations with most of the other Mellons tend to be less than cordial. Certainly that holds true within his own family: Scaife has only one sibling, Cordelia Scaife May, and he has not spoken to her for the past seven years.

One small insight into Scaife's personality is provided by Pat Minarcin, a former editor of the now-defunct *Pittsburgher* magazine, which Scaife financed. "We were talking one time after a meeting and I said to him, 'Is money power?'" Minarcin recalls. "He paused three or four seconds and looked at me really hard. He's just not used to people speaking to him on that level. He said, 'I didn't use to think so, but the older I get the more I do.' "

Certainly money is very much the stuff of which Mellon family history is made. Judge Thomas Mellon, the son of an Irish immigrant farmer who settled in the Pennsylvania countryside, rose to prominence in Pittsburgh during the latter half of the nineteenth century through shrewd real estate investments and a lending business that became the Mellon Bank. In time, the family holdings came to include, in addition to the bank, substantial blocks of stock in Gulf Oil and Alcoa, among other companies. By 1957, when *Fortune* magazine tried to rank the largest fortunes in America, four Mellons, including Scaife's mother, Sarah Mellon Scaife, were listed among the top eight.

In 1965, when his widowed mother died, Richard Scaife — in his early thirties, married, and the father of the first of two children — had no real career. After flunking out of Yale (he later finished at the University of Pittsburgh), Scaife had followed in the footsteps of his father, a retiring man from a local industrial family, and been given a variety of titles but little real power in several Mellon enterprises.

Just looking after his personal affairs could have become a full-time job. At the time of the last public accounting, in 1978, Scaife was the second-largest stockholder (after his second cousin Paul Mellon) in the Mellon Bank, one of the top twenty banks in the country. Until 1978, he was a bank trustee, having been elected to that post at the age of twenty-six. Among Scaife's other personal sources of wealth is the income from two trusts set up for him by his mother — probably amounting to around $8 million a year. He has homes in Pebble Beach, California, and in Pittsburgh, and a large estate in Ligonier, Pennsylvania, and he flies from coast to coast in a private DC-9 — a plane so big that in commercial service it carries up to 100 passengers.

After his mother's death, Scaife began to take an increasingly active role in the family's philanthropic activities. Scaife family entities currently engaged in giving money to charity include the Sarah Scaife Foundation, set up by Scaife's mother; the Allegheny and Carthage Foundations, set up by Scaife; and the Trust for Sarah Mellon Scaife's Grandchildren (who number only Scaife's two, because Cordelia Scaife May has none). Taken together, these four groups have assets of more than $250 million, and current annual income of at least $12 million. (Eventually, Scaife's children will get the income from their trust, as Scaife now gets the income from his trusts.)

Gulf Oil company stock makes up a large part of the Scaife fortune. If one were to count in not just Richard Scaife's personal holdings in Gulf, but also those of the various Scaife charitable entities, the total would probably rank as the second largest holding (after Paul Mellon) in the company. By the same rough yardstick, Scaife and Scaife family entities account for about 6 percent of the stock (all nonvoting) of First Boston Corporation, a major investment banking firm. Scaife was elected to the First Boston board last year. The Mellons and Scaifes as a whole hold about 13 percent of the First Boston stock, an investment second in size only to that of Financière Credit Suisse.

THE SMALL-BORE PUBLISHER

It was newspapers, however, not the world of finance, that eventually captured Richard Scaife's interest. In 1969, he made a successful offer of almost $5 million for the Greensburg, Pennsylvania, *Tribune-Review* (daily circulation: 41,500), which was part of an estate being handled by the Mellon Bank. Greensburg, a town of 20,000 people about thirty miles east of Pittsburgh, is the county seat of Westmoreland County, which is a curious mix of, on the one hand, working-class, mob-infiltrated towns, and, on the other, rolling hills where Mellons ride to hounds.

Scaife apparently has not scrimped on costs at the paper, including salaries. He has lured at least two people from the Pittsburgh dailies, and his Harrisburg bureau chief, J. R. Freeman, says that it is his understanding that he can "go anywhere in the world and stay as long as I want." The paper, housed in an attractive, modern building on a Greensburg side street, routinely features staff reports on Pittsburgh politics as well as local affairs, depending on the wires for most national coverage.

Despite his vast resources, Scaife has not moved into the big leagues of publishing. During the Nixon years, he was urged by at least one high official in the White House to bid for *The Washington Star*, but he never did. Pittsburgh acquaintances say that several years ago Scaife talked about buying *The Philadelphia Inquirer;* however, Sam McKeel, president of Philadelphia Newspapers, Inc., the Knight-Ridder group that owns the *Inquirer*, says Scaife never made any overtures. Last year, Scaife entered into negotiations to buy *Harper's* magazine, but nothing came of those talks.

Instead, Scaife has settled for a modest collection of holdings which include, in addition to the *Tribune-Review*, the *Lebanon* (Pennsylvania) *Daily News* and *Sunday Pennsylvanian;* two Pennsylvania weeklies, *The* (Blairsville) *Dispatch* and the *Elizabethtown Chronicle;* until recently, a city magazine, *Pittsburgher*, which folded early this year; and a new monthly business Sunday supplement called *Pennsylvania Economy*, which began publishing last October. Elsewhere, he owns half of two weeklies in California and half of *The Sacramento Union*, his largest (circulation: 106,000) and only nationally known acquisition. Scaife bought the half interest in late 1977 from John McGoff, a Michigan publisher who is under investigation by federal authorities in connection with alleged secret payments by the South African government to permit him to buy news properties.

Various explanations are offered for Scaife's failure to acquire a major national publication. Some acquaintances speak of his dislike of publicity;

others of his unwillingness, despite his wealth, to spend the sums required. Pat Minarcin, the former *Pittsburgher* editor, suggests another aspect of Scaife's personality that may be relevant. "Here is a man who is as rich or richer than any other man in the country, who has a hunger to be accepted as a journalist and a responsible member of society," says Minarcin. "Yet he has this fatal flaw — he keeps shooting himself in the foot."

In the case of the *Tribune-Review*, the "shot" was Scaife's firing of a young reporter, Jude Dippold, in October 1973, two days after Dippold had remarked to the newsroom upon reading of Spiro Agnew's resignation as vice-president, "One down and one to go." Within hours of Dippold's firing, ten of the paper's twenty-four-person editorial staff resigned. They charged in a statement that Scaife (a $1 million contributor to Nixon's re-election campaign and a $47,500 contributor — according to Justice Department records — to the illegal Watergate campaign fund known as the Townhouse Operation) had "continually, in the opinion of the professional staff, interjected his political and personal bias into the handling of news stories."

Six years later, another chapter was added to the "Citizen Scaife" saga. This time it involved the firing of a young editorial cartoonist, Paul Duginski, at *The Sacramento Union.* According to Duginski, on December 3, 1979, he was called in by editor Don Hoenshell, who has since died, and shown a letter from Scaife complaining about several unflattering cartoons Duginski had drawn of California's conservative lieutenant governor, Mike Curb. According to Duginski, the letter instructed Hoenshell to restrict Duginski to doing cartoons on local issues. Duginski accepted the restriction but told his story to *feed/back*, the San Francisco State journalism review. Shortly after *feed/back* published an article on the matter last spring, Duginski was told that he was being laid off for economic reasons.

As in the case of Jude Dippold, Duginski's colleagues rallied to his defense. In addition to presenting him with a T–shirt that announced "I've been Scaifed," twenty-seven of them signed a petition offering to donate part of their salaries so that Duginski could continue to be employed. Management declined the offer. Duginski still has not found another full-time cartooning job.

Scaife's one foray into international publishing represents perhaps the most curious of his publishing enterprises. In 1973, he became the owner of Kern House Enterprises, a U.S.-registered company. Kern House ran Forum World Features, a London-based news agency that supplied feature material to a large number of papers around the world, including at one time about thirty in the U.S. Scaife abruptly closed down Forum in 1975, shortly before *Time Out*, a British weekly, published a purported 1968 CIA memorandum, addressed to then-director Richard Helms, which described Forum as a CIA-sponsored operation providing "a significant means to counter Communist propaganda." The Forum-CIA tie, which lasted into the seventies, has been confirmed by various British and American publications over the years, and it was confirmed independently by a source in connection with this article.

Helms is a member of the same country club near Pittsburgh as Scaife. "Unfortunately," Helms says, "I really don't know him." On the matter of Forum and a possible CIA link, he adds, "I don't know anything about it. And, if it were true, I wouldn't confirm it."

Scaife's involvement with Forum began at a time when he seems to have begun to recognize that newspapering might not represent the most effective way to make his mark on the world. Perhaps it was frustration at his lack of clout as a publisher that led Scaife to cast around for other areas in which to play a public role. This search coincided with the birth of a powerful new movement, one that was to culminate in the election of Ronald Reagan — the New Right.

OVERLOOKED MAECENAS TO THE NEW RIGHT

Many leaders of the New Right are, like Scaife, men in their thirties and forties who, for one reason or another, see themselves as outside the old conservative establishment. They share not just a traditional free-market, anti-Communist view of the world, but also a sophisticated ability to analyze the forces that shape American society. This analysis has led to the creation of myriad New Right lobbying groups and think-tanks whose techniques are drawn directly from citizens groups and New Left organizations of the 1960s. ("Ten years ago the liberals kind of had a copyright on organizations outside of government," says Leon Reed, an aide on defense matters to Senator William Proxmire. "At some point the Right realized that all of the things like shareholder resolutions and testifying before Congress can be used by anyone.") This analysis also accounts for the tremendous emphasis the New Right puts on the news media, particularly television. No longer, as in Spiro Agnew's day, are the media seen simply as the enemy; rather, they are regarded as an institution which, like any other, is capable of being influenced as well as intimidated.

Scaife, with his money, his interest in politics and the media, and his long-held conservative views, quickly became a key New Right backer. Indeed, the rise of the New Right coincided with a substantial increase in Scaife's power to assist it. In 1973, he became chairman of the Sarah Scaife Foundation; within a year, a total break occurred between him and his sister. Since their mother's death, Cordelia Scaife May had tried to restrain her brother from shifting family charitable donations away from Sarah Scaife's priorities — population control and art — and toward conservative causes. After the break, she apparently gave up.

Scaife beneficiaries take pains to draw a distinction between Scaife as an individual and the Scaife charitable entities, each of which is presided over by several trustees, of which Scaife is but one. The virtually complete shift from Sarah Scaife's priorities to Richard Scaife's is, however, clear evidence of his overriding influence. The New York-based Population Council, for example, has been given no further Scaife funds since 1973, after receiving nearly $16 million during the previous thirteen years.

The Sarah Scaife Foundation, the Carthage Foundation, and the Allegheny Foundation, whose donations are a matter of public record, do give to many civic projects as well as to Richard Scaife's political charities. The Allegheny Foundation in particular has been a generous benefactor of such local causes as a major restoration now in progress in Pittsburgh. But the clearest indicator of which charities lie closest to Richard Scaife's heart is the giving pattern of the Sarah Scaife Grandchildren's Trust. Trusts, unlike foundations, do not have to give any public accounting of how they spend their income. According to information privately made available, the grandchildren's trust has virtually ceased giving to organizations other than conservative and New Right groups.

Total donations from Scaife entities to conservative causes currently run about $10 million a year. (This amount, of course, does not reflect any personal contributions Scaife may make, about which no information is publicly available.) Among better-known conservative funders, the John M. Olin Foundation gave a total to *all* causes of $5.2 million in 1979, while the Adolph Coors Foundation gave away $2.5 million. Among funders perceived as left of center, Stewart Mott, heir to a General Motors fortune, gives away, through a trust, an average of between $700,000 and $1.3 million a year, according to an aide, while the Haymarket Peoples Fund gave $191,400 in 1979.

Sometimes, of course, a small amount of money at the right time is of more value than millions later on. Since 1973, Scaife entities have provided seed money to as many as two dozen New Right organizations.

The power of Scaife money is well appreciated by those who come up against it. An official of a large foundation concerned with arms control says whenever he and other foundation executives interested in military issues discuss new projects, they "always inevitably think about all that Scaife money and what it's doing." The official adds that the conservative groups "have a heck of a lot more influence [in defense matters] than the left-wing groups.

"A group like the National Strategy Information Center, which invites young academics to Colorado every year, can reach a lot of people very effectively," he says. "There is no analogous program on the left. The left-wing groups are constantly scraping for money. And they're badly splintered. The only thing that is anything like a match for the right-wing groups is the Institute for Policy Studies." The IPS budget for 1980 was $1.6 million.

DRAWING UP THE AGENDA

Military and intelligence think-tanks and academic programs like the National Strategy Information Center have been particularly favored by Scaife; a catalog of Scaife recipients over the past few years would contain virtually every significant conservative defense-oriented program in existence in the U.S.

WHERE THE MONEY GOES

Some of the larger or better-known conservative and New Right groups to which Richard Scaife has given substantial funding since 1973 are listed below. Amounts, which include grants from the Carthage and Sarah Scaife

Foundations and the Trust for the Grandchildren of Sarah Mellon Scaife, are approximate.

DEFENSE

The Center for Strategic and International Studies, Georgetown University (Washington, D.C.)	$5.3 million
The Committee for a Free World (New York)*†	$ 50,000
Committee on the Present Danger (Washington, D.C.)†	$360,000
Hoover Institution on War, Revolution and Peace, Stanford University (Stanford, Calif.)	$3.5 million
Institute for Foreign Policy Analysis (Cambridge)*†	$1.9 million
National Security Program, New York University† and National Strategy Information Center (New York)†	$6 million

ECONOMICS

Foundation for Research in Economics and Education (Westwood, Calif.)	$1.4 million
International Center for Economic Policy Studies (New York)†	$150,000
International Institute for Economic Research (Westwood, Calif.)*†	$300,000
Law and Economics Center, originally at Miami University, now at Emory University (Atlanta)*†	$3 million
World Research, Inc. (San Diego)	$1 million

MEDIA

Accuracy in Media (Washington, D.C.)	$150,000
Alternative Educational Foundation (*The American Spectator* magazine, Bloomington, Ind.)	$900,000
The Media Institute (Washington, D.C.)*†	$475,000
WQLN–TV (Erie, Pa.)	$500,000

THINK-TANKS

The Heritage Foundation (Washington, D.C.)*†	$3.8 million
The Institute for Contemporary Studies (San Francisco)*†	$1.7 million

POLITICAL RESEARCH/EDUCATION GROUPS

American Legislative Exchange Council (Washington, D.C.)†	$560,000
The Free Congress Research and Education Foundation, Inc. (Washington, D.C.)†	$700,000

LEGAL GROUPS

Americans for Effective Law Enforcement (Evanston)	$1 million
National Legal Center for the Public Interest, plus six affiliates (Capital Legal Foundation, Washington, D.C.; Mountain States Legal Foundation, Denver; Mid-Atlantic Legal Foundation, Philadelphia; Great Plains Legal Foundation, Kansas City, Mo.; Mid-America Legal Foundation, Chicago; Southeastern Legal Foundation, Atlanta)*†	$1.8 million
Pacific Legal Foundation (Sacramento)†	$1.9 million

---

†Denotes that the group recently received a contribution equal to 10 percent or more of the current or most recent available budget, as based on public or private records and/or confirmation by organization.

*Denotes that the group is known to have received seed money from Scaife.

Groups devoted to free-market economics—like the Law and Economics Center at Emory University, which has provided all-expenses-paid economics courses for 137 federal judges—have been the second-largest beneficiary since 1973.

Because they have been able to attract big names—people like former Navy Secretary Paul Nitze, now chairman of policy studies of the Committee on the Present Danger, and economist Milton Friedman, a frequent lecturer at the judges' seminars—many Scaife-funded defense and economics organizations command media attention. This attention has increased with the movement of a number of people from New Right groups into the Reagan administration—among them Interior Secretary Watt, from the Mountain States Legal Foundation, and presidential counselor Edwin Meese, one of the founders of the Institute for Contemporary Studies. Both groups describe Scaife as their largest donor, and the institute says Scaife provided its seed money of $75,000 in 1973.

Not just names but numbers count. With so many conservative groups active in defense and economic matters, vast quantities of facts are constantly being generated and large numbers of seminars and briefings are constantly under way. "You can't underestimate the effect of a simple paper avalanche," says Leon Reed, the Proxmire aide. "One of the most important things groups like this can do is to give information to the people in Congress who support you. Groups can also provide people to speak at press conferences, testify before committees, things like that."

One example of the kind of "paper avalanche" to which Reed refers is the number of facts and figures generated by conservative groups at the time of the start of the 1979 congressional debate on the SALT II treaty. A quick check reveals at least eight studies of the issue, all critical, by groups that receive substantial Scaife backing. In addition, the Scaife-assisted Georgetown Center for Strategic and International Studies held a two-day briefing for twenty key European journalists on the issue, and The Heritage Foundation held an all-day session for members of the U.S. press. According to Herb Berkowitz, Heritage director of public relations, that press briefing "really kicked off the debate." The arms limitation treaty was not ratified.

Other examples of the potential impact of names and numbers abound.

● In its September 17, 1979, issue, *Time* devoted two pages to a report on a Brussels conference on NATO sponsored by the Georgetown Center and chaired by Henry Kissinger, a counselor in residence at the center. The article gloomily asserted: "The North Atlantic Treaty Organization received a thorough physical and psychological checkup last week and was found to be less than robust at age 30. The general diagnosis: flabby nuclear muscle and a creeping inferiority complex."

● In August 1980, a United Features Syndicate column by Virginia Payette reported that "Terrorism has become a fact of American life." The article went on to explain, "It doesn't have to be that way, according to Dr. Samuel T. Francis, an expert on international terrorism of The Heritage Foundation . . . Not if we give the FBI and the CIA a chance to stop it . . . The way things are now, he warns, the FBI and the police are not only hamstrung by red tape, they are themselves being hauled into court for violating the civil liberties" of known terrorists.

• On December 15, 1980, the *New York Times* carried a full-column report, datelined San Francisco, which began: "A group of conservative black businessmen and educators, meeting here over the weekend with representatives of President-elect Ronald Reagan, advocated a reduction in the minimum wage, the elimination of rent control laws and a thorough reorganization of many social programs." In the seventh paragraph, the article reported that the sponsor of the conference was the Institute for Contemporary Studies (to which Scaife is the largest donor).

• Among a plethora of news articles last year on weakened U.S. military capabilities — which appeared at the same time as Scaife-backed organizations were turning out at least a dozen studies on the subject — probably the most breathless was an October 27 *Newsweek* cover story entitled "Is America Strong Enough?" The article, which quoted few people by name, depended heavily on such sources as "defense experts" and "a respected American military analyst." It reported in apocalyptic Pentagonese that "experts say Soviet advances in missile guidance now threaten the security of Minuteman ICBM's that constitute the land-based leg of America's nuclear triad — opening a 'window of vulnerability' that threatens to subject the United States to nuclear blackmail, if not a Soviet first strike, by as early as 1982." The only expert named in a two-page spread entitled "Sizing up the Soviets' Might," was Jeffrey Record from the Institute for Foreign Policy Analysis. In the old days, Record explained, "Our nuclear superiority gave the Russians pause because they knew we could blow them out of the water. Now our trump card has been canceled." Scaife provided the largest single portion of the institute's seed money ($325,000) in 1976, and continues to be the institute's single largest donor, providing about one third of its current $1 million budget.

Such examples suggest how layer upon layer of seminars, studies, conferences, and interviews can do much to push along, if not create, the issues which then become the national agenda of debate.

A BEAD ON THE MEDIA

While the defense and economics groups funded by Scaife court the news media and, by the very nature of what they do, attract coverage, Scaife has also shown himself to be interested in groups that specifically produce or scrutinize news or try to affect the newsgathering process itself. Contributions in this area do not approach those going to the other two areas; but they are substantial, and growing.

Some insight into the thinking of Scaife's advisers regarding the media is provided by George Mair, formerly of the Foundation for American

Communications. "They always wanted me to tell them about how things work at CBS," Mair recalls. "They seemed fascinated by the media and loved to hear all the gossip. But, at the same time, they had a conspiratorial view of how the media work."

To date, FACS has received more than $700,000 from Scaife, including about 20 percent of its current $650,000 budget. According to FACS president Jack Cox, Scaife remains the organizations' single largest donor. Besides sponsoring conferences which have been attended by close to 500 journalists, FACS runs seminars for nonprofit organizations and businesses on how to deal with the media. Cox estimates that 3,000 to 4,000 executives have attended these sessions. FACS also sends a newsletter free to about 6,000 people, including the op-ed editors of all metropolitan dailies and all news directors of commercial radio and television stations.

Recent events sponsored by FACS include an April seminar for business executives cosponsored by the UCLA Graduate School of Management (itself the recipient of a $1 million grant from the Sarah Scaife Foundation three years ago), and a December conference for journalists on nuclear energy cosponsored by the Gannett Newspaper Foundation.

Jack Scott, president of the foundation, describes FACS as "a balanced organization" with no perceptible bias. "Cox is a conservative; there's no blinking at that," Scott says. "But he is very reluctant to project his political opinions. I don't think that as an organization they have a philosophy."

Llewelyn King, publisher of *The Energy Daily*, based in Washington, D.C., was a panelist at the December nuclear conference. He says that he believes that the reporters at that conference, whom he describes as having come, by and large, from small papers, "would have liked to have heard more from people opposed to nuclear power." At the same time, he says, "I don't think anybody got brainwashed."

Michael Rounds, a business reporter for the *Rocky Mountain News* who attended a FACS seminar on economics last year, says, "I felt it was very well done. Where else would I get a chance to meet Paul Samuelson?" He adds, "I saw it as business-supported – that's why I went. The economists weren't what I would call liberals. The organizers were trying to educate a bunch of journalists like me, trying to give them and me a sense of how business works and to deal with perceived anti-business bias."

Education of journalists is also a part of the work of another Scaife-backed media group, the Washington-based Media Institute. The institute's president, Leonard J. Theberge, also was a founder of the National Legal Center for the Public Interest, the umbrella group for six conservative legal groups funded by Scaife. Institute board members have included Herbert Schmertz, vice president, public affairs, of Mobil, and J. Robert Fluor, chairman of Fluor Corporation. Scaife's assistance began with a $100,000 donation in 1975, the first year of the institute's existence, and is around $150,000 this year, or about 15 percent of the budget.

Frank Skrobiszewski, second in command to Theberge, describes the main objective of the Media Institute as being "to improve the quality of economic reporting, particularly on network television." To this end, the institute has published, for example, a study of television news that concludes that the networks have increased the public's fear of nuclear power. It also runs lunch seminars for journalists and puts out a newsletter.

The institute's newest project is the Economic Communications Center, which began operating last October. Its purpose, according to Skrobiszewski, is to provide journalists with quick analyses of current economic issues and easy access to experts in the field. "For example, when news comes out on something like the wage-price index, we can have an analysis prepared in one-and-a-half to two hours and have an economist ready to discuss it," Skrobiszewski explains. "Journalists often complain that they have no one to go to outside of government. This closes that gap." Skrobiszewski cites as an example of the center's quick acceptance the fact that its analysis of Iranian assets prompted interviews with the expert who prepared it by, among others, ABC, the AP, and UPI.

Scaife's funding not only makes possible a critical scrutiny of television programs; it also helps to create programs. Between 1976 and 1977, Scaife entities supplied $225,000 (the second-largest grant after Mobil) to WGBH, the Boston public broadcasting station, for a series that examined topics including the CIA, defense, and foreign policy. Scaife later supplied $110,000 in pre-production grants for a series on intelligence issues, based on a script by former CIA deputy director Ray Cline, now a top official at the Georgetown Center for Strategic and International Studies. According to Peter McGhee, WGBH program manager for national productions, the series currently is in limbo because only half of the needed $2 million has been raised. He says he is unsure how much of that, if any, was pledged by Scaife.

Closer to Pittsburgh, Scaife supplied $500,000 to public television station WQLN in Erie, Pennsylvania, to help underwrite *Free to Choose*, a ten-part series featuring Milton Friedman.

On the print side, Scaife has helped to underwrite a number of magazines. In the past decade, for example, Scaife has given more than $1 million to the publishers of *The American Spectator*, a monthly whose views range across the conservative spectrum.

The most prestigious of the periodicals with which Scaife has been associated is *Daedalus*, the journal of the American Academy of Arts and Sciences. Three years ago, Richard Pipes, a Harvard historian who is now a member of the National Security Council staff, approached *Daedalus* with a proposal for a special issue on U.S. defense policy, with himself as guest editor. Pipes also provided a proposed backer, in the form of a Scaife charity that was willing to put up $25,000 immediately and $25,000 to $50,000 later.

Pipes was keenly interested in defense policy, having been chairman of the so-called B-team, a group of ten outside experts convened by George Bush while Bush was CIA chief to make an assessment of Soviet military strength. The B-team conclusions, delivered in late 1976, included an estimate of Soviet defense spending that was twice as high as previous government estimates and an assertion that the Russians were bent on nuclear superiority. The conclusions, which were widely accepted as official, played a major role in shaping the current defense debate.

The *Daedalus* project proposed by Pipes was agreed to, but funding was sought from the Carnegie Endowment for International Peace to provide balance to the Scaife donation, and the issue of Pipes's editorship was left unresolved. As the essays began to come in, according to one source close to the project, it became evident that many were "under the influence of Pipes and the B-team mentality. It became clear that this was to be the B-team's riposte to earlier liberal critics." Eventually, it was agreed that the project would have a board of advisers but no guest editor.

At some point following that decision, Scaife withdrew from the agreement to supply additional funds and insisted that the Scaife name not be associated with the project. Stephen R. Graubard, *Daedalus*'s editor, says his recollection is that Scaife aides were unhappy about several things, especially a time delay in the publication of what turned out to be two special issues, Fall and Winter 1980. "They never said Pipes had to be guest editor or we'll take our marbles and go home," Graubard says. Others recall things differently. A second source close to the project says, "The Scaife people said their understanding was that Pipes was to be the sole guest editor and strongly implied bad faith. They were, in effect, trying to dictate what was to be in the magazine. They wanted to give the cold-war hard line.

In the end, it is difficult to say what lessons, if any, can be drawn from the story of Richard Mellon Scaife and his activities. While such a recounting suggests that journalists should treat the rich and their creations—the foundations, the trusts, the charitable organizations—with as much curiosity and skepticism as they treat government and political groups, the fact is that the size of Scaife's fortune and the narrowness of his interests make him unusual, if not unique.

Beyond this, the fact that Scaife—virtually unnoticed—has been able to establish group after group whose collective effect has been to help shape the way Americans think about themselves and their nation's problems raises a concern addressed by Walter Lippmann nearly sixty years ago. "On all but a very few matters for short stretches in our lives, the utmost independence that we can exercise is to multiply the authorities to whom we give a friendly hearing," Lippmann wrote in *Public Opinion*. "As congenital amateurs our quest for truth consists in stirring up the experts, and forcing them to answer any heresy that has the accent of conviction. In such a debate, we can often judge who has won the dialectical victory, but we are virtually defenseless against a false premise that none of the debaters has challenged, or a neglected aspect that none of them has brought into the argument."

By multiplying the authorities to whom the media are prepared to give a friendly hearing, Scaife has helped to create an illusion of diversity where none exists. The result could be an increasing number of one-sided debates in which the challengers are far outnumbered, if indeed they are heard from at all.

WINNERS/LOSERS

Now that the nation is headed in a radically New Right direction, in opposition to the American Consensus of half a century, let us look at winners/losers in the economic game of life. Here are examples of New Right imperatives of economic power:

> *Get the federal government out of the private sector.*
>
> *Maximize free enterprise; minimize regulation.*
>
> *Lower taxes on the rich, and that will help the poor.*
>
> *Eliminate the minimum wage to give more people jobs.*
>
> *Increase productivity, replacing welfare with workfare: No Work, No Food.*
>
> *Get women back home and out of the job market.*
>
> *Preserve tax-exemption for churches and tax-related schools.*
>
> *Don't do business with the communists.*

Even two years before the 1980 elections, almost no one in national power dreamed the Radical Right could win control of America. The new battle of faiths now being waged in the White House and the Congress concerns drastic cuts in the federal budget, massively increased military appropriations for the years ahead, and unprecedented cuts in the taxes of individuals and corporations.

What's ahead for the economy? Who can best advise us concerning this? Political and religious leaders of the New Right frequently cite William E. Simon and Nobel Laureate Milton Friedman. Their role in relation to our economic future is appraised in a Speak Out *selection on "The Conservative Onslaught" by John Kenneth Galbraith, the liberal economist and author who served as the United States Ambassador to India. His most recent book is his autobiography,* A Life in Our Times.

Galbraith is followed by Lester Thurow, Professor of Economics and Management at the Sloan School of Management at the Massachusetts Institute of Technology. A probing analyst of economic life, Thurow, author of The Zero Sum Society, *has succeeded Paul Samuelson as economic columnist for* Newsweek. *Looking at the long-range effects of the Reagan administration's redirection of national income, expenses, and productivity, Thurow dares to describe "How to Wreck the Economy."*

The Conservative Onslaught

JOHN KENNETH GALBRAITH

In economic and social affairs we value controversy and take it for granted; it is the essence of politics, its principal attraction as a modern spectator sport. This regularly keeps us from seeing how substantial, on occasion, can be the agreement on a broad range of ideas and policies within which the political debate proceeds.

Such has been the case with economic and social policy in the industrial countries since World War II. There has been a broad consensus in the United States extending to most Republicans and most Democrats. Similarly as between Christian Democrats and Social Democrats in Germany and Austria, the Labour and Tory parties in Britain, Liberals and Progressive Conservatives in Canada. Policies in France, Italy, Switzerland, and Scandinavia have generally conformed. The rhetoric in all countries has been diverse. The practical action has been similar.

There have been three points of convergence. All governments in all of the industrial countries, although differing in individual emphasis, have agreed that:

- There must be macroeconomic management of the economy to minimize unemployment and inflation. This, at least in the English-speaking countries, was the legacy of Keynes.

- There must be action by governments to provide those services which by their nature are not available from the private sector or on which, like moderate-cost housing, health care, and urban transportation, the private economy defaults.

- There must be measures — unemployment insurance, welfare payments, old-age pensions, medical insurance, environmental protection, job safety and product safety regulation — to protect the individual from circumstances with which he or she cannot, as an individual, contend. Much of this last has been thought of as smoothing and softening the harsh edges of capitalism.

No accepted term exists for the consensus which these policies comprise. Keynesian policy refers too narrowly to macroeconomic action; liberal or social democratic policy has too strong a political connotation for what has been embraced in practice by Dwight D. Eisenhower and Gerald Ford, Charles de Gaulle, Edward Heath, and Konrad Adenauer. I will not try to devise a new term; instead I will refer to the broad macroeconomic, public-service, and social-welfare commitment as the economic and social consensus or just the consensus. It is the present attack on this consensus — notably by Mrs. Thatcher's government in Britain and by numerous of Ronald Reagan's supporters in the United States — that I wish to examine.

The ideas supporting the economic and social consensus have never been without challenge. Keynesian macroeconomic management of the economy, the first pillar of the consensus, was powerfully conservative in intent. It sought only to correct the most self-destructive feature of capitalism, the one Marx thought decisive: its tendency to recurrent and progressively more severe crisis or depression. It left the role of the market, current income distribution, and property rights unchallenged. But numerous conservatives, especially in the United States, long equated Keynesian economics with subversion. There was some conservative discomfort when, thirty years after Keynes's *General Theory* was published and the policy it prescribed was tending visibly to obsolescence, Richard Nixon, in an aberrant moment, was led to say that all Americans, including Republicans, were Keynesians now. A reference to the social welfare policies of the consensus has always encountered a slightly disapproving mood: something expensive or debilitating was being done for George Bernard Shaw's undeserving poor. The need to compensate for the failures of capitalism in providing lower-cost housing, lower-income health care, and mass transportation has been accepted in all countries; but in the United States at least not many have wanted to admit that this is an unavoidable form of socialism. In all countries at all times there has been much mention of the cost of government, the level of taxes, the constraints of business regulation, and the effect of these on economic incentives.

It has always been likely, one should note, that an attack on the economic and social consensus would be taken to reflect the views of a larger section of the population than was actually the case. That is because articulate expression on public issues is strongly correlated with income, and the consensus is of the greatest importance for those of lowest income. Also the perception of a movement in political attitudes can be as important in its effect on politicians as a movement itself. These matters deserve a special word.

That a large share of all economic comment comes from people of comfortable means will not be in doubt. High social, business, and academic position gives access to television, radio, and the press. And professional access to the media also gives a relatively high income. It follows that the voice of economic advantage, being louder, regularly gets mistaken for the voice of the masses. On the need for tax relief, investment incentives, or a curb on welfare costs, the views of one articulate and affluent banker, businessman, lawyer, or acolyte economist are the equal of those of several thousand welfare mothers. In any recent year the pleas by Walter Wriston of Citibank or David Rockefeller of Chase Manhattan for relief from oppressive taxation, regulation, or intrusive government have commanded at least as much public attention as the expressions of discontent of all the deprived of the South Bronx. So the voice of affluence being resonant, it is frequently thought to be the voice of the masses. And since it is so interpreted by politicians, it has much the same effect on legislatures and legislation as a genuine shift of opinion.

In the last thirty-five years we have had many such shifts of opinion — all drastically to the right. Immediately after World War II, Professor Friedrich Hayek emerged as the messiah of a modern and comprehensive rejection of the state. His *Road to Serfdom* was hailed as the new sacred tablet. In 1964, Senator Goldwater was thought to represent a growing conservative mood that was sweeping the country. Messrs. Richard Scammon and Ben Wattenberg then identified this conservative mood with an unpoor and distinctly unradical Dayton housewife; this lady was for some months the new American archetype.[1] The applause for Spiro Agnew was taken to mean the rejection, at long last, of the liberal elite. George Wallace was once thought to have a highly conservative message for the American people. Based on all past experience, it is the beginning of wisdom to doubt the depth and durability of great shifts of American opinion to the right.

However, even after an appropriate discounting, it seems certain that not only in the United States but in other industrial countries as well there is now an attack on the economic and social consensus that has a deeper substance. Mrs. Thatcher and Mr. Reagan have won elections. Much, if not most, of Mr. Reagan's success must be attributed to President Carter's economists — to the macroeconomic management that combined a severe recession with severe inflation, with a drastic slump in the housing industry, with particular economic distress in the traditional Democratic industrial states — and all these in the year of the election. Economists do some things with precision. But effective macroeconomic management was one part of the consensus. Obviously there is something wrong with the way it now functions.

There is, indeed, substance to the conservative attack on the economic and social consensus. It strikes at genuine points of vulnerability. This, however, is not true of all of the attack; some of it is merely a rejection of reality — or compassion. The conservative onslaught we now witness needs careful dissection and differentiation.

Three different lines of attack can be identified, and the relevant nomenclature readily suggests itself. There is the *simplistic*, the *romantic*, and the *real* attack. These terms, needless to say, are intended to be purely descriptive; they have no pejorative connotation.

The *simplistic* attack consists in a generalized assault on all the civilian services of modern government. Education, urban services, and other conventional functions of government; government help to the unemployed, unemployable, or otherwise economically incapable; public housing and health care; and the regulatory functions of government are all in the line of fire. People, in a now famous phrase, must be left free to choose.

In its more elementary form this attack on the consensus holds that the services of government are the peculiar malignity of those who perform them; they are a burden foisted on the unwilling taxpayer by bureaucrats — public servants. The most eloquent American spokesman for this view is William Simon, once a prominent Cabinet prospect under Mr. Reagan. "Bureaucrats," Mr. Simon has said, "should be assumed to be noxious, authoritarian parasites on society, with a tendency to augment their own size and power and to cultivate a parasitical clientele in all classes of society." There must, he urges, "be conscious, philosophical prejudice against any intervention by the state into our lives."[2] If public services are a foisted malignancy — if they are unrelated to need or function — it follows that they can be reduced more or less without limit and without significant social cost or suffering. This is implicit, even explicit, in this case.

Other participants in this line of attack are, superficially at least, more sophisticated. Professor Arthur Laffer of the University of Southern California has supported the case with his now famous curve, which shows that when no taxes are levied, no revenue is raised, and that when taxes absorb all income, their yield, not surprisingly, is also zero. Taxes that are too high, as shown by a curve connecting these two points, have at some point a reduced aggregate yield. The Laffer Curve, which in its operative ranges is of purely free-hand origin, has become, in turn, a general case against all taxes. Let there be large horizontal reductions and the resulting expansion of private output and income — supply-side economics for those who will believe anything — can be great enough to sustain public revenues at more or less the previous level. For the less gullible, the Laffer Curve still argues for a large reduction in the cost and role of government.[3]

Yet another attack on the public services comes from Professor Milton Friedman and his disciples. It holds that these services are relentlessly in conflict with liberty. The market accords to the individual the sovereignty of choice; the state, as it enlarges its services, curtails or impairs that choice. And its tendency is cumulative and apocalyptic. By its acceptance of a large service and protective role for the state, democracy commits itself to an irreversible descent into totalitarianism and communism. Professor Friedman is firm about the prospect. "If we continue our present trend," he has said, "and our free society is replaced by a collectivist society, the intellectuals who have done so much to drive us down this path will not be the ones who run the society; the prison, the insane asylum, or the graveyard would be their fate."[4] "Or," he has asked, "shall we have the wisdom and the courage to change our course, to learn from experience, and to benefit from a 'rebirth of freedom?'"[5]

I have called this attack on the social consensus simplistic; it could, by the untactful, be called purely rhetorical. That is because it depends almost wholly on passionate assertion and emotional response. No one, after reflection, can easily conclude that publicly rendered services are less urgently a part of the living standard than privately purchased ones — that clean water is less needed than clean houses, that good schools for the young are less important than good television sets.

Public services are not rendered in most countries with high efficiency, a point worthy of real concern. But no way has ever been found for seriously reducing outlays for either efficiently or inefficiently rendered services without affecting performance. Public bureaucracy has a dynamic of its own, but so does private bureaucracy. As road builders promote highways and public educators promote public education, so private weapons firms promote weapons and other corporate bureaucracies promote automobiles, alcohol, toothpaste, and cosmetics. This is the common tendency of organization, as we've known since Max Weber. Good education, health, and law enforcement do not impair liberty or foretell authoritarianism. The entire experience of civilized societies is that they are consistent with liberty and enlarge it. Professor Friedman's belief that liberty is measured, as currently in New York City, by the depth of the uncollected garbage is, as I've previously observed, deeply questionable.

Taxes on the affluent do reduce the freedom of those so taxed to spend their own money. "An essential part of economic freedom is freedom to choose how to use our income."[6] But welfare payments, unemployment compensation, and old-age pensions serve even more specifically to increase the liberty of their recipients. That is because the difference for liberty between considerable income and a little less income can be slight; in contrast, the effect on liberty of the difference between *no* income and *some* income is always very, very great. It is the unfortunate habit of those who speak of the effect of government on freedom that they confine their concern to the loss of freedom for the affluent. All but invariably they omit to consider the way income creates freedom for the indigent.

The differential effect of taxes and public services on people of different income is something we must not disguise. Taxes in industrial countries are intended to be moderately progressive; in any case, they are paid in greatest absolute amount by people of middle income and above. Public services, in contrast, are most used by the poor. The affluent have access to private schools; the poor must rely on public education. The rich have private golf courses and swimming pools; the poor depend on public parks and public recreation.

Public transportation is most important for the least affluent. So are public hospitals, public libraries, and public housing. So are the services of the police and other municipal services. Unemployment and welfare benefits are important for those who have no other income. They have no similar urgency for those who are otherwise provided. In California an estimated two thirds of the tax saving under Proposition 13 accrued to individual corporations and large property-owners. The services curtailed (or which would have been curtailed in the absence of state rescue action) were most used by those with the lowest incomes.

We hesitate in these careful days to suggest an opposition of interest between the rich and the poor. One should not stir the embers of the class struggle. To encourage envy is uncouth, possibly even un-American. But any general assault on the public services must be understood for what it is; it is an attack on the living standard of the poor.

The *romantic* attack on the social consensus, to which I now turn, has superficially a more powerful intellectual base. It calls on the two-hundred-year-old tradition of classical and neoclassical economics which holds that all possible economic decision should be left to the freely competitive market. No other system is socially so efficient or responds more genuinely to the will of the consumer. None rewards more reliably the competent response or punishes more reliably the incompetent one. The social consensus has impaired the operation of the market in two ways: first, by enlarging the public sector, it has diminished, *pro tanto*, the market sector of the economy; second, by accepting and encouraging a large and varied range of regulation, it has interfered with the free operation of markets. So for this reason too government must be reduced in scale. And, more specifically, it must remove the regulatory shackles from private enterprise and restore the market. In the recent campaign this demand was strident. It is an appeal that can be counted upon to arouse the interest of numerous, otherwise quite placed economists. Here is the opportunity to protect or retrieve the textbook market to which the intellectual capital of much of the profession is still firmly mortgaged.

I have called this attack on the consensus romantic; that is because it ignores the historical forces which make practical steps to restore the market deeply unappetizing. And it makes them especially unappetizing to the very people who urge reestablishing the primacy of the market.

Specifically, the greatest historical force against the market is the modern great corporations. Of these, a couple of thousand now produce around 60 percent of all private product in the United States. This is not exceptional; the concentration is similar in the other industrial countries. These corporations have substantial discretion in setting their prices. They extensively influence the taste of consumers. They similarly organize their supplies of raw materials. With all of this they erode the power of the market. And, given the scale of their investment and the long-term horizons involved, this is what corporations must do. Planning in a partially controlled setting is essential for modern corporate operations. Such planning the classical market does not allow.

But a crusade against corporations does not attract the free-market philosophers. One does not turn the guns on one's own cavalry. So it must be pretended that the modern corporation does not exist. Or with equal implausibility it must be urged that General Motors, Shell, IBM, Philips, and Nestlé are only a slightly enlarged manifestation of the classical atomism of the market. Mobil is just the corner grocer grown up. This latter effort, regularly undertaken by corporate spokesmen, serves principally to cultivate the suspicion that the large corporation somehow lacks legitimacy. Something must be fishy when corporate spokesmen (or compliant economics professors) are forced to argue that Exxon and the friendly neighborhood news vendor are the same economic institution — that each is governed by the same inexorable competitive forces; each is subordinate to the same impersonally determined market prices; neither has a significant political role in the state.

A few of the devout who seek the revival of the market do call for vigorous action to restore competition — for action to arrest and reverse the trend to industrial concentration. But that again is to turn the guns on one's own troops. It also requires action by the government — an alliance with the enemy. And even for the passionate, the antitrust laws, which are the traditional instrument, are a serious strain on faith. We have had them now for ninety years; how much longer do we have to wait before they become effective against industrial concentration?

So, in one way or another, those who defend the market must contrive to ignore the modern great corporation and conglomerate — not an easy thing to do. And few of the other forces degrading the classical market are attractive as political antagonists. Farmers in all the industrial countries have replaced their market with state-supported minimum prices. But few conservatives wish to take on the farmers, and farmers are often conservative too. OPEC has set the market aside for oil. But OPEC is beyond reach. Trade unions powerfully influence their own wage claims and set the pattern for wages in general. But unions fight back. So it comes about in the United States that practical action against the forces infringing upon the free market regularly ends up (as predictably in these last weeks) in proposals for reducing or reforming the minimum wage. An attack on the minimum wage, the poor man's union, is, almost uniquely, safe.

The elimination of other government regulation that interferes with the free expression of market forces also encounters the difficulty that much of it is very much wanted by those who most protest their devotion to the market. The crusade against unnecessary, crippling, costly, and otherwise repressive government regulation goes hand in hand with a desperate effort by the trucking companies to preserve licensing and otherwise to restrict competition in interstate transport. It goes along with a parallel effort by the steel companies to have target prices and to regulate steel imports; and with an effort by the textile companies to keep quotas on cloth imports; and with a demand by the auto industry to ease the competition from Japanese cars; and with a keen wish by all who fly that there be nothing casual about government standards of maintenance for the DC–10. Even in Southern California, the home turf of the New Right and Ronald Reagan, there is no urgent demand for more air pollution. Thus it emerges that unnecessary regulation is what those urging regulation do not happen to need.

The conflict with reality in which those opposing regulation find themselves in a highly organized, highly technological, interdependent society could not be better illustrated than in the case of nuclear power. Just as the advocates of nuclear freedom were gearing themselves up a year and a half ago for a major campaign against government regulation came the accident at Three Mile Island. And just as they recovered their equilibrium came the recent trouble at Indian Point, New York. Ideology is a wonderfully flexible thing; it gives its exponents a wide range of choice. Circumstance, in contrast, is very confining. And it is circumstance that largely governs. This the Reagan years will admirably reveal.

The market, none should doubt, continues to render highly useful service. In economics there are no absolutes. But the only possible policy toward the market, either for conservatives or liberals, right or left, is one of open-minded pragmatism. Where it works, the market should be allowed to work. Where it doesn't, regulation has to be accepted.

I come now to the attack on the economic and social consensus which I called *real*. It holds that expenditure on public welfare services has involved no careful judgment on need or cost; more has been believed to be better. And that the quality of public administration has been seriously deficient. And finally and most importantly it holds that the macroeconomic management of the consensus no longer works. On all three points the attack seems to me justified; on all three the economic and social consensus is vulnerable.

On public welfare and social expenditure — for housing, health care, various forms of direct welfare support, education, and public services in general — active exponents of the consensus have indeed taken the position that the more the better. The basic test has been what conservatives could be made to accept.

For so long as whatever was done by way of social insurance, welfare payments, health care, housing, was elementary or limited, this was a workable test. But it was workable only under conditions of general insufficiency. Thereafter an objective consideration of opportunity cost was needed. The effect of public outlays on such a direct and widely used levy as the property tax needed especially to be considered. It cannot be thought reactionary that such tests be applied. On the contrary, the older working assumption that more is always better was certain at some point to become intellectually and politically discrediting. I do not suggest, however fashionable it might be at the moment, that our public-service and social-welfare expenditures are too high, and certainly not for those who use or need them most. Comparing generally the quality and extent of the public services with the extent and variety of private consumption, one can be certain that the balance wonderfully favors the latter. I argue only for better tests of sufficiency — tests that, at a minimum, contribute to a better defense of social expenditures than we have now.

The second vulnerable point of the economic and social consensus concerns the quality of public management. When they are judged by the same standards, public bureaucracy is not obviously inferior either in moral tone or even in efficiency to private bureaucracy. Incompetence and failure in the leadership of private corporations are commonplace. So is dishonesty. Chrysler has for many years had a reputation in automobile circles for cloning inadequacy. This is now conceded; its advertising speaks of the "new" Chrysler Corporation. No public agency ever descended to a deeper level of incompetence than Penn Central in its final years. In these last months NBC, one of the guardians of our public virtue, has been contending with the imaginative larceny of its own unit managers.

Many years ago I divided my efforts between Time Inc. and the federal government. One could not doubt that it took more people earning more money to do less work in New York than in Washington. One had a blessed feeling of relaxation on returning to private enterprise. Expense-account writing at Time was a small creative art, so discussed. Everyone dealt righteously with the U.S. Treasury. When an important and articulate man in the State Department wore out or was too obviously dissolving in alcohol, he was made ambassador to a minor country or the consul-general in Naples. At Time, if similarly important, he was promoted to corporate vice president and put in charge of looking into new publishing opportunities.

But none of this excuses inferior performance by the public agency. It is under far more rigorous scrutiny by both those whom it serves and those who pay for it. And more attention is paid to training for private management than for public. Business schools train private administrators by the thousands. No comparable effort goes into training in the theory and practice of public administration. Performance in public office, as in sex, is still believed to be extensively a matter of basic instinct.

The solution is without novelty. Defenders of the consensus must be far more concerned with the quality of public management and address ever more seriously the development of a force of public managers of the highest level of intelligence and proficiency. They must be men and women who believe in public service and public enterprise, who take pride in seeing performance that improves on private capitalism, and who take a substantial part of their reward in their own sense of accomplishment.

The important, indeed decisive, failure of the consensus has been in the macroeconomic management of the economy — its failure to deal effectively with inflation and unemployment. This was a major part of its promise. No one can doubt that an attack here is justified — that this is a point of conspicuous vulnerability. There is verification in the fact that in those industrial countries which have succeeded in combining high employment with stable prices, West Germany and Austria being the notable examples, the economic and social consensus has remained invulnerable.

In the two decades following World War II, the primary need of macroeconomic management was to counter deflation and unemployment. In the United States and elsewhere this was done by increasing expenditures and reexpenditures from borrowed funds through low interest rates and easy lending conditions — monetary policy. And it was accomplished by increased public services and expenditure or by reduced taxes and increased private expenditure — fiscal policy. None of these measures involved any serious political conflict with any important economic interest. Nor do lower interest rates, lower taxes, or higher public expenditures encounter any serious public objection. Since prices were relatively stable — a not surprising thing in the context of the concern for deflation and unemployment — union wage settlements and their effect on prices were not a matter for great anxiety. Everything was pleasant in those years for economists and economic policy. It was something to which economic policy makers became accustomed.

But in those years — roughly from 1948 to 1969 — changes were in process that drastically altered both the economic and the political context of macroeconomic policy. Corporate concentration, a singular and indubitable feature of capitalist development, however sophisticated the denial, continued. So did the power of corporations to hold and increase prices — to escape the discipline of the market. Trade unions were still of only slight power in the United States at the beginning of World War II. In the other industrial countries they had been weakened by depression or suppressed by fascism. Now, after the war, they asserted their claims everywhere with increasing confidence and effect and, as earlier noted, set the pattern for all wages. Corporations, in turn, after ritualistic objection, passed the cost of wage settlements on to the public. Farm prices in the industrial countries were also now supported by governments. And with OPEC, third world countries entered the game.

The game, in effect, was to set aside the market and win the power to raise prices and incomes. When used, this power became the new and intractable form of inflation. Prices could still rise as a consequence of strong demand. But prices now also rose as the result of the strong upward pressure of corporations, trade unions, farmers, oil producers, and other organized power.

This new development was admirably designed to weaken the economic and social consensus and encourage attack. With inflation the costs of government go up and so do taxes. When taxes, property taxes in particular, are relatively stable, they are much less noticed. When they are going up, they are greatly visible and much resented. This resentment is then transmuted into an attack on all public services. And the inability to control inflation conveys a further impression, not unjustified, of government inadequacy or incompetence.

As damaging to the consensus were the measures which were taken to deal with inflation. Monetary policy was the first resort. This requires no legislation, only a pliable central bank. Here Professor Friedman, the omnipresent and, by a wide margin, the most eloquent figure in the great conservative revolt, comes to the foreground again. Control the money supply, have it increase only as the economy expands, and you control everything. There may be some initial discomfort and unemployment; presently all will be well.

Unfortunately central banks have not yet learned to control the money supply with any precision. Nor under modern circumstances, when money can be anything from currency to bank deposits to savings deposits to unused lines of credit, is it at all clear what is to be controlled. Controlling what you don't know you are controlling is difficult. And running through all monetary action is a disconcerting uncertainty about the relationship between action and effect. In 1979 in the United States there was an intense discussion over whether tighter bank lending and higher interest rates would cause a recession. The most self-confidently learned participants said it would and were wrong. Then in 1980 there was a further tightening, and the experts turned out to be right. Thus the recession that coincided so admirably for the Republicans with the election. There is a strong case against a policy that has a largely random result.

Going on from the uncertainty of the connection between action and effect, monetary policy has other adverse consequences. It discriminates sharply against those industries, housing being the notable case, which rely on borrowed money. Strong corporations (unlike Chrysler) with capital from earnings and the ability to pass costs along in prices are much less affected. Working against inflation through a reduction in investment spending, monetary policy has a highly adverse effect on productivity. And most important, it works against the inflation caused by corporate, union, and other organized power only as it creates enough unemployment to soften union claims and enough idle plant capacity to make it difficult for corporations to raise prices. To get price stability in this way requires very strong monetary action. Even though the recent recession was painful, politically and otherwise, it did not arrest — has not arrested — inflation. This, given the new power of organization, was altogether predictable.

The reliance on monetary policy has thus been deeply damaging to the economic and social consensus. Fiscal action which controls demand by controlling private and public consumption would have been less so. It is more predictable in effect, it does not favor the large firm over the small, and, since its restraining effect is on consumption, it is not directly damaging to productivity. Unfortunately fiscal policy — higher taxes, reduced public expenditure — is, to put it mildly, politically inconvenient. For this reason policy makers in recent times, looking as ever for soft solutions, have been reluctant to use it. Instead we have combined inflation with tax reductions and compensated with ever more severe monetary policy.

But fiscal policy also works against the inflationary pricing of strong corporations and strong unions only as it creates a substantial amount of idle capacity and of unemployment — until a recession becomes the restraining influence on wages and prices. Economic change — corporate concentration, trade union strength, other power to influence income — has thus rendered all of the measures of the old consensus against inflation ineffective except as they induce idle capacity and unemployment. Such has been the fate of the macroeconomic management which was one of the three pillars of the consensus.

The arrival of the Reagan administration in the United States will not be very useful to those who would like to move on from the consensus. That is because its design for economic management incorporates all of the old elements of failure in a somewhat exaggerated form. As a result, adherents to the old consensus will be able to accumulate negative capital merely by sitting quietly and awaiting the failures. Specifically, the Reagan administration promises higher defense expenditures, which are certain. And it promises lower taxes, which are almost certain. And it promises to reduce *total* federal expenditure by reducing the relatively small volume of noncontractual civilian expenditures, i.e., expenditures other than for interest, social security, and the like.

This it cannot do; and the consensus not being vulnerable in respect of these residual expenditures the administration will make itself wonderfully unpopular if it seriously tries. With lower taxes and public spending as high as or higher than before, fiscal policy under President Reagan will, if anything, be more inflationary than in the past. The new administration promises further that the present rather primitive arrangements for restraining wages and prices will be abandoned; indeed, these cannot be tolerated by scholars for whom all forms of government regulation are repugnant — for whom the market, however deteriorated, is still a totem. So there will have to be greater reliance than ever before on monetary policy. As the arch-exponent of monetarism, Professor Milton Friedman has great days ahead.

This will not be his unalloyed good fortune. There are grave disadvantages in being associated with a policy that, however persuasively it is defended, does not work. Professor Friedman has already been forced to dissociate himself from Chile and Israel where he was once celebrated as a prophet. And the Friedman policy in Britain has so far produced only high inflation, deep internal stagnation, the highest unemployment since the Great Depression, and some indication that Professor Friedman would like to detach from Mrs. Thatcher as well. But deep as is my compassion for an old friend, my present concern is for the effect on the adherents to the consensus. Their tendency will be to relax comfortably in the discovery that monetarism means either high unemployment and high rates of inflation or a little less unemployment and yet more inflation. Were it otherwise, were there here a simple formula for solving our troubles, it would have been in general use long before now.

What will be needed by defenders of the consensus is not relaxation but a vigorous effort to bring it abreast of the changes that rendered it vulnerable. This means, as noted, better tests of what is sufficient and affordable in public services and public welfare. It means all possible steps to ensure better public management. But it requires, most of all, acceptance of the logic of modern corporate, union, and other organized power and its effect on price-making and inflation.

A firm resourceful use of fiscal policy is still necessary. When demand presses on resources, there must be increased taxes, and these must be primarily on the affluent. This is the alternative to the excessive — and disastrous — reliance on monetary policy to limit demand or a heartless manipulation of the public services to the poor. I would urge increased use of indirect taxation on objects of upper-income or luxury consumption; it is hard to have tears for those who must pay more for luxury automobiles, furniture, housing, attire, or entertainment. Even those so taxed have some reluctance in pleading hardship. There must also be a general stand against tax concessions to the rich, and this applies to virtually all talk of incentives. Lurking behind the word incentives, we must never forget, is always the wish of someone for more income.

Corporations now have an admirable tendency to invest when they foresee a profit; tax reduction does not turn a prospective loss into a profit. It is the pride of the modern corporate executive that he gives his all to his enterprise; it is insulting to him to suggest that he grades his effort to his after-tax income. And he would be fired were he thought to do so. Taxes on unearned income and inheritance are good for the work ethic; over time they return the rich and their offspring to useful toil. It is one of the oddities of our time that we think the work ethic to be particularly ethical for those in the lower income brackets. A well-considered use of leisure by the affluent is a mark of civilized behavior.

But we must also have direct action to hold wages and salaries to what can be afforded at current prices. And likewise, and as firmly, there must be action, enforced as necessary by law, to restrain industrial prices where market power is great. No market principles are violated when the state moves to fix those prices that, as the product of industrial concentration, are already fixed. And other income that is subject to organized enhancement must similarly be subject to restraint. This is not as great a task as is sometimes imagined. The centralization of market power by corporations, unions, and farm organizations that causes inflation in its modern form greatly reduces the number of firms and organizations that must be controlled. It is not the classical market that is being replaced. That has obviously gone forever and that is the problem.

Thus the task. The consensus must, of course, be defended at its positions of present strength. But here there will be great support from circumstance. The real task is to repair, renew, and redesign it at its points of present failure.

NOTES

1. Richard Scammon and Ben Wattenberg, *The Real Majority* (New York: Coward McCann, 1970).

2. William Simon, *A Time for Truth* (New York: Reader's Digest Press, McGraw-Hill, 1978), pp. 219, 218.

3. Professor Laffer's inspired use of purely fortuitous hypotheses, it is only fair to note, has been a source of some discomfort to some of his more scrupulous conservative colleagues.

4. Professor Friedman's foreword to William Simon's *A Time for Truth*, p. xiii.

5. Milton and Rose Friedman, *Free to Choose* (New York: Harcourt Brace Jovanovich, 1979, 1980), p. 7.

6. Friedman, p. 65.

How to Wreck the Economy

LESTER THUROW

Reagan is proposing to increase defense expenditures by $142 billion, from $162 billion for the fiscal year 1981 to $304 billion in fiscal year 1985, the last budget of his first term. If re-elected he is planning a further $39 billion increase, to $343 billion in fiscal 1986.

This $181 billion increase over five years can be understood only if it is compared with the build-up of military spending during the Vietnam War. In the five years between 1965 and 1970 military spending rose by $24.2 billion, and soon after rose to a peak of $26.9 billion. After correcting for inflation, a $26.9 billion increase then would be equivalent to a $59 billion increase now.

As a result the military build-up that is currently being contemplated is three times as large as the one that took place during the Vietnam War. Whether an increase of this magnitude is really necessary depends on an analysis of foreign affairs and military readiness that is beyond this review. Some defense experts and legislators are questioning whether many items in the new military budget are actually needed and whether some of them endanger national security more than they protect it. Such questions are certainly important and must be raised. But if such a build-up is necessary, then it is important that it be done in such a way that it does the least possible damage to the economy.

The Reagan budget has not been clearly understood because, perhaps deliberately, it has been presented as a set of subtractions from or additions to the Carter budget. The policies of President Carter are now irrelevant. It makes no difference what he proposed. Everything that is in the budget is now a Reagan proposal. The only questions to be resolved turn on what President Reagan wants.

In addition to the increase in the military budget, civilian expenditures are scheduled to rise by $76 billion — from $493 billion to $569 billion. After correcting for inflation, we can see that civilian expenditures are down substantially by 16 percent, although they rise in money terms. As a result the total budget increases from $655 billion in fiscal 1981 to $912 billion in fiscal 1986. In addition, President Reagan is proposing a 16 percent reduction in federal tax collections — $196 billion in fiscal 1986 — in order to stimulate savings and investment.

President Johnson's refusal to raise taxes to pay for the Vietnam War is legitimately remembered as one of the key factors leading us into our current economic mess. He wanted both the Great Society and the war. But if he was to have both and not wreck the economy, his only option was to raise taxes sharply. He chose not to do so, and he wrecked the economy.

President Reagan wants both dramatic tax cuts to encourage investment and an even more extensive military build-up. But he cannot have both without wrecking the economy further unless he is willing to raise taxes dramatically on private consumption. He has chosen not to do so. If his current program is carried out, he too will wreck the economy.

Military spending is a form of consumption. It does not increase our ability to produce more goods and services in the future. While it may be necessary, it is consumption nonetheless. And as in any private budget, if you allocate more to one form of consumption, you must allocate less to some other form of consumption.

This means equivalent cuts must be made in other forms of consumption. The proposed military increase is so large that it cannot be fully paid for with cuts in civilian expenditures unless the president is willing to abolish major social programs such as Social Security. If he is not willing to do this, taxes must be raised to cut private consumption.

While President Reagan is only preparing for war and not actively engaging in one, the economic problems of military spending spring from the rapid production of weapons, not from their use. The capacity to produce capital goods and equipment, skilled manpower, and raw materials must all be quickly redirected to military production. In shifting both human and capital resources from civilian to military activities tremendous strains are placed on the domestic economy, unless measures are taken to restrain private consumption. Without tax increases the military can get only the necessary capital capacity, skilled manpower, and raw materials by paying more than the civilian economy is willing to pay. This drives up prices and creates civilian shortages.

The problem is compounded if tax breaks are to be given for investment, as is contemplated by Reagan's economic plan. The capital goods industries cannot produce enough equipment to build both military factories and civilian factories. The investment tax reductions therefore encourage private investors to get into a bidding war with the military for the industrial equipment that is available. The result would be a rapid rate of inflation in capital goods that would eventually lead to inflation in consumer goods. Inflation would break out, as it did during the Vietnam War, but this time the United States would be adding inflation to an economic system that already has an 11 percent rate of inflation rather than to a system that had an inflation rate of less than 2 percent.

Unfortunately the negative effects of such a military budget and such a tax policy do not emerge quickly. Remember the acceleration in inflation during the Vietnam period. It was very slow but very persistent. During 1965 inflation stood at 1.7 percent per year. From there it rose to 2.9 percent in 1966–1967, to 4.2 percent in 1968, to 5.4 percent in 1969, and to 5.9 percent in 1970. President Nixon temporarily stopped inflation with wage and price controls in 1971, but when those controls were lifted inflation broke out in an even more virulent form, and has continued to this day.

As with President Johnson, the mistakes of President Reagan will only become obvious long after they have been made. By the time they are obvious, it will be too late to correct them. If the mistakes are to be corrected and the undesirable effects avoided, the correction must be made now — not two to three years from now.

President Reagan talks as if his cuts in civilian government consumption are going to pay for the extra military spending. But he also talks as if those civilian budget cuts are going to pay for the loss in revenue from business tax cuts and from the 30 percent cut in personal income taxes called for by the Kemp-Roth plan. But the sums that will be spent and saved do not match. A $138 billion cut ($43 billion of which has not yet been announced) in civilian expenditures — not an absolute cut but one relative to the Carter budget — simply does not counterbalance a $196 billion tax cut and a $181 billion increase in military spending

If the Reagan administration were to carry out its current plans, it would have no rational alternative to a large tax increase on private consumption. If we were actually to fight World War III, we would instantly increase taxes to pay for it. If we want quickly to buy the equipment the administration claims is necessary to fight World War III, we have to be willing to do the same.

If the administration is unwilling to raise taxes on private consumption, it will repeat the Vietnam experience. Initially output will rise and unemployment will fall. But eventually a sustained inflation will result from the economy's inability to produce both the civilian and military goods that are being demanded of it. But the economic problems of a large increase in military spending go far beyond that of simply keeping total consumption under control. The defense department does not demand exactly the same commodities that civilians give up when their after tax income goes down. Even if taxes are raised by the requisite amount, essential supplies will have to be directed to military uses without completely disrupting the civilian economy.

To do this, most countries when they decide to wage war or prepare for war traditionally impose controls over production, wages and prices, raw materials, and capital equipment. In this respect, the Korean War is a model of what to do. The Vietnam War is a model of what not to do.

During the Korean War America raised taxes dramatically at the beginning of the war and imposed a full range of wartime controls. When the war proved to be smaller than was first expected, those controls could be gradually eased with no disruption to the civilian economy. Instead of rising during the war, inflation fell from 6.6 percent in the first year of the war to 1.6 percent in the last year of the war.

By contrast, during the 1960s the U.S. did none of the things that would have been necessary to fight the Vietnam War without economic damage. Military spending reached a peak of 13 percent of the gross national product during the Korean War and only 9 percent in the Vietnam War, but the economic damage was far greater during the Vietnam War. The economics of war production calls for planning for the worst possible economic effects and then being pleasantly surprised if the worst does not occur. Perhaps our economy will be able to take the current build-up without being wrenched out of shape, but no one should count on it.

The economic problems of the military build-up planned to take place between 1981 and 1988 are complicated by the current weakness of the American economy and the economic strength of the countries that are our military allies but our economic adversaries. When a nation such as the U.S. sharply increases its military forces, it generally does so at a time when its industrial competitors are also attempting to increase their own military establishments, and are experiencing comparable economic strains. But the Reagan build-up is to take place in a time when our allies are not raising their military expenditures at anything like our pace. Germany has just announced plans to cut back on its defense budget.

This difference poses the problem of how the U.S. can maintain the industrial strength to compete with other countries in civilian production and sales. The basic problem here is not so much one of obtaining critical raw materials and equipment, although there may be shortages of both, but is one of skilled workers — craftsmen, engineers, and scientists. Such people will tend to be attracted to military production. Defense contractors will entice workers away from civilian firms by paying higher salaries as they build up their work forces on a crash basis. But even if the salaries were identical there would be a tendency for the most highly qualified people to move into defense. For most engineers, such work is simply more exciting.

Would the typical engineer rather work on designing a new missile with a laser guidance system or on designing a new toaster? To ask the question is to answer it. Military research and development are more interesting since they are usually closer to the frontiers of scientific knowledge and are not limited by economic considerations such as whether the product can be sold in the market. The military is willing to pay almost any premium to have a superior product. The civilian economy is not. As a result the most skilled technicians and scientists move into defense.

But suppose you own a civilian computer firm in Boston and many of your best people leave to work in Boston's higher paying and more exciting aerospace firms. How do you compete with Japanese computer firms that will not be losing their most brilliant employees? The Japanese engineer might also like to work on missiles but he does not have the opportunity to do so. The result is that you cannot compete; the Japanese computer industry could well drive the American computer industry out of business.

A military build-up of the magnitude proposed by President Reagan almost demands that the U.S. insist that its military allies, who are also its economic competitors, engage in a similar military build-up. From the point of view of equity, the American taxpayer cannot be expected to accept a large reduction in his standard of living while taxpayers abroad continue to improve their standards of living. But even more importantly, America cannot afford to destroy the competitive strength of its none-too-strong domestic economy. If the skilled workers and funds that are used for defense here are used for civilian production abroad, it should not come as a great surprise if we are driven out of civilian markets. What will happen to the United States if the industries that manufacture semi-conductors, micro-processors, and computers are forced out of business while the nation is busy rearming itself? What good does it do us to dominate the world in missile production if we are at the same time being defeated in toasters? In the long run, a civilian economy that consistently fails in competition abroad will be unable to produce missiles for an effective military economy.

According to the Reagan economic scenario, the burden of total government spending will shrink not because of a decrease in that spending, but because there will be an explosion of economic output. After we correct for inflation, output is supposed to grow 23 percent during the next five years.

This explosion in output is predicted for an economy where growth in productivity has been gradually slowing down since 1965 and has in fact been negative during the last three years. The Reagan administration assumes that productivity is going to return to a 3 percent rate of growth almost instantly, but what will make this happen? Such an increase in productivity has never happened before in our history, and there are good technical reasons for believing that it will not happen now.

Our slowdown in productivity is caused by many factors, including an increasing movement toward services, and sharp declines in construction and mining productivity. These are not going to end suddenly. And the same slow transition will occur in the part of the economy on which the Reagan administration is focusing most of its attention – investment. New investment takes time. Major new industrial facilities typically take from five to ten years to complete, so we will have no output from them for five to ten years. Consequently they will not be raising productivity for five to ten years.

If a little extra investment would cure our productivity problem we would not have such a problem at all. When productivity was growing at more than 3 percent per year, from 1948 to 1965, Americans invested 9.5 percent of their GNP in industrial plant and equipment. While productivity was falling 0.5 percent a year from 1977 to 1980, Americans invested 11.3 percent of their GNP in industrial plant and equipment. We need more investment, but investment cannot cure the productivity problem in the short run.

But in planning a major military build-up, a wise economic general does not argue about whether there will, or will not, be a dramatic rebound in the growth of productivity. He plans such a rapid increase on the conservative assumption that there will not be a sharp change in productivity and hopes to be pleasantly surprised if productivity does in fact dramatically improve. No permanent damage occurs if he plans for slow productivity and finds that productivity is actually growing rapidly. He can always easily cut taxes if the economy has extra unused productive capacity. But if he plans for rapid growth in productivity and it does not occur, the economic damage will be great. Taxes can be raised later on, but as the Vietnam War demonstrated, a tax increase in 1969 does not substitute for a tax increase that should have occurred in 1965.

If vigorous growth resumes, as the Reagan administration assumes it will, the defense budget will generate the kinds of economic stress that we experienced during the Vietnam War. Under Reagan's assumptions about economic growth, the military budget will consume an extra 1.5 percent of the Gross National Product. Vietnam consumed an extra 1.7 percent. But if vigorous growth does not resume, the strains will be far more serious. The military will be absorbing an extra 2.4 percent of the GNP. As a result we should plan for those larger stresses but hope for the smaller ones.

These economic difficulties will also be magnified by the plans for the civilian budget. A 16 percent cut in taxes is supposed to stimulate savings and investment but it is directed at the wrong targets. Any across-the-board tax cut such as Kemp-Roth must confront the fact that the average American family saved only 5.6 percent of its income in 1980. Past experience strongly suggests that given a $100 tax cut, the average American will save and invest $5.60, but will also consume $94.40. In view of our needs for investment and of the military program the administration demands, we simply cannot afford to add private consumption of this magnitude to our economic system. We should be cutting consumption.

Similarly, many of the investment tax cuts proposed by Reagan are poorly conceived. A cut in the capital gains tax that includes both investment in plant and equipment and speculative investment — in land, homes, gold, antiques, paintings, etc. — may suck investment funds out of productive investments and into speculative investments, since speculative investments pay off faster than productive investments. But we need productive investments, not speculative investments. If supply-side economics were to make sense, it would include tax increases for speculative investments.

The current proposal for accelerated depreciation on a "10-5-3"[1] basis gives the largest breaks to commercial buildings and may well encourage the construction of more shopping centers rather than industrial factories. Here again the largest tax breaks should favor new industrial facilities.

The administration's cuts in the civilian budget have relatively little to do with economics. They are good or bad depending upon your view of what constitutes adequate provision for the needy in a good society. My ethics tell me that there is something wrong with cutting nutrition programs for poor pregnant women. Mr. Stockman's ethics tell him that they are precisely the group whose benefits should be cut. Perhaps that is the difference between learning one's ethics and economics in a department of economics rather than at a divinity school.

There is, however, one major economic problem with the proposed cuts in expenditures. Most of the cuts focus on the working poor — essentially the group that is above the poverty line but within $3,000 of it. This group is going to be faced with a choice. The Reagan administration assumes that a cut in the social welfare benefits for the working poor will force them to work more. It is more likely that it will encourage them to work less to regain eligibility for the programs that they have just lost.

Suppose you are one of the working poor and have a sick child. One choice is to work harder — perhaps by taking a second job — in order to pay the necessary medical bills. Another is to quit working to make yourself eligible for Medicaid. To pose the choices is to give the likely answer. If the second choice prevails, the remaining social welfare programs will have to expand and will cost more than expected. The cuts in the civilian budget will therefore be smaller than the ones now projected. The result will be that the grave strains imposed on the economy by Reagan's military build-up will become graver still. The dangers of this budget are such that I can think of no priority higher for the nation's economic welfare than close and skeptical scrutiny of all new military expenditures to determine whether they are really needed.

NOTES

1. This means that autos and light machinery can be depreciated over three years; other, generally heavier, machinery over five years; and a variety of real estate over ten years.

POLITICS

The American Counterrevolution brought to pass by the election of President Reagan had as a persistent campaign slogan: "Get the government off our backs." From the standpoint of the program of the religious New Right, the general and special imperatives of power providing guidance for policy implementation, amidst storms of transition, include counsel both to weaken and to strengthen action by government:

> Stop busing children to get racial equality.
>
> Bring prayer back to the public schools.
>
> Enforce stronger laws against marijuana.
>
> Mete out capital punishment for capital offenses.
>
> Register Christians to vote and take them to the polls.
>
> Make the Bible the foundation of our government and our laws.

Joined with exhortations to back the citizens' tax revolt against Big Government are counsels to foster a religious revival so our nation can survive. Behind both imperatives are others that bare the overall political objectives of the New Right:

> Replace liberals in all major American institutions.
>
> Become the permanently dominant power in the Congress, the Courts, and the White House.

The electoral triumph of the New Right in 1980 has raised questions about the impact of the evangelicals. Our selection, "The Election and the Evangelicals," disputes the claim that the religious New Right had a discernible effect on the election that swept conservatives into the Senate, and elected Ronald Reagan President. Seymour Martin Lipset, Professor of Political Science and Sociology and Senior Fellow of the Hoover Institution, Stanford University, was joined by co-author Earl Raab, Executive Director of the Jewish Community Relations Council of San Francisco. The University of Chicago has now issued an updated paperback edition of a classic they co-authored, The Politics of Unreason: Right-Wing Extremism in America.

The thesis of our Lipset-Raab selection has been questioned by James M. Wall, editor of the interdenominational weekly The Christian Century. Wall holds that Lipset and Raab developed a false definition of an evangelical, which led them to dissociate the nation's movement to the Right from the political action of the New Religious Right. Wall reads the election returns as "the reawakening of the fundamentalist right to its potential in the political arena." He asserts that Lipset and Raab would have us believe that such defeated liberal senators as George McGovern in South Dakota, John Culver in Iowa, and Frank Church in Idaho were merely victims of the nation's move to the Right in quest of a strong economy and a more assertive America. He concludes: "The three men named above, all of whom faced vicious, religiously bigoted campaigns — including references to 'baby-killing' (abortion) — are not likely to agree with this assessment . . . Until we see evidence to the contrary, we will have to acknowledge that the religious New Right played a major role in pushing this country to the right in 1980."

Wall is the author of our next selection, "An Ominous Threat to Books." Immediately after the 1980 elections, the rate of library censorship leaped 500 percent according to the American Library Association, which reports that efforts to ban books arose from four per week to four per day. The ALA's Office for Intellectual Freedom publishes a monthly Newsletter on Intellectual Freedom providing reliable reports on this dimension of America's new battle of faiths. Judith F. Krug, Director of the Office and co-editor of the Newsletter, gives figures on the New Right crusade to target library books: "We have had 148 titles challenged in 34 states. And that does not take into account that some titles, like Our Bodies, Ourselves, have each had a dozen or more challenges."

Among the works most often attacked are many American literary classics and best-sellers that have been circulating for years: Catcher in the Rye, Brave New World, Black Like Me, To Kill a Mockingbird, and Diary of Anne Frank. Despite the stature of these books, the fact is that censorship has been rising in the United States for the past ten years. Making It with Mademoiselle was banned by one school board, which reversed its decision when its members learned it was a how-to pattern book on dressmaking. It is not unusual for censoring authorities to ban books they have not read. Moreover, it is not to be expected that this new battle of the books will be readily won in the courts. So far the book protesters have been holding their own in most court proceedings.

America's new battle of faiths involves a series of church-state issues. Therefore, we include "The Separation of Church and State" by Dr. Leo Pfeffer, Special Counsel to the American Jewish Congress and Professor of Constitutional Law at Long Island University. Dr. Pfeffer is the author of major works in this field, including Church, State and Freedom: Creeds in Competition (with Anson Phelps Stokes), Church and State in the United States, and God, Caesar, and the Constitution. Drawing on this background, as well as his history of the Supreme Court of the United States, This Honorable Court, Dr. Pfeffer describes for Speak Out what appears to him to be an unholy triple alliance encompassing the Reagan administration, a hard-core right-wing faction of Congress under the leadership of Senator Jesse Helms of North Carolina, and Moral Majority, Inc.

The Election
and the Evangelicals

SEYMOUR MARTIN LIPSET & EARL RAAB

Since the 1980 presidential campaign many political observers have expressed deep concern over the growing political power of orthodox Christian groups in this country. According to one election scenario, it was the evangelical TV preachers who played a decisive role in the 1980 election. Not only did they elect Reagan to the Presidency, but, even more alarmingly, they also managed to unseat a number of liberal Senators through a massive, well-financed campaign to brand their targets as un-Christian political sinners. This campaign mobilized the fundamentalist constituency which was so decisive a factor in the conservative tide that swept the nation. And the worst — so the scenario concludes — is yet to come.

This version of recent events, while not entirely inaccurate, contains several crucial flaws. For one thing, it critically misstates the relation between religious beliefs and political attitudes among the evangelicals themselves. For another, it seriously overrates the political strength of organizations like the Moral Majority. And furthermore, it distorts the real meaning of the election results by placing much too narrow and short-sighted a construction on their significance.

Who are the evangelicals? One of their leading periodicals, *Christianity Today,* describes two general categories: "orthodox" and "conversionalist." The orthodox evangelicals are distinguished first by their belief in the literal word of the Bible, and second by their belief that Jesus is divine and the only hope for personal salvation. According to a *Christianity Today* Gallup Poll, taken in 1978, over 40 percent of the adult American population qualifies as evangelical according to orthodox criteria. These are the people commonly referred to as fundamentalists.

The conversionalist evangelicals differ from the orthodox in having had an explicit religious experience in which they asked Jesus to be their personal savior. These are the "born-again" Christians, and they need not be fundamentalists. A little over a third of American adults qualify as conversionalists by this criterion.

Both the fundamentalists and the conversionalists share a commitment to reaching out with the message of salvation and doing their best to convert others (in accordance with the Greek root of the term "evangelical" which means messenger).

All told, then, there are three criteria for qualifying as an evangelical: belief in the literal word of the Bible; a born-again experience; a commitment to proselytizing activity. Various polls taken in 1980 have found that between 20 and 25 percent of American adults qualify on all three counts. This tallies up to over 30 million adults.

Of these 30 million people, about 10 percent are Catholic, about a quarter are black, and a little more than one-third are male. About half live in the South, and about a quarter in the Midwest. Compared with the total population of the United States, they are somewhat less likely to be college graduates or to be in the upper income brackets, though factors of race, region, and sex account for more of this socioeconomic discrepancy than does the religious variable. Male Southern white high-school graduates who are evangelical, for example, will show about the same economic pattern as male Southern white high-school graduates who are not. Still, the fact remains that white evangelicals have an aggregate economic/ educational position slightly below that of the rest of the country. If there is an economic pinch, they are the ones who feel it most.

In the areas of political, economic, and social/cultural attitudes, there are some issues on which the evangelical population differs from its non-evangelical neighbors, and others on which it does not. On general economic and political issues, the evangelicals are themselves substantially split. When asked by a Gallup Poll in August, for example, whether there should be more government programs to deal with social problems — a flag-question for philosophical conservatives — slightly over half the country's evangelicals answered in the *affirmative*. Presented with two other such flag-questions — about support of firearm registration and support of ERA — slightly over half the evangelicals again replied positively. In fact, the poll showed that there was no statistical difference between evangelicals and nonevangelicals on attitudes toward firearm registration and nuclear power plants. Some differences were recorded on support of ERA (53–66), and increased defense spending (78–68), but they were by no means of tidal significance.

One lesson to be drawn from these figures is that the term "evangelical" is rather meaningless when interpreting reactions to general political issues. Blacks, for example, are disproportionately evangelical, comprising from one fifth to one quarter of the nation's evangelical population. Yet black evangelical attitudes toward the flag-questions differed sharply in the liberal direction from those of their co-religionists. And if the effect of the blacks' religious orthodoxy is submerged by their other life circumstances, then the political effect of the whites' religious orthodoxy cannot be assumed, either. Their other life circumstances must be taken into account as well.

The picture becomes a bit sharper, however, when we come to the area of social and cultural attitudes. The Survey Research Center (SRC) of the University of California once did a study attempting to correlate religious beliefs with attitudes toward the role of the state in economic affairs and toward cultural change, specifically in the area of manners and morals. Members of "fundamentalist" denominations (which include most Baptist groups as well as the Missouri Synod of the Lutheran Church) were compared with members of "liberal" denominations (Presbyterians and Methodists). In general, the SRC survey found that fundamentalist-church members were somewhat more conservative on economic issues than liberal-church members, although the difference between the two groups tended to flatten out when one adjusted for educational attainment. But in the matter of cultural conservatism, the story was very different. At each educational level, the gaps between fundamentalist-church adherents and others were much greater than in the area of economic attitudes. The overall percentage of cultural conservatives with a high religious commitment was radically larger than the percentage of those with a low religious commitment (62–6).

By the same token, while the total evangelical population is evenly divided on such indicators of political conservatism as state intervention in economic problems, it is fairly united on certain measures of cultural conservatism — especially those directly related to religious belief. Thus, about four out of five evangelicals would require prayers in the public schools and would also bar homosexual teachers from the schools, according to the September 1980 Gallup survey. Only a bare majority of non-evangelicals favor these policies.

We must bear in mind that religious fundamentalism and cultural conservatism have long gone together in this country. Religious identity is, after all, bound up with cultural tradition as part of a total way of life. When the security and status of that way of life appear threatened, its religious and moral content typically become rallying points of defense. Political figures who seem indifferent or hostile to these values will be seen as messengers of wickedness, while those politicians who appeal to them are likely to be invested with an aura of moral goodness.

This has been a recurrent pattern in American history. It was not in 1980 but in 1800 that a pamphlet was published with the ominous title, *Serious Considerations on the Election of a President, and a Voice of Warning to Christians in the Ensuing Election.* It warned that immorality would flourish if Thomas Jefferson were to be elected. Another pamphlet of the period predicted that Jefferson's election would mean "the consequent wonderful spread of infidelity, impiety, and immorality."

A similar note was sounded in a presidential campaign a hundred years later, when William Jennings Bryan ran against McKinley. As James Q. Wilson has noted recently in *Commentary*,[1] "Bryan's appeal was as much cultural and moral as economic and political. Fundamentalist Protestants were outraged over the moral decay of urban life . . . Bryan called not simply for a new economic order, but for the purification of society." So, too, in the 1920's the second Ku Klux Klan attracted heavy fundamentalist Protestant support while inveighing as much against immorality as against immigration. As Arnold Rice put it in his history of the KKK: "The 1920's meant 'modernism.' And 'modernism' among other things meant the waning of church influence, the breaking down of parental control, the discarding of the old-fashioned moral code."[2]

Even more important, "modernism" also meant rapid urbanization and industrialization, which implied in turn that more immigrants would be entering the country and demanding their share of political and economic power. The old world was breaking up and the older established population was losing control. The group most vulnerable to these changes was the fundamentalist Protestants — not because they were fundamentalist, but because they were by region, history, and education the group most rooted in the past, the one with the least capacity for adjusting to change. More significant than their religion and morality was their traditionalism. They were taking a stand against the whole sweep of modernity itself, and all the changes it signified, and in doing so they spoke for many other traditionalists who did not share their particular religious beliefs.

In different forms and under varying circumstances, this reaction has occurred over and over again in American history. It suggests that political orientation is not just an economic question, but is also a matter of mood. Negative political sentiment has often been generated by a sense of imminent deprivation, or diminishing status on the part of a substantial segment of the population.

Clearly, it was while in such a mood that many Americans, most of them not evangelicals, made their election choices this past fall. Even if their own status was not in question, many voters were registering displeasure at the diminishing status of America itself in the world. They were protesting American humiliation, and not even by another superpower but by a group of petty Middle Eastern despots.

Even the economic issues which dominated the campaign can be seen in this light. For most of us, inflation is more than just a pocketbook issue. It erodes the household budget but it also, more subtly, undermines past achievements. In the same way, the decline in American productivity and the growing superiority of foreign imports over our own products may be seen as issues of national status as much as of economics.

Actually, these issues of status far outweigh the factor of moral backlash that has been the subject of so much worried speculation since the election. Voters in 1980 were certainly expressing revulsion at what they perceived as an assault on traditional moral values. That particular beachhead, however, had been established over a decade before, and the evangelical preachers had been fighting ever since to enlarge it, with no great success. Not until a general backlash mood swept the country, precipitated by such matters as the Persian Gulf and the inflation rate, did the moral issue became an election factor, symbolizing for many the whole downward drift of the nation.

In attempting to ascertain the role of religion in all this, we must bear in mind that frustration over loss of status is concentrated — as it always has been — mainly in that sector of the white Protestant population that is disproportionately evangelical in religious persuasion. This population, as already noted, is much more conservative culturally than the rest of the country. But — except when it feels especially vulnerable or threatened — it is no more conservative politically. Thus, the evangelicals supported Franklin D. Roosevelt heavily in all four elections, they voted for Adlai Stevenson (as Albert Menendez's precinct study shows[3]) in the same proportion as the rest of the nation — and incidentally in a higher proportion than white nonevangelical Protestants — and they backed Johnson over Goldwater, again in the same overwhelming pattern as the rest of the country. They did not prefer Kennedy in 1960, but this was largely because of the Catholic issue.

The most drastic defection of the white evangelicals from the Democratic party occurred in the late '60s and '70s, in the era of the counterculture. During this turbulent period their votes for Humphrey and McGovern dropped to around one-third or less. Carter, by contrast, received about two-fifths of their vote in 1976, clearly because he was perceived as one of their own by many small-town evangelicals and white Southerners of similar background.

In sum, the traditionalism of the evangelicals does not impinge on their political orientation except when some aspects of modernity radically threaten their status and security. Then, more than others, they tend to express themselves in terms of outraged morality, which comes to symbolize everything they feel they are losing. But while the terms in which they couch their protest may be somewhat different from those of the rest of the country, they are not alone in their larger sense of loss. Certainly they had a lot of company in 1980.

To be sure, it is precisely this recourse to moralistic expression which gives rise to so much apprehension where the evangelical movement is concerned, echoing, as it does, the language of past right-wing extremist movements. But even more ominous than its moralistic terminology to historians of extremism is the connection frequently made in current evangelical doctrine between morality and political ideology. Jerry Falwell, the head of Moral Majority, makes such a link when he says that "What's happening to America is that the wicked are bearing rule." Christian Voice, another of the evangelical-political groups, makes the tie even more explicitly when it proclaims in its official statement of purpose: "We believe that America, the last stronghold of faith on this planet, has come under increasing attack from Satanist forces in recent years . . . that the standards of Christian morality . . . are now under the onslaught . . . launched by the 'rulers of darkness of this world' and insidiously sustained under the ever more liberal ethic."

What is alarming about these pronouncements is their fanaticism. If a political opponent is just wrong, or stupid, or misguided, he can presumably be dealt with in the marketplace of ideas. But when his political opinions arise from deliberate moral wickedness, as this kind of rhetoric implies, a case can be made that he does not deserve to be in the debate at all. It is only one step from here to a full-fledged conspiracy theory, wherein a cabal of evil men conspires secretly to thwart the popular will. This, of course, is the very model of political extremism, waiting only to be completed by the designation of one or another ethnic or religious group to represent the cabal.

There is every reason for nerves to jump at such an approach to politics. Inevitably, it recalls groups like the clergymen affiliated with the Ku Klux Klan in the 1920s or the Reverend Gerald Winrod's Defenders of the Christian Faith in the 1930s. Winrod, a fundamentalist preacher whose organization received wide support up until World War II, dwelt on the breakdown of morality in America, denouncing both political parties, though mainly the Democrats, for the country's moral turpitude. In 1938, he entered the Kansas Republican senatorial primary, and received 22 percent of the vote. Much of his animus was directed against the Jews, whom he called "contaminators in the moral realm as well as despoilers in the business field," but he was also strongly anti-black and anti-Catholic.

Today's evangelical groups have made it a point to avoid this kind of hatemongering. Though there is no denying that many evangelicals today are still wary of the Catholics, and have great theological problems with the Jews, and though one may argue further that the Moral Majority's focus on "Christian" values undermines the healthy pluralistic tone of the nation, nevertheless that organization has never even come close to incorporating in its platform the nativism and overt bigotry central to earlier groups. For the Reverend Gerald Winrod to have accepted an award from a national Jewish conclave, as Jerry Falwell recently did, is unimaginable. Indeed, so sensitive is the Moral Majority to Jewish fears that it has requested a "dialogue" with representatives of every major Jewish organization "to make the Jewish community aware that we are not an anti-Semitic group and that we probably are the strongest supporter of Israel in this country."

But it is not just in the absence of overt bigotry that today's evangelical Right has been more moderate than its predecessors. Though its public agenda calls for action on a whole range of domestic and international questions — from socialized medicine to relations with Taiwan and Zimbabwe — its real goals seem to be more limited. One observer, writing in the *Congressional Quarterly*, reports the movement's most concerted lobbying efforts to date have been the battles for voluntary school prayer and for an amendment restricting federal intervention in private, mainly Christian, schools[4] — important issues, but hardly global in their scope. Another observer, writing in the *National Catholic Reporter*, notes that the real core of the platform is Senator Paul Laxalt's Family Protection Act.[5] This bill, too, confines itself to fairly narrow questions — prayer in the schools, parental review of textbooks, elimination of tax laws requiring married couples to pay more than singles living together, and a number of other sections concerning gay rights and abortions.

In other words, thus far at least, the activity of right-wing evangelical political groups has centered on moral issues rather than on general political ones. As we have seen, these are the only matters on which the positions of the evangelical political groups have reflected the opinions of the general evangelical population. Whenever attempts have been made to stretch the Christian dimension beyond these specific religion-linked issues, they have provoked internal dissension. When, for example, the Harris Poll of October 6, 1980 asked whether it is impossible to be both a political liberal and a good Christian, both the general population and the white evangelical population disagreed overwhelmingly, as did a number of evangelical leaders.

Some, if not all, of these leaders have themselves been careful to make a distinction between moral questions and political ones. Thus, Carl Henry, a leading evangelical theologian, warns against making the jump from "individual spiritual rebirth to assuredly authentic and predictable public policy consequences . . ." He reminds his hearers that "equally devout individuals may disagree over the best program for achieving common goals."[6] Making the same point, an editorial in the most widely read evangelical journal, *Christianity Today*, said: "We get the impression that some evangelical lobbies on the political Right as well as liberal lobbies on the Left want us to believe that theirs is the only true Christian position on all issues. How can a policy board of evangelical Christians without access to vast amounts of intricate political data emerge from a meeting and announce that it has arrived at *the* Christian or moral position on lifting sanctions against Zimbabwe, for example?"[7]

If the right-wing evangelicals are not effective in seriously influencing their coreligionists on general political issues, what is the import of their activity? Perhaps they should be thought of not as evangelical groups but as straight right-wing political groups which happen to have an evangelical bent. Perhaps they are best seen organizationally as a part of the so-called New Right network.

That network includes Richard Viguerie and his famous computer in Falls Church, Virginia; Paul Weyrich and his Committee for the Survival of a Free Congress; Terry Dolan and his National Conservative Political Action Committee (NCPAC); and E. E. McAteer and Howard Phillips of the Conservative Caucus. These loosely knit groups had begun to see the usefulness of the "moral issues" to their cause well before the evangelical preachers got into the political business. In an interview in 1976, Viguerie predicted: "The next major area of growth for conservative ideology and philosophy is among the evangelicals." In a speech four years later at the National Press Club, Viguerie described how he, E. E. McAteer, Robert Billings, and Howard Phillips had devised and successfully implemented a plan to move "preachers-into-politics."

In 1978, Warren Billings, former head of the national Christian Action Coalition, which was then a school lobby, impressed both the evangelicals and the New Right when he used the mailing list of the Old Time Gospel Hour (whose minister was Jerry Falwell) to mobilize a massive letter-writing campaign opposing efforts of the IRS to remove the tax-exempt status of Christian schools which were not racially integrated. Weyrich, an Eastern-rite Catholic, helped form the Christian Voice with one of his close associates as its legislative consultant. Billings and Weyrich, along with Howard Phillips, a Jew, helped to establish the Moral Majority, with Jerry Falwell at its head. (Billings was at one time both the executive director of the Moral Majority and Weyrich's deputy at the Committee for the Survival of a Free Congress.[8])

While the sheer amount of time and money expended by this New Right apparatus may indeed have had some practical political consequences, especially in primaries and in targeted congressional districts where name-recognition was a factor, it is important, in attempting to understand the 1980 election, not to overstate that effect. Perhaps the most striking case in point is the results of the presidential vote itself. One of the consistent messages of the politicized preachers was that their evangelical constituency should vote for Reagan. But according to the *New York Times*/CBS election-day poll of voters as they left the booths, a slightly *smaller* percentage of born-again white Protestants (61 percent) than of other white Protestants (63 percent) actually voted for Reagan. A comparison of the 1976 and 1980 votes indicates as well that Carter lost less support among his fellow born-again Protestants than among others. In the election-day study, he retained a larger proportion (82 percent) of white evangelicals who said they had voted for him four years earlier than of other white Protestants (78 percent). This was true of the South as well (where the proportions were 86 percent to 76 percent). The drop-off in Carter's support among Catholics and Jews was somewhat greater than among the born-agains.

Results of the Senate elections cast further doubt on the assumption that the politicized evangelical groups and their New Right allies had much impact on the outcome. NCPAC, as we know, targeted five Northern liberal Democratic Senators — Bayh, Church, Cranston, Culver, and McGovern — and all of them except Cranston were defeated for reelection. But the decline in their vote was *almost identical* with that of the Democratic senatorial candidates in eighteen non-targeted states in the North. The average vote for the five liberal Senators fell from 54.5 percent in 1974 to 48 in 1980; the Democratic senatorial vote in the eighteen other Northern contests declined from 55 percent to 48. As Ronald Roberts, a staff member on the Republican Senatorial Campaign Committee, has pointed out, there were conservative victories in states like Wisconsin and New York, where the New Right and the politicized evangelicals were not very active, and liberal victories in states on New Right target lists, like California and Missouri.

It is harder to evaluate the impact of the political/religious Right on House races, given the large number of candidates involved, and the difficulty of measuring the effort actually expended in the various local constituencies. But it may be noted that NCPAC officially endorsed candidates in 103 contests, 57 of whom lost compared to 46 who were elected, a result which parallels closely the party distribution for all 435 House seats.

Strikingly enough, a number of Republican candidates who were supported by fundamentalist groups believe that they were not helped, and may even have been harmed, by these allies. James Abnor, who trounced George McGovern in the South Dakota senatorial race, denies that New Right groups were influential in the state and has even complained to the Federal Election Commission about the unauthorized use of his name by NCPAC. Charles Grassley, who defeated Senator John Culver in Iowa, also feels that the activities of the New Right groups had nothing to do with his success. An aide to Steven Symms, victor over Frank Church of Idaho, told the press that NCPAC had actually helped Church by making "erroneous charges" against him, emphasizing that "if anything, groups such as NCPAC probably hindered Steve Symms." Dan Quayle, who defeated Birch Bayh in Indiana, argued publicly late in the campaign that "New Right groups might cost the Republicans the election" in a number of states.

Statewide opinion surveys reinforce these judgments. In Indiana, polls show that the public had little familiarity with NCPAC slogans, and surveys taken for Symms in Idaho supported the claim that NCPAC, on balance, hurt him by a few percentage points.[9] Similar conclusions have been reached by Arthur Miller, a study director of the University of Michigan's Survey Research Center. Basing his judgment on interviews with 10,000 people, Miller believes that the impact of fundamentalist groups on the election outcome was much exaggerated. So too does Louis Harris who argues that the right-wing moralists actually hurt rather than helped the GOP cause, since "the country has moved slightly to the conservative side in opposing nearly all new government regulatory measures on economic matters, but has not moved at all to the Right on the social issues that are such an emotional concern to the die-hard right-wing conservatives."[10]

So far as the specific role of the TV preachers goes, that too seems to have been overestimated. A national Los Angeles *Times* survey in early September found that, among the half of the nation's evangelicals who watch or contribute to TV preachers, there was about a 3-to-2 majority favoring a constitutional amendment to ban abortion. Evangelicals who do *not* watch or support the TV preachers were evenly split on that question. In each group — the TV-watching and the non-watching evangelicals—three out of five agreed that the ERA was an attack on the American family. Interestingly enough, on general political issues, the watching and non-watching evangelical groups were equally agreed (3-1 in both cases) that the Vietnam war was *not* a noble cause and that the U.S. should maintain its informal relations with Taiwan instead of upgrading them, as advocated by candidate Reagan and organizations such as the Christian Voice and the Moral Majority.

Finally, a survey taken among "likely voters" by NBC News and the Associated Press in early October found that when interviewees were asked whether an election recommendation by a member of the clergy would "make you more likely to vote for that candidate, less likely to vote for that candidate, or wouldn't make a difference," only 3 percent replied "more likely," 8 percent said "less likely," and 88 percent answered, "no difference." Only 3 percent reported having "been asked by a member of the clergy to vote for a specific candidate in this fall's election."

It remains, of course, true, that the area in which the Republicans gained strikingly, the South, is the one in which evangelicals are strongest. But the region has been moving away from the Democratic party ever since 1948, to the point where, by 1981, the GOP holds eleven out of the twenty-two senatorial seats in the once Confederate states. These changes reflect a process of party realignment by Southern whites as they react to the conflict between their dominant economic, cultural, and racial values and those of the national Democratic party.

What all these findings seem to indicate is that the efforts to mobilize a religious constituency for political purposes in America had no measurable effect on the 1980 elections. Instead, the available evidence appears to sustain the thesis that the electoral swing toward conservatism and the emergence of a political evangelical movement were parallel developments which may have been mutually reinforcing rather than related to one another as cause and effect.

The political evangelical groups worked hard at increasing turnout, an activity which was particularly important in the South where less educated evangelicals have relatively low voting records. But the seeming success of such work did not create the Republican landslide. Rather, it reflected the country's conservative political swing, which occurred among all groups — and more, as we have seen, among nonevangelicals than among born-agains.

To fail to acknowledge that the growth of support for the GOP and conservatism is a consequence of general social processes is to give groups like the Moral Majority more credit than they deserve and to run the risk of a self-fulfilling prophecy. If politicans become convinced that the Moral Majority is a decisive force in American life, they are more likely to treat it as such, just to be on the safe side. A more important danger of overestimating the Moral Majority's role is that it can serve to blur the meaning of what *has* happened. For many liberals, who cannot quite believe that the American people, blue-collar and all, have turned conservative of their own free will, it would seem preferable to believe that some sinister manipulative force is at work which has turned large segments of the population into robots. But this is self-delusion — the facts state otherwise.

In attempting to keep the Moral Majority in perspective, it may be useful to acknowledge that moral backlash is not necessarily a pejorative term. If it "belongs" to the evangelicals, this is because other organized religious groups have not claimed it, which may explain why fundamentalist churches, in recent years, have been growing at a 2 percent annual rate while mainstream churches have been declining at 1 percent per annum. Only 40 percent of the adult population attends church regularly as of

1980, the lowest figure recorded since pollsters started inquiring about this subject.

In spite of this decline, however, it is important to remember that with the exception of Ireland, America is still the most religious country in the Western world. In 1977, a sample of youth between the ages of eighteen and twenty-four was asked by Gallup affiliates in different countries whether religion should be "very important" in life. Over 40 percent of the Americans interviewed answered affirmatively, as against less than 10 percent of respondents from Japan, Germany, France, and Great Britain respectively.[11] Nor are these views limited to the young. Gallup surveys of the entire population have shown that Americans generally are more likely than are the residents of twelve other developed countries to consider religion important. A larger proportion of Americans (94 percent) report a belief in God, and — even more strikingly — the only two countries in which a majority said they believed in "life after death" were the United States (71 percent) and Canada (54 percent). Less than two-fifths of the French, West Germans, and Scandinavians shared this belief.[12]

Traditional religious belief, moreover, need not be connected to actual church attendance. A 1978 Gallup survey indicated that 41 percent of the American people are unchurched. But while there are doctrinal differences between those who do and those who do not attend church, 76 percent of the unchurched reported that they pray to God and hold to traditional values. Nine out of ten, in both the churched and the unchurched groups, said they would welcome more traditional family ties than now exist. About the same percentage in both groups said they would also prefer greater respect for authority in society.

Given such statistics, the interesting problem is not to account for the revival of backlash moralistic politics, but rather to explain its relative weakness. Part of the explanation undoubtedly lies in the fact that despite the recent rise in membership in orthodox churches, they still have considerably fewer members today than in the 1920s and 1930s. And this decline is linked with numerous structural changes in American society which have weakened the base of the fundamentalist-traditionalist forces. The ranks of farmers in America have fallen greatly since the '20s and '30s, and so has the proportion of small-town residents. At the same time, the number of people engaged in pursuits which require advanced education has increased substantially.

The Americans who "turned Right" in the last election did not by any means agree with the Moral Majority or New Right programs. These Americans were not supporting specific political solutions any more than they usually do. They wanted a government that would more demonstrably reflect their *mood*: a more assertive America on the world scene, and on the domestic front a serious campaign to fight inflation and refurbish American industry. That is the extent of their political conservatism.

Contrary to some allegations, they are not now captive to any political movement, fundamentalist or otherwise, extremist or otherwise. They are shopping. But the attention of these Americans will not be regained by liberal political forces which are more preoccupied with advancing their own conspiratorial explanation of events than with formulating a compelling pragmatic solution to genuine moral and political problems.

NOTES

1. "Reagan and the Republican Revival," October 1980.

2. *The Ku Klux Klan in American Politics* (Public Affairs Press, 1962), p. 116.

3. *Religion at the Polls* (Westminster Press, 1977).

4. Bill Keller, "Lobbying for Christ: Evangelical Conservatives Move from Pew to Polls, But Can They Sway Congress?," *Congressional Quarterly Weekly Report*, September 6, 1980, p. 2627.

5. James W. Michaels, Jr., "Conservative Christians Spread Influence, Attract Political Attention," *National Catholic Reporter*, August 15, 1980, p. 8.

6. "Evangelists Out of the Closet, But Going Nowhere?," *Christianity Today*, January 4, 1980, p. 21.

7. "Getting God's Kingdom Into Politics," *Christianity Today*, September 19, 1980, p. 11.

8. L. W. Davis, "Conservatism in America," *Harper's*, October 1980, pp. 21–26.

9. See Bill Keller, "New Right Wants Credit for Democrats' Nov. 4 Losses but GOP, Others Don't Agree," *Congressional Quarterly Weekly Report*, November 15, 1980, pp. 3372–3373.

10. Louis Harris, "Reagan Leading as Election Heads into Its Final Hours," *ABC News-Harris Survey*, November 2, 1980, p. 2.

11. *Public Opinion 1978* (Scholarly Resources, 1980), p. 339.

12. *Public Opinion*, March/May 1979, pp. 38–39.

An Ominous Threat
to Books

JAMES M. WALL

The darker side of the conservative mood affecting this nation now reaches into our schools and libraries and threatens to impose restraints on books and reading. At its best, conservatism has sought to preserve what is valued and cherished in a culture. But what we are witnessing in this newer version of "conservatism" is a move by right-wing activists to dictate to schools and libraries a particular world view by blocking what they term "objectionable" books — and in some instances, films — from public and school view.

I

This development was to be expected as the religious New Right and its secular allies, including Phyllis Schlafly's Eagle Forum, gained media attention and political clout. They have frequently insisted that society should not tolerate books containing material, particularly that related to sex, which is contrary to what they term "traditional American values." Their campaign is widespread and well orchestrated, and it follows a pattern of intimidation of local and state school and library officials.

The goal of these forces is to reverse a trend they call "permissiveness" in public schools, and in the application of the First Amendment's protection of our right to read. They have found a favorable public climate, for there is no doubt that major changes have occurred in life styles and sexual attitudes over the past two decades. These changes have shocked parents who find it difficult to relate to a younger generation that not only rejects but at times ridicules older values. But censorship is not the answer to changing values. The prudish Victorian era, as just one example, produced some classic pieces of pornographic literature. Repression does not eliminate an interest in sex; it merely drives it underground.

Schools do need to be sensitive to material made available to young people, especially that which contradicts prevailing cultural standards. But sensitivity does not mean repression. What groups like the Moral Majority and Eagle Forum propose to do is turn back the cultural clock, raiding schools and libraries and demanding adherence to a narrow, limited view of sexuality. There is growing evidence that they are succeeding.

A coalition of religious and secular groups has joined in a National

Coalition Against Censorship (NCAC) to alert the rest of us to this threat. In a recent issue of *Censorship News,* published by the NCAC, editor Leanne Katz reports on several cases now moving through the judicial system, each of which, if successful, could point to a drastic rearrangement of how the issue of the right to read is treated.

Even as we examine these cases, we have to acknowledge that there are certain rights parents have regarding the type of education their children receive. The public is not entirely at the mercy of schools and libraries regarding available reading matter. In this, as in all matters of public life, there is a tension between individual rights and group rights, a tension basic to a pluralistic society. But fundamental to any free people is the right of access to printed matter, regardless of its worth. The First Amendment was added to our Constitution in part to protect words and ideas which the majority might find objectionable. These are protected under the amendment because freedom is a precious commodity that flourishes best in an atmosphere of openness.

II

Among cases that have emerged in recent months, editor Katz cites a March 3 decision by Judge Jon O. Newman which calls for a fact-finding trial growing out of the removal in 1976 of nine books from school libraries in Island Trees, New York. The local school board, having acted to remove the books, then requested dismissal of a suit that sought to overturn its decision to remove the books. Judge Newman, in calling for a trial, said the books' removal posed a "sufficient threat to the free expression of ideas within the school community to establish a First Amendment violation." The books involved were not pornographic, and in many school libraries would be considered modern classics: works by Bernard Malamud, Kurt Vonnegut, Eldridge Cleaver and Desmond Morris. Until the case is settled, these books remain off the shelves.

In Alabama four parents appeared before the state board of education, requesting that the board remove a six-volume textbook series, *Justice in America,* then being used in classrooms throughout the state. Objections varied, but they included claims, according to NCAC, that the books "undermined parental values, taught disrespect for law, encouraged dependence on welfare, contained profanity, included discussion of abortion and divorce, were anticapitalist and pro-labor, were hostile to the Bible, supported equal rights for women, and did not stress that the United States is 'a republic and not a democracy.'" Testimony from teachers found the textbooks to be realistic, fair and valuable. The board voted to remove the books from the state's approved list.

III

The Moral Majority of Washington Legal Foundation, acting on behalf of a group of parents, filed a complaint in December 1980 against Mead School

District No. 354, in the state of Washington. The complaint asks that Gordon Parks's book *The Learning Tree* be permanently removed from use in the district's schools. No decision has been reached on the complaint, which alleges that teaching of *The Leairning Tree* "tends to inculcate the anti-God religion of Humanism, which is antithetical to plaintiffs' beliefs and which violates the free exercise and no establishment clauses." In other words, this particular book offends the sensibilities of *some* of the citizens in the area.

And in another Washington case, Moral Majority filed suit against the state library, demanding disclosure of the names of public schools that had borrowed *Achieving Sexual Maturity*, an award-winning sex education film. Apparently having made its point, the organization asked the court for "dismissal with prejudice" of its own case and promised to go to individual schools to determine which ones were using the film.

In Illinois, a bill pending before the General Assembly would make librarians criminally liable for "harmful" materials that might be read by children. Again, the motive would appear to be worthwhile: the protection of children. But it is obvious that this is one of those bills that are designed not to protect children but to intimidate librarians. Its language is too extreme, its categories too vague, to be enforceable. Ironically, this bill introduced by legislators who usually favor getting the government "off our backs" would establish a huge, unworkable monitoring system that would require numerous bureaucrats just to define what is "harmful."

IV

The pattern is clear. A narrow view of human sexuality is to be imposed on all of the public. A method of intimidation is unfolding, and from other reports it appears that local school boards and libraries are finding it easier to give in to the threats of lawsuits than to stand firm against encroachments upon the U.S. Constitution.

There is no doubt that parents grow frustrated over the content of books to which children are exposed in our public educational system. And not every book on the shelf of a public library is to the taste and preference of every citizen. But nothing is more reprehensible on the printed page than the word "censorship," a word denoting an act which violates individual rights and determines the tone of a society from the perspective of a limited few.

The Moral Majority and its allies are exploiting a public which is uneasy over cultural changes, and longs for a return to old ways. Not all of the new is better, of course, but public tastes and preference should be shaped, not controlled. What these forces seek to do is to control our schools and libraries through intimidation. If we prefer freedom over repression, and want to resist this alarming trend, we have an alternative. We can stand up for freedom when school and library board elections are held, and we can speak up for pluralism when hearings are announced. It should not take costly court cases to determine that the real majority in this nation prefers to protect the right to read, not to repress it. The religious New Right wants to intimidate public officials. The way to meet intimidation is not to yield to it, but to insist on public dialogue. Truth has always been its own best advocate.

The Separation
of Church and State

LEO PFEFFER

The concept that true religious freedom mandates a separation of church and state is peculiarly American. It was written into the Constitution as the first words of the First Amendment because the American people, under the intellectual and moral leadership of Jefferson, Madison, Tom Paine and George Mason, would not otherwise accept the Constitution and declare it to be the supreme law of the land.

Under our system of separation of powers, the judicial system, and ultimately the Supreme Court, became the final arbiter in relation to the meaning of the Constitution and all its parts, and this included the First Amendment, the opening words of which mandate that "Congress shall make no law respecting an establishment of religion or prohibiting the free exercise thereof." It was Jefferson who first used the phrase "the separation of church and state" to describe the meaning of the phrase, although it was Paine who, earlier, in *Common Sense*, epitomized the unity of church-state separation and religious freedom in the statement that, "as to religion, I hold it to be the indispensible duty of our government to protect all conscientious professors thereof, and I know of no other business which the government hath to do therewith."

American history establishes that on the whole our people and their government have been remarkably loyal to that mandate, more so than to the others in the same Amendment relating to the freedom of speech and the press and the right to assemble and petition for a redress of grievances. Yet, during periods of war and the threat of war, even the integrity of the religious freedom guaranty has at times been imperiled, as is indicated by the sad history of the Jehovah's Witnesses during World War II. It is in such periods of war that the Supreme Court has on the whole ennobled itself in the cause of First Amendment freedoms by keeping its head while all others lost theirs.

We are not now at war as that term is used to define actual armed conflict. We are, however, in a period of intense preparation for an actual war which, should it come, could well be the war that ends all war and leaves the world in the peace of universal death. It is therefore not surprising that the American people seem to have lost their heads in voting into power an administration that promised to curb galloping inflation by radically reducing governmental spending and then giving it unlimited license to expend their money to purchase arms no matter what they might cost.

My concern in this essay is not with militarism or with economic issues generally, but with the constitutional principle of church-state separation. Here we find what appears to be a holy triple alliance encompassing the Reagan administration, a hard-core right-wing faction in Congress under the leadership of Senator Jesse Helms of North Carolina, and the fundamentalist Moral Majority and similar but less-publicized rightist religious groups. The political power of this coalition manifested itself even before the 1980 election, when Mr. Reagan caused deletion from the Republican Party campaign platform of a promise to work for ratification of the Equal Rights Amendment, and this even though the measure could not have received the necessary two-thirds vote in each house of Congress without the support of the Republican members.

The Equal Rights Amendment is not, at least as of now, part of our Constitution, but the Equal Protection Clause of the Fourteenth Amendment is, and the Supreme Court has shown a modest but, nevertheless in a sense, revolutionary inclination to interpret it as securing some degree of gender equality. This it has done notwithstanding the strong opposition not only from fundamentalists within Protestantism but also those within American Catholicism and Judaism. It has, moreover, done this in disregard of a prior opinion by a Supreme Court Justice who had asserted that "Man is, or should be, woman's protector and defender . . . The paramount destiny and mission of woman are to fulfill the noble and benign offices of wife and mother. This is the law of the Creator." (Under our system of church-state separation it is generally assumed to be the function of the clergy rather than the courts to determine what is "the law of the Creator.")

One cannot question the right of a presidential candidate (or anyone else) to express opposition to the Equal Rights Amendment or any other proposed constitutional amendment. Indeed, he should be commended for doing so while he was yet a candidate for nomination by a party that previously had taken the opposite position. However, sanctioning and encouraging evasion of what actually is in the Constitution is an entirely different matter. Every person, once elected or appointed, whether to the presidency or to any other governmental office from that of Senator representing North Carolina to a member of the police force in a small hamlet, must take an oath of office that he will uphold the Constitution as it now reads and not how he would like it to read.

For better or for worse, this means upholding the Constitution as it is construed by the Supreme Court, and the Court has construed it to bar prayer and religious instruction in the public schools, the use of tax-raised funds to finance parochial schools, and governmental restrictions on abortion, at least during the first trimester of pregnancy.

Let us start with prayers in the public schools. In 1962 and 1963 the Supreme Court ruled these practices violative of the Establishment Clause.

Reagan, Helms, and the Moral Majority have not been happy with these decisions, but they were not the first to manifest their unhappiness. In the almost two decades since the decisions have been handed down, numerous efforts were made towards the adoption of a constitutional amendment overruling the decisions. All have proved unsuccessful and because during this period the Supreme Court has shown no indication of itself either overruling the decisions or sanctioning ill-disguised efforts to evade them, the pro-prayer forces are now seeking to achieve their purpose through what has become known as the Helms amendment. This was so called because it was first employed by Helms in April 1979, before the Republicans won control of the Senate and adoption of a measure authorizing prayer in the public schools could not be achieved directly. Nor for that matter, could it be achieved indirectly (as in the case of the Hyde amendment, dealing with medicaid funding of abortion) by cutting off federal funds from public schools that allow prayer.

What Helms did was to attach to a bill creating a new department of education a rider that would remove suits challenging state-sponsored prayer from the jurisdiction of the federal courts, including the Supreme Court. The effort has so far proved unsuccessful, but now that the Republicans control the Senate and, through alliance with the conservative southern Democrats, the House as well, it is quite likely that the Helms amendment will be enacted by Congress and receive the President's approval.

The purpose of the amendment is to leave the question of constitutionality exclusively in the hands of state legislatures and courts. Legislators, and, to a somewhat lesser extent, judges who are not appointed for life but must look to the voters for re-election, are far more amenable to political pressures than are federal judges and particularly Supreme Court justices. It is, therefore, almost a certainty that many state courts, especially in the South, will uphold public school prayer. Adoption of the Helms proposal would thus mean the frustration of what has heretofore been deemed a binding determination by our highest tribunal that public school prayer violates the First Amendment, not in some but in all states.

Many, perhaps most constitutional lawyers believe that if the Helms amendment were adopted, the Supreme Court would hold it unconstitutional. Nothing, however, is certain in law, and we must consider the possibility that the measure would survive court challenge. What then?

The language of the amendment is restricted to "voluntary" prayer in public schools. Presumably that means that if any pupil or the parents of any pupil whose religious conscience forbids participation objects thereto, prayer would nevertheless be continued but the child must be excused, else a lawsuit to achieve exemption could be brought. The result would be to divide public school pupils into those who do and those who do not engage in public prayer. This would inevitably impose a badge of inferiority not unlike that in respect to racial segregation in public schools, held unconstitutional under the equal protection clause, in the historic 1954 decision of *Brown* v. *Board of Education*.

There is another significant parallel between racial segregation and prayer in the public schools. In both, a decision of the Supreme Court declaring unconstitutional long-standing practices in many of the nation's public schools encountered efforts on the part of local school authorities and state legislatures to evade or frustrate the court's mandate. These efforts threatened the integrity not only of the specific constitutional guarantees of the First and 14th Amendments, but perhaps even more important, the mandate of Article VI declaring that the Constitution is the supreme law of the land and imposing upon all government officials, state no less than federal, the obligation to support it.

Fortunately, the struggle to restore prayer to the public schools has been considerably more pacific than the efforts to retain racial segregation. The pattern in prayer cases has been not outright defiance, as often was the case in respect to racial segregation, but evasion and avoidance. Heretofore, the federal courts have been no more sympathetic to efforts to retain or restore religious segregation in public schools than they have been in respect to racial segregation. It is because of this fact that Helms seeks to exclude federal court review of religious segregation in the public schools. But how can we be certain that a rider will never in the future be successfully utilized to return racial segregation to the public schools in states whose legislatures would like to achieve that end?

Helms has charitably limited his proposal to encompass only "voluntary" prayer. There is, however, nothing to prevent him or some other senator from using the same rider device to enact a school prayer statute that is not limited to "voluntary" participation. Although the Helms device deals only with prayer, it could, if successful, be used to restore religious instruction or devotional Bible reading, held unconstitutional in *McCollum* v. *Board of Education* (1948) and *Abington School District* v. *Schempp* (1963). There is no reason that Helms and the Moral Majority would not press for that too, and efforts to achieve this have already begun notwithstanding the fact that as of the present writing it has not yet succeeded even in respect to public school prayer.

Only recently, the Supreme Court declared unconstitutional, as violating the mandate of church-state separation, a Kentucky law authorizing the posting of the Ten Commandments on the walls of public school classrooms. Under a Helms-type law Kentucky and like-minded states could effectively restore the Ten Commandments to accompany prayer recitation, religious instruction, devotional Bible reading, the posting of other religious symbols such as crosses or crucifixes and displaying the Holy Manger in public schools.

That is not all. Somewhat more than a half-century ago not only the United States but much of the rest of the world followed, I am sure with some amusement, the course of the Scopes or "monkey" trial. Involved was a Tennessee law forbidding public school teaching of evolution or any other explanation of the origin of man inconsistent with the account in Genesis.

The prosecution of Scopes, a public school teacher charged with teaching evolution, was conducted by three-time presidential candidate William Jennings Bryan; the defense, by Clarence Darrow, a noted and successful criminal trial attorney. Scopes was convicted, and the state's supreme court upheld the validity of the statute but hinted strongly to the state officials not to make fools of themselves or the state by seeking to enforce the law by further prosecutions.

In 1968 the issue did reach the Supreme Court in a suit by Susan Epperson, a public school teacher in Little Rock, Arkansas, who challenged a statute similar to Tennessee's "monkey law." The Court held unconstitutional, as a violation of the Establishment Clause, any law that seeks to protect religious orthodoxy from what the legislature might consider dangerous secular teachings, and the Arkansas law did just that.

It was not to be assumed that the religious right would accept this decision as final and determinative. Almost as soon as it was handed down, efforts were launched to return Genesis to the public school curriculum, at least in states whose legislatures could be induced to accept it. The protagonists realized that even in the most backward of the states, public schools could not be barred from teaching evolution; were Arkansas to try to do so, it would, like Tennessee before it, become the laughing-stock of America and would make it difficult for its high school graduates to gain admission in out-of-state colleges. The most they could expect to achieve was a compromise by legislating what, in respect to radio and television, was called the fairness doctrine, that is, mandating equal time for both sides of a controversial issue.

After several vain efforts to achieve this by lawsuits, the religious right succeeded, in March of 1981, in inducing the Arkansas legislature to vote, and the governor to sign into law, a measure entitled the "Balanced Treatment for Creation-Science and Evolution-Science Act." The act did not forbid the teaching of "Evolution Science" (it could hardly do so in view of the Epperson decision); it said only that if the schools did teach Darwinism, they must equally teach Genesis.

Because of what its defenders asserted was obvious fairness, and because the political powers of the Moral Majority and Helms extend beyond Arkansas, similar measures were introduced in other states, including some northern states such as Colorado, Illinois, Iowa, Michigan and Minnesota. Indeed, almost as soon as the Arkansas law was adopted, a similar one became law in Louisiana. The American Civil Liberties Union has already instituted a suit in a federal court challenging the Arkansas statute on the principal ground that it violated the Establishment Clause, and a similar one is highly likely in respect to the Louisiana law.

Joining in the Arkansas suit as co-plaintiffs were parents of public school children, prominent Christian clergymen (including the Bishop of the Catholic Diocese of Little Rock) and organizations — such as Arkansas Education Association, the National Association of Biology Teachers, the National Coalition for Public Education and Religious Liberty (National

PEARL), the American Jewish Congress, the American Jewish Committee and the Union of American Hebrew Congregations.

The fate of these lawsuits may well depend upon what happens to the Helms amendment. Should that become law, there can be little doubt that a similar measure relating to evolution will be adopted by Congress and signed by Mr. Reagan. The President is a staunch advocate of states' rights and would welcome a measure that would give states the last say on the constitutionality of laws affecting public school curriculum, prayer, Bible reading, Ten Commandments and evolution, among others.

One should, however, not assume that the Moral Majority and its allies will be content with local option. Nor will they be content with limiting their efforts to legislation affecting only public schools. Their concern now encompasses governmental funding of religious schools as well, and, as will be discussed later, to arenas having no direct relationship to education at all, such as that of abortion.

For many years the staunchest opponents of governmental financed aid to parochial schools have been southern Protestants. The sponsors of the measure to provide aid that is now most forcefully urged upon Congress, with the blessings of Mr. Reagan, are Senators Packwood and Moynihan, who represent respectively the northern states of Oregon and New York, and who are both moderately liberal in their politics. However, the Supreme Court's exclusion of prayer and the rigorous federal court enforcement of the *Brown* v. *Board of Education* segregation decision have impelled reconsideration by many right-wing legislators and fundamentalist churchmen in the South of their anti-aid position.

Reconsideration has resulted in a comparatively new phenomenon in American education, the southern fundamentalist parochial school that welcomes prayer and Bible but manages to escape from the Blacks. When the Court handed down its 1962 decision forbidding prayer in the public schools, the response by Representative George W. Andrews of Alabama was typical. "They put Negroes in the schools," he said, "and now they've driven God out." These schools are seeking and sometimes getting governmental funding not merely in the form of tax-exemption (a suit by Bob Jones University, now before the Supreme Court, challenges revocation of its tax exemption because it forbids interracial marriage or dating among its students) but also of subsidization, either in cash or its equivalent. This trend is manifested in a suit by Americans United for Separation of Church and State challenging a grant by the federal government to the Valley Forge Christian College of some 77 acres of land and buildings with an assessed value in excess of $1,000,000. Another that may also be on its way to the Supreme Court—*Decker* v. *United States Department of Labor*—is one sponsored by the American Civil Liberties Union, that seeks an injunction against use of CETA funds to finance instruction in parochial schools.

These cases involve federal action, and the Helms device will obviously not do. It is hardly likely that a Republican Congress will pass, or the President will approve, a measure that nullifies all constitutional law respecting Supreme Court jurisdiction beginning with John Marshall's 1803 decision in *Marbury* v. *Madison*. Even where a Helms barrier would apply, the Moral Majority and other constituents of the new right, are certainly not going to be content with it. What they aim for are laws affecting all people in all states, north no less than south of the Mason-Dixon line. They want devotional Bible reading and prayer recitation even in states where the legislatures will not enact permissive laws or where the state courts would declare the laws unconstitutional. If parents will not insure salvation for their children, the government must do so, with or without the cooperation of state courts or legislatures.

Nor, for that matter, are they content with legislation affecting education. They seek governmental action, by law and law enforcement agencies, which will remove pornographic magazines from newspaper stands, peep shows from Times Square, and immoral books from libraries and book stores.

They want also an end to abortion and here (as in the case of aid to religious schools) they have joined Catholic Church leadership in efforts to achieve this. In the 1973 case of *Roe* v. *Wade*, the Supreme Court ruled that a state may not restrict abortions during the first trimester of pregnancy. However, it later ruled that it is not unconstitutional for federal or state governments to refuse to finance abortions for women who cannot economically afford them.

This, however, does not satisfy the anti-abortionists. Their aim is not merely to bar governmental financing but to forbid the procedure itself, even to those who can manage to scrape up the money for it. What they want is an act by Congress defining the term "life," wherever used in law, as encompassing the fetus from the moment of conception. This would make abortion the legal equivalent of murder, to be treated as such, even to the extent of capital punishment in states where it has not been abolished. Logic, at least, impels such a conclusion. The same logic impels the conclusion that the measure, if adopted, would criminalize not only abortion, as that term is usually understood, but also the morning-after pill, which is generally considered contraceptive rather than abortive. Its effect would be to nullify the Supreme Court's decision in *Roe* v. *Wade* and make murderers not only of women who resort to the procedure but also physicians who perform it and associations that aid or abet it.

I have already referred to gender equality and sexual discrimination (most recently manifested in the Supreme Court decision upholding the power of Congress to exclude women from the compulsory military registration law). Related to this is the subject of homosexuality, a mortal sin in the Bible. While it is not likely that the religious right could reinstate the death penalty for commission of this sin, its opposition to decriminalization or removal of civil disabilities is intense.

The 14th amendment guarantees to all "persons" the equal protection of the law. The Civil Rights Act of 1964 expressly forbids discrimination by reason of sex and makes no exception in respect to homosexuality — although it is hardly likely that those in Congress voting to enact the measure had homosexuality in mind at that time. Nevertheless, like it or not, the Moral Majority can hardly deny that homosexuals are persons, and that discrimination against them is discrimination on account of sex.

Judicial challenges to laws penalizing or discriminating against homosexuals have generally been based either upon the Equal Protection Clause or upon the right to privacy. (The latter has been read into the Constitution by the Supreme Court, at least in respect to sexual relations in the 1965 case of *Griswold* v. *Connecticut* which dealt with contraception.) When, in 1980, the Supreme Court upheld the power of Congress to exclude abortion from governmentally financed medical procedures, it expressly rejected the claim that the statute violated the guaranty of church-state separation in that it was based upon religious prohibition to the procedure. It is, therefore, highly probable that in a case challenging the constitutionality of laws relating to homosexuality, it will not invalidate them on the ground that they are founded upon Leviticus. Yet, it is even more probable that sooner or later the Court will uphold the rights of homosexuals (and this will occur even if a majority of the Court will be Reagan appointees), but it will do so on the basis of the right to privacy or to the equal protection of the laws, rather than freedom from an establishment of religions. When that happens one can expect, with a reasonable degree of certainty, that the Moral Majority will push for another Helms amendment barring the federal courts from taking jurisdiction of any case concerning homosexuality.

In this instance as well as the others mentioned in this chapter, the measure will represent an effort on the part of the radical right coalition not only to repeal the provision in the Constitution declaring that it is the Supreme Law of the land but also to transform what is now the Supreme Court into a very inferior court, at least in respect to the fundamental freedoms of the American democratic system.

PEACE/ WAR

Since the survival of our species is at stake with respect to issues of peace and war, we must weigh the value of New Right imperatives of power meant to guide American foreign policy. They are three:

Abandon detente, a disaster for the West.

Triple our expenditures for nuclear and other arms.

Be the number-one world military power.

New Right leaders warn that America is decadent and in danger of collapse and that the Communists have always had the goal of destroying American capitalism and taking over the country. Why reduce tensions with respect to an enemy who wants to bury you and the rest of the free world? The Moral Majority is not alone in insisting that the future of the nation depends upon restoring our primacy of military power.

Rather than to reply directly, point by point, to the now actively proceeding military build-up which has been advocated by such groups as The Committee on the Present Danger, Speak Out *addresses the peace/war problem by presenting alternative scenarios of the world situation. Two of the following selections are by former United States Ambassadors to the Soviet Union: a noted IBM executive, Thomas J. Watson, Jr., and George F. Kennan, a diplomatic historian who wrote a classic* Foreign Affairs *article on Soviet containment under the name of Mr. X. Our first* Speak Out *selection, however, is by Helen Caldicott, President of Physicians for Social Responsibility (PSR).*

Dr. Caldicott's words concerning "This Beautiful Planet" are indicative of the message being communicated in leading cities such as Seattle and New York, San Francisco and Cambridge, Albuquerque, Chicago, and Los Angeles in a series of PSR symposia on the medical consequences of nuclear weapons and nuclear war. Members of a rather cautious profession conclude that the health professionals and existing health facilities will be utterly unable to provide the medical care which will be needed in the event of a nuclear holocaust, which they call "The Last Epidemic." Our pediatrician author has now left her positions at Harvard Medical School and Children's Hospital so that she may give undivided attention to the most dangerous threat to our children. Our Speak Out *selection was the Phi Beta Kappa oration to the Harvard Chapter in 1981.*

Our second Speak Out *selection on peace/war is by Thomas H. Watson, Jr., who succeeded his father as President of IBM and who championed the switch from cog-and-gear office machines to the field of electronic computers, in which IBM rapidly became an international pace-setter. This non-Utopian executive warns us of the illusion that one side can start a nuclear war and win it. Watson delivered his words at the 1981 Harvard Commencement.*

Our third Speak Out *selection reiterates and amplifies this same ultimate concern. "Cease This Madness!" exclaims George F. Kennan, who presents an alternative scenario contrasting strongly with the growing American New Right Counterrevolution respecting United States–Soviet Union relations. His words are presented in two parts, arising from different occasions. First comes "A Modest Proposal," which America's most distinguished diplomatic historian delivered on the occasion of receiving the award of the Albert Einstein Peace Prize. Professor Kennan, of the Institute for Advanced Studies at Princeton University, was chosen the Einstein Peace Laureate because of his continuing efforts to ease tensions between the United States and the Soviet Union. The second part of his presentation consists of the historic address Dr. Kennan delivered to the Second World Congress on Soviet and East European Studies held in 1980 in Germisch, Germany. The text is included in full in order to convey the actual international context in which people East and West are called upon to* Speak Out *and to act to reverse the trends that have brought such high danger to the present moment of peace/war.*

This Beautiful Planet

HELEN CALDICOTT

This beautiful planet of ours is terminally ill. Unless we face it and do something about it, almost certainly it will die along with us and the whales. It is important to examine this terminally ill planet, which presently is infected with lethal "macrobes," the nuclear weapons, which are mestastisizing rapidly.

The nuclear age began in the late '30s and early '40s when Einstein wrote to President Roosevelt telling him that he thought Hitler was developing nuclear weapons and that America should be doing the same thing. This led to the Manhattan Project which was funded by huge amounts of government money and through which many scientists became involved in the challenge of their lifetime.

A film shown on PBS, "The Day After Trinity," described the history of the experiment. It took the scientists about three years to develop enough enriched uranium and plutonium to make three bombs. Even after it became apparent that Hitler, in fact, was not going to make nuclear weapons, and even after VE day, when Germany surrendered, they kept going. Some of the scientists had a meeting to discuss whether they should proceed, but because they were absolutely fascinated by what they were doing, they decided it would be better to make the bombs and use them to show mankind how dreadful they were, and then they would never be made again.

The first bomb was named Trinity and it was called a "gadget." The "gadget" was hoisted to the top of a tower in Almagordo Desert in July 1945. On a stormy night with lightning everywhere, the "gadget" exploded. One scientist described how he felt when it blew up. He said, "The noise went on, and on, and on, like thunder, never stopping. The desert suddenly became small."

They were not sure before they blew up the bomb that the whole atmosphere would not go critical. They were worried about this probability, so they redid their calculations and the probability remained the same. It was not extremely small. One technician was upset to hear Enrico Fermi taking side bets as the "gadget" was hoisted to the tower, that New Mexico would be incinerated.

After the explosion, the radioactive cloud hovered overhead for some time, worrying the scientists, because if it did not blow away in the direction they had prescribed, it could have killed them or injured them severely. However, it did eventually blow away. That night the scientists had a party.

The next bomb was blown up or tested over a human population on August 6, 1945, at 8:15 in the morning. In fact, the air force had been told to spare two cities in Japan so that we could see the effects of these weapons on human populations. The bomb was dropped from a plane called the Enola Gay, which flew over Hiroshima. Men looking up saw one parachute opening and they were pleased because they thought the plane had been shot down. Another parachute opened adjacent to the first. Then there was a blinding flash and tens of thousands of people were vaporized. People, in fact, when they disappeared, left their shadows on concrete sidewalks behind them. Children were seen running along streets shedding skin from their bodies like veils; a man was standing in a state of acute clinical shock holding his eyeball in the palm of his hand; and a woman lay lying in a gutter with her back totally burnt with her baby suckling at her breast as she lay dying.

Some people who escaped Hiroshima migrated then to the only Christian center in Japan, Nagasaki, thinking that it would never be bombed by the Americans. They arrived three days later, just in time to receive the second bomb. Many Japanese will say, if you visit there, "We can sort of understand the first bomb, but why the second?" One of the physicists who celebrated at the party the night after Trinity, recounted in "The Day After Trinity" how he felt after the bomb in Hiroshima was used. He said, "I was so nauseated that night I had to go to bed, and I was profoundly depressed. We are scientists. We never thought of human beings as matter."

After the war, Robert Oppenheimer thought that if the nuclear secret were shared with Russia, neither country would develop the weapons. But it was decided that the secret should remain. This, he said, was the beginning of the Cold War. However, several years later Russia developed the secret and the arms race began. Oppenheimer was interviewed 20 years later in the PBS documentary. The then gaunt man was asked, "What do you think?"

In a very didactic, scientific way, puffing on his pipe, he said, "It is too late."

"What should have happened?" the filmmakers asked.

He said, "It should have been stopped the day after Trinity."

This was in the sixties. Today we have tens of thousands of hydrogen bombs on this planet, with more being built every day.

During the sixties, Robert McNamara, who was Secretary of Defense, determined that if America had 400 one megaton bombs, this would be an adequate deterrent. A one megaton bomb is equivalent to one million tons of TNT. The bomb used on Hiroshima was equivalent to approximately 13,000 tons of TNT. The maximum payload any plane could carry during the Second World War was four tons of bombs. The four hundred bombs would be sufficient to kill one third of the Russian population and destroy two thirds of their industry. I thought about that statement the other day from an ethical, moral and medical perspective and I realized that the last person who spoke like that in my lifetime wrote a book called *Mein Kampf*. To kill one third of the Russian people is to kill nearly one hundred million human beings. We have been anesthetized and we practice psychic numbing. We listen to the Pentagon jargon which is, I think, meant to confuse. It is rather like the medical jargon which we use to confuse the patients, so they do not understand what is actually wrong with them.

That is the history of this terminally ill planet. At the time 400 bombs were determined to be an adequate deterrent force, the air force had control of all the nuclear weapons, but traditionally the army and navy have rivalries, and they were jealous. It was then decided to develop a triad of nuclear weapons, so everybody could have them. The arms race really began in earnest. Also, at that time it was decided to nuclearize all forms of conventional weapons. So now there are atomic bombs in torpedoes and in land mines, and men who go into battle with 18-inch howitzers on their shoulders, carry with them atomic bombs.

What is the physical condition of our planet today? America now has some 30 to 35 thousand hydrogen bombs. The Pentagon says, however, there are only five thousand worthwhile targets in the Soviet Union. According to the Pentagon's estimates, there are enough weapons in this country to overkill (a Pentagon word) every Russian human being 40 times. There are, in fact, enough weapons on one Trident submarine to destroy every major city in the Northern Hemisphere, and America is building 11 Trident submarines.

The Soviet Union has some 20,000 hydrogen bombs which are bigger than the American bombs because they are less accurate. The Soviets have enough weapons to overkill every American human being some 20 times. Collectively, the superpowers can overkill every human being on earth 12 times.

I have heard statements recently that America is behind Russia. I do not understand that statement. How can one be behind or ahead when both countries can kill each other many times over? I have heard talk of Russian expansionism, and I investigated that thoroughly. I found that, according to the Pentagon, America has 200 major bases in 45 nations in the world and 20 major ports; the Soviet Union has none.

The world spends over $600 billion a year on the arms race. That is over a million dollars a minute. Incidentally, the cost of one third of one Trident submarine would eradicate malaria in the world. Two thirds of the world's children are malnourished and starving. Over half the scientists in this country work for the military-industrial complex.

What, therefore, is the prognosis of our terminally ill planet? It is gloomy. In 1975, the Joint Chiefs of Staff testified before a Senate Committee and predicted a 50–50 chance of a nuclear war occurring before 1985. A Harvard/MIT study done later verified that prediction. *The*

Bulletin of the Atomic Scientists, which commenced publication during Einstein's era, has a doomsday clock on its cover. Its hands have been moved only ten times since 1945. During the years of detente when there was some relaxation and a little bit of confidence and hope about the future, the clock was at nine minutes to midnight. After Afghanistan, it was moved to seven. In January 1981, the hands moved to four minutes to midnight.

Dr. George Kistiakowsky, Professor Emeritus of Chemistry at Harvard University, who was Eisenhower's science advisor and who devised the implosion, or triggering, mechanism for the first atomic bomb, has serious doubts that we will survive to the year 1990. Presidential advisors, some of them coming from Harvard, at the moment are making statements that we must psychologically prepare ourselves for a nuclear war. As a physician who knows something about psychiatry, I am not sure how one does that. Other advisors are writing articles in *Foreign Affairs* saying it is possible to fight and win a nuclear war. Let me describe the terminal or agonal event of this planet if such a war should occur.

A nuclear war between the superpowers, using only strategic weapons, would take about half an hour to complete. In fact, the weapons on the submarines off the coast of this country and the Soviet Union need only ten minutes to a quarter of an hour to reach their targets. The reason for this is that once the weapons are launched, they go out into space, reenter the earth's atmosphere at 20 times the speed of sound and land accurately on target. Meanwhile, the other country's satellites, radar and other instruments detect the attack and the button is pressed on the other side. The weapons cross mid-space, practically. And they land within about half an hour.

According to the Arms Control and Disarmament Agency, there are enough weapons to target every town and city with a population of ten thousand people or more. Apparently the nuclear reactors are also targeted. Inside each thousand megawatt nuclear reactor is as much long-lived radiation as that released by 1,000 Hiroshima-sized bombs. Apparently the major airports, the major oil refineries, and industry are also targeted.

Let me describe now a 20 megaton bomb dropping on Boston, using a series of articles published in *The New England Journal of Medicine* in 1962. A 20 megaton bomb is equal to 20 million tons of TNT. That is four times the collective size of all the bombs dropped during the Second World War. It is a small sun. It explodes with the heat of the sun. It will do this to Boston: It will carve out a crater about half a mile to a mile wide and 300 hundred feet deep. Everything in that volume will be converted to radioactive fallout. Every human being within a radius of six miles from the hypo-center will be vaporized, as will most buildings. Concrete and steel will burn. Out to a radius of 20 miles, most people will be dead, or lethally injured with tens of thousands of severe burn victims, when there are only facilities for 2000 acute burn victims in the whole of the United States of America. There will be injuries such as compound fractures, ruptured lungs from the overpressure, ruptured internal organs and massive hemmorhage. What was left of the building will be lying in what is left of the streets. Most hospitals will be destroyed, most medical personnel dead or injured. If one doctor works for two weeks, 18 hours a day, he or she will only be able to see each patient once for a ten-minute period during that time, meaning every patient would die. If you happen just to glance at the blast from 35–40 miles away, the flash would instantly burn the retina and blind you. It will create a fire storm of 15,000 to 30,000 square miles, in which everything will spontaneously ignite, creating a holocaust fanned by hurricane force winds, so if you were in a fallout shelter, you would be pressure-cooked and asphyxiated as the fire used all the oxygen. The explosion will create an electromagnetic pulse damaging all electronic equipment and all communications equipment.

As most towns and cities in this country are so targeted, what happens if you are in a rural area that is not targeted? Now you must not be asleep. You must be listening to the radio or television to hear the emergency signal. You sometimes hear it tested, don't you? "Oooooooooh, we are testing the emergency signal." This time I guess they will tell you you have 15 minutes to run to the nearest shelter. Medically, you will not be able to re-emerge for 2 to 6 weeks because the short-lived isotopes in the fallout will be so intensely radioactive that you will die within days of acute radiation sickness if you are exposed to it.

When you re-emerge, the world will be different. This building will be gone; Harvard will be gone. All the magnificent architecture we have inherited from our ancestors will be destroyed. The Bach, the Handel, the Beethoven will be gone from the planet. The art, the literature, the poetry, everything will be gone. There will be no one to come and help as there was in Hiroshima because most people will be dead. There will be nobody to bring medical help, because doctors will be dead or injured. There will be no drugs for the dying patients. Just last year the Boston *Globe* reported that President Carter was stockpiling huge quantities of opium just in case there was to be a nuclear war. Of course, that would be used for euthanasia, if anyone knew where it was.

The National Academy of Science did a study in 1975 that stated if the superpowers used only 10 percent of their nuclear arsenals, that could destroy 50 to 80 percent of the ozone layer in the Northern Hemisphere and 30–40 percent in the Southern Hemisphere because of the nitrous oxide released in the explosions. Some scientists predict that if only 30 percent of the ozone layer (which protects the earth from the ultraviolet radiation of the sun) is destroyed, it could blind every organism on earth, including the insects and bees, which literally means the death of the ecosphere as we know it. If people stay in the sun for half an hour, they will get third degree sunburn, which is lethal, and be blinded. Survivors will die of a synergistic combination of acute radiation sickness, sunburn, blindness, starvation and epidemics of disease (as bacteria mutate and multiply in the millions of dead bodies, to become more virulent while our immune mechanism is depleted by background radiation) and people die of grief.

In the symposia that Physicians for Social Responsibility hold on the medical consequences of nuclear war, addressed by some of the most famous physicians in this country, it is predicted that within 30 days after an all-out nuclear exchange, 90 percent of American human beings will be dead. And not just in America, you know, but in Canada, Mexico, all of Europe, all of England, all of Russia, and much of China.

What is the etiology or cause of the present situation, our terminally ill planet? It is psychiatric. We are causing the illness. We are very intelligent, but we are motivated by our emotions. How did we let it happen? One of the reasons we have let it happen, according to Robert Lifton, is that we practice psychic numbing. We block it out. We push it back into our subconscious because we do not like to think about it. Because if, in fact, we take this on emotionally, it is as if I have told you just now that you have a terminal illness. You, the planet, us. If you have a cancer, you might die in a year. If you understand this fact emotionally, you enter the stages of grief which are, first, shock and disbelief. "She must be mad. Anyway, one of her facts is wrong, so I will discount the lot." The next stage is profound depression. You would prefer to feel the pain of a fractured arm than the pain of the depression, followed by profound anger, followed perhaps eventually, by adjustment. The human being would do anything to avoid those feelings, so we practice psychic numbing and avoid the feelings.

During the early sixties, the days of atmospheric testing and the Cuban missile crisis, we were not psychically numbed, but then we developed the partial test ban treaty, and the bombs were tested underground. Out of sight is out of mind. The Vietnam war was unthinkable, Watergate was a little bit of fun, if not very serious, and we forgot that the weapons were being made, and that this country makes or recycles 3 to 10 new hydrogen bombs per day.

We also practice adaptation. When animals are in the jungle and are threatened with some stimulus they perceive to be life-threatening, they will immediately be alert. But if the stimulus persists and nothing bad happens, they adapt and move on to receive new stimuli which may be threatening. Adaptation is what we have done with the threat of nuclear war.

Another thing we do is project the fear of the nuclear age. The fear is profound. I am sure we have all had nuclear nightmares. I am sure some of you in the '50s and '60s used to practice hiding under your desk in schools in case a bomb exploded, or put bits of paper on your head so that you would be protected from the flash. The fear is so profound that we normally tend to project it onto other people. At a recent meeting of physicians from 11 countries, we worked out that we are projecting that fear onto the Russians. The fear is so profound in the nuclear age that in our fear, the Russians, or whoever, become inanimate objects. If they are inanimate objects, we can talk about killing tens or hundreds of millions of them and it does not feel bad at all. In so doing, we have lost our own humanity.

The other thing we tend to do is use what I call the "but what about the Russians" syndrome. When I talk on television about the medical effects of nuclear war, the first question that comes back to me is "But what about the Russians?" It is as if the people have streamlined all the information so it goes over their heads, and the fear is still projected onto the Russians. Therefore, I say I am not worried about the Russians, I am worried about you and your children being incinerated. It is rather like telling a patient, you have a bad disease and if the patient does not comply medically with what you prescribe, you are psychologically a little more brutal at the next appointment.

What about the adolescents? The Harvard psychiatrists' recent study of 1,000 adolescents in Boston shows that one of the main reasons they think the children are taking drugs and drinking alcohol is that most of these children expressed a profound fear of the future and a feeling that they probably won't grow up and will probably never survive to have children.

It is interesting treating children, which is what I do. Children can face death more openly and readily than adults. I think they are less conditioned. They are less like Pavlovian dogs than we are.

What about the scientists, the leaders of the countries of the world, and the industrialists who make the weapons. Partly these people are stuck in old thinking. They see nuclear weapons as they saw bows and arrows or conventional weapons. The more one has, the safer one is, because you can destroy your enemy and rebuild from the rubble. There are very few leaders in the world who have seen a hydrogen bomb explode and seen battle ships become like splinters in the water or felt the heat or the blast. In their imaginations, can they possibly foresee what that is like? So they think of more hydrogen bombs as providing more security, when in fact this thinking is leading us to total insecurity. Einstein put it best. He said, "The splitting of the atom changed everything save man's mode of thinking, thus we drift toward unparalleled catastrophe."

America's leaders also practice psychic numbing. During the SALT hearings, they talked about how many bombs the Russians have and how many more we need to counter them. They sound like nine-year-old boys, a little like my younger son.

I called the Senate Foreign Relations Committee and asked, "Why hasn't anybody testified about the medical consequences of thermonuclear war?"

They said, "The senators don't like to hear that sort of thing, it makes them feel uncomfortable."

I think many politicans are practicing power games or projecting their dark sides onto other people, which we all tend to do. It takes much more courage for men and women to face their own anger, fear and hostility and understand where it comes from and grow emotionally than it does to project one's fear and anger onto other people and blame them.

I also think there is another mechanism that is operating. We all have a profound fear of our own death, which we don't think about. Some people cope with that by using a counter-phobic mechanism by dealing in death or playing with it. Perhaps that is what the scientists and engineers are doing as they make these weapons for mass genocide without contemplating the end result of what they are actually doing.

What would be the pathogenesis of the terminal event, or of nuclear war? If you look back through history, you see that wars are often started for totally illogical reasons, inane reasons. Often wars are started by sane men. Adolf Eichmann when psychoanalyzed after the war, was found to be, psychiatrically, totally sane. Moreover, a third world leader could initiate a nuclear war. Libya's Colonel Qaddafi is financing a Pakistani bomb program and so he will soon have his own nuclear weapon. I don't know what will happen then in the Middle East.

Nuclear war could be initiated by pathology within leaders of the world. In medicine, we see pathology a lot. I have seen sane people develop an acute psychosis suddenly, under severe stress. Or the president of either country or the chairman of the Soviet Union could develop a cerebral tumor and, before getting a CAT scan, could do something which is totally insane.

A nuclear war could be started by accident. Over the last 18 months, computers within the Pentagon and elsewhere have made 151 errors that predicted that nuclear weapons were coming from the Soviet Union. One such error was started by a man who plugged a war game tape into the fail-safe computer at the Pentagon in November 1979. The computer detected weapons coming from Russia. The whole world went on nuclear alert for six minutes. Some planes took off with nuclear weapons heading toward the Soviet Union. At the seventh minute, the President was to be officially notified, but he could not be found. If the error had not been determined at that time, in 14 minutes we would have been annihilated.

What is the therapy for this planet, and for us? First, as physicians, we must shatter people's psychic numbing. It is inappropriate for any person on this planet to be psychologically comfortable in this day and age. As the psychic numbing is shattered, people will enter the phases of the grieving reaction. This then motivates individuals to become active in doing something about the problem. The anger can be very profound. It is therapeutic to do something, it feels better. We must also deal with our own dark side and stop projecting it like children onto other people and stop blaming other people for things we ourselves can fix and for which we are responsible.

We must also have a total commitment to save this planet. Now, a marriage or a relationship with two people will never work unless each partner is totally committed to that marriage. If there is so much as one toe out the door, saying if you don't do this I will leave, the marriage will eventually disintegrate, because neither partner will go through the pain and humiliation of personal growth to reach the stage where the relationship matures. Similarly, both superpowers must be totally committed to saving this planet. For nothing else really matters. War is no longer appropriate. Even conventional war is no longer appropriate because of nuclear reactors and huge nuclear radioactive waste dumps everywhere that would produce, to a degree, genetic suicide. These weapons are biologically inapplicable and cannot be used. The only weapon we have at our disposal in this day and age is the larynx.

Kübler-Ross studies people who are terminally ill. Many people who are terminally ill find it very hard to die. The people who find it hardest to die and are clinging on to life are those who have never really loved and given and who have been selfish and greedy. Often the people who die with grace and dignity and at peace are those people who have given to other people and loved. In other words, the way to true happiness is through helping other people on this planet, not to make yourself happy. Therefore, our challenge today is to help each other and to help the planet survive. It does not really matter if you get a good job; it does not really matter if you have children and make sure they clean their teeth and eat good, nutritious food, if we don't survive. In fact, if we continue practicing psychic numbing, we are passively suicidal. If a patient comes into my office who is suicidal, I hospitalize him immediately because this is an acute clinical emergency.

This is the ultimate in preventive medicine, because nuclear war will create the final medical epidemic for which there will be no cure. We as physicians are extremely concerned about this. The American Medical Association has passed a resolution against nuclear war. We are also negotiating with Soviet physicians now. Dr. Chazov, Soviet President Brezhnev's personal cardiologist, said recently, "You know, the politicians are our patients."

Governments were instituted partly because of our medical knowledge. Our knowledge has produced hygenic sewage systems, clean water supplies and immunization programs, but the vectors of disease today are not flies, rats, mosquitoes and poor sanitation. They are us. They are the scientists who make the weapons, the industry who build them, and the politicans who use them for power. We must confront these vectors of disease.

This is the greatest challenge the human race has ever had since we stood on our hind legs and developed the opposing thumb to use weapons. Unless we mature and stop behaving like children, we will not survive.

I saw a bumper sticker the other day that said, "God Bless America," but every person on earth is the son or daughter of God, including the Russian people. We are together on a small, fragile planet. We will either live together or we will die together.

What is our responsibility toward evolution? To continue this beautiful life process. If you take this on, life becomes very precious. Even the things you dislike most about your life become precious. Go outside and look at a rose and smell it, or look at a baby to know what I mean.

We are curators of all life on this planet. We hold it in our hands. It is a beautiful planet, maybe the only life in the whole universe, and I refuse to believe we are silly enough to destroy it.

What Future Lies Ahead?

THOMAS J. WATSON, JR.

What future lies ahead? There are many things to be optimistic about. The view from the Kremlin is bleak, with nearly everyone on the Soviet border hostile. The view from Washington sees mostly friends, admirers, or neutrals.

On the other hand, an anthropologist writing the history of the past forty years since the first atomic explosion might well conclude that we human beings have been preparing for our own demise. Like many extinct species we have had a massive change in our environment. We have finally invented the ultimate weapon, and in a mad technological race have connected thousands of them to two buttons — one in Washington and one in Moscow. With two very slight pressures we can literally do away with the world's two most powerful nations, and leave much of the rest of our planet unfit for human habitation.

Is that our future? The answer hinges on many things. But it hinges above all on us: on the United States' policy on nuclear weapons — on what we and our leaders do about that policy in the days and months immediately ahead.

Let me start out by speaking to those of you who are young. Throughout the past half-century, young people have played many heroic roles. You went to World War II and brought down fascism. You fought and died in the mountains of Korea. Spurred by the challenge of the Russian Sputnik, you made brilliant contributions to American science and engineering, keeping America in the forefront of technology. You fought heroically in Vietnam. And you worked courageously within the system, joined it in large numbers, became a potent political force, influenced public opinion, and helped bring that tragic war to an end.

We need — and shall always need — this kind of courage and conviction. And especially we need today the courage and conviction of youth to face up realistically to a change of course as a nation — our course on strategic arms control and our whole handling of the nuclear equation.

The hour is late. The imperative of realism and reason is urgent. And we confront many illusions.

First is the illusion of victory — the illusion that one side or the other can start a nuclear war and win it. Sober common sense analysis will tell anyone that this is impossible. Consider this illusion in its most popular package: The Soviets launch a surgical first strike and destroy most of our Minutemen and Titan missiles in their underground silos. Thus they leave us few weapons capable of retaliation in kind — of wiping out their remaining underground missiles. Thus they force us to a choice: attack Soviet cities with our submarine missiles and bombers, thereby provoking a counterattack on American cities from Boston to Seattle; or surrender.

What's wrong with this picture? Lots of things. It assumes — against all common sense — that the Soviet leaders, notoriously cautious about security, would bet their total nation on at least four foolhardy all-or-nothing gambles:

• the gamble — against all technological likelihood — that their first strike would be essentially perfect — that it would leave few if any Minutemen or Titans to retaliate in kind;

• the gamble that we would not use some of our remaining underwater and airborne weapons, nearly three fourths of our total warheads, to attack the thousands of vulnerable military targets in the Soviet Union other than missile silos;

• the gamble that when our President learned the Soviet missiles were flying our way, he would freeze and do nothing — that he would not send those targeted Minutemen and Titans flying towards Russia's remaining silos before the enemy missiles landed;

• and the ultimate gamble: That in desperate retaliation we would not rain down total destruction on Soviet cities, even though that might mean our own destruction as well.

Make no mistake: That scenario defies all sober analysis. It would be the most risky and ultimately costly gamble in history. By overwhelming odds, the result of any use of nuclear weapons would not be victory. It would be all out war and total destruction. And in the words of President Kennedy, "The living would envy the dead."

The illusion of Soviet preemptive victory has a corollary: the illusion of achievable American superiority — the illusion that like the Red Queen in *Through the Looking Glass* we can outrace the danger by going "faster, faster"; outproducing the Soviets in nuclear arms; playing a multi-billion-dollar shell game in the desert; hoping that somehow with exotic weapons we can erect a protective umbrella over our country. So-called nuclear superiority assures no safety — not for the Soviet Union; not for us; because what counts is not superiority but sufficiency — the guaranteed power to destroy the other side under all circumstances. And we both have it.

A quarter century ago Donald Quarles, then Secretary of the air force and a wise scientist in a Republican administration, put it succinctly:

> Beyond a certain point, the prospect is not the result of rela-
> tive strengths of the two opposing forces. It is the absolute
> power in the hands of each . . .

Think of it this way: Would you, if you sat in the Kremlin, attack the United States, even knowing that you could knock out 95 percent of our weapons, but realizing that the remaining five percent could destroy literally the whole Soviet Union?

Would you, sitting in Washington, attack even a smaller country which had only a thousand warheads knowing that if you missed only ten percent they could wipe out a hundred American cities?

You know the answer: There is no safety in numbers. The war planning process of the past has become totally obsolete. Attack is now suicide. Yet the pursuit of the mirage of superiority persists. And over the years the two superpowers have piled weapon on useless weapon.

In 1945, when we exploded our first atomic bomb at Hiroshima, we had a four-year lead over the Russians. In 1952, when we exploded our first H-bomb, we had a ten-month lead. The Soviet Union closed the gap despite having a country severely torn by the ravages of a war of a ferocity never visited on our country. It has kept up in the race, despite the burden of a hopelessly inefficient economy, by ruthlessly channeling its resources, and by calling upon the Soviet people for an endless acceptance of sacrifice.

Between us, our two countries now have explosive power equal to a million Hiroshima A-bombs. We have between us some 15 thousand "city killing" weapons — one bomb, one city. Bigger stockpiles do not mean more security. Enough is enough. And we are far beyond that point now.

There is a third illusion, rooted in the belief that nuclear victory is possible and strategic superiority attainable. It is the illusion of nuclear omnipotence — that if we just have more weapons we can use nuclear threats to deter Soviet misbehavior anywhere in the world. I can think of no quicker prescription for disaster. Our nuclear weapons are useless except for their mission of preventing direct attack on us.

Fourth is the illusion of futility: the illusion that we cannot sign treaties with the Russians because they systematically violate them. Let us be clear about this: there are major differences between our two countries. Soviet values are diametrically opposed to ours. Contention between us on a global scale is a fact of life. Suspicion is the keynote or our relations. But having said that, let me add this: on the evidence, the Soviets do keep agreements provided each side has an interest in the other's keeping the agreement; and provided each side can verify compliance for itself.

Look for example at the 1972 Anti-Ballistic Missile Treaty and the Interim Agreement — the two parts of SALT I. The Soviet Union has violated neither. These treaties do not depend on trust or good will. They depend on cold self-interest and unilateral verifiability.

Fifth is the illusion of benign neglect, the idea that if we just muddle along, in the phrase of Dickens' Mr. Micawber, "something will turn up"; that the current aging Soviet leadership, for example, will soon be replaced by enlightened and reasonable men; that the Soviet system will crumble from within; or that we can indefinitely stall on serious negotiations, let the Soviets cool their heels waiting, and use the intervening time for our own advantage — to arm up.

Let us not delude ourselves. We can take no comfort from all these kinds of wishful thinking. To be sure, the average Soviet Politburo member today is sixty-nine years old, but I have met many of the possible successors, and I can tell you: I foresee no real change. I do not see the Soviet Union becoming more pro-American. I do not see a revolution around the corner. I do not foresee the demise of the rigid system or the rigid thinking that runs it. I see no chance that the Soviet leaders will be hoodwinked by protracted negotiations while we try to jump ahead in strategic arms.

Finally, we confront the illusion of softheadedness; that anyone who favors an end to the arms race must be soft on U.S. defense or even soft on Communism. And we confront its corollary: the simplistic formula "arm up and stand firm," though war would mean losses of 50 to 75 percent on each side. The illusion of softheadedness is thermonuclear McCarthyism. Because the search for a way out of this morass — the search for an avenue of negotiation and survival instead of confrontation and weaponry — has a long and honorable heritage. That heritage includes Republicans and Democrats; military and nonmilitary leaders, among them some of the greatest and most tough-minded of our time. It began in 1946 under President Harry Truman with the proposal of a hardheaded financier, Bernard Baruch, for international U.N. control of atomic energy. It continued with President Dwight Eisenhower, who in his first major foreign policy address denounced the tragic waste of armaments, and in his farewell message warned against the power of a military-industrial complex. It includes another great five-star general, Omar Bradley, who nearly a quarter century ago called for the country to turn away from "the search for peace through the accumulation of peril."

That heritage embraces the last legacy of President Kennedy, the nuclear test ban treaty of 1963; the SALT I accords under President Nixon; and the SALT II treaty initiated by President Nixon, continued by President Ford, and completed by President Carter. SALT II was guided to completion in large part by former Secretary of State Cyrus Vance, for whom I was proud to serve in Moscow. Though the U.S. Senate has not ratified the treaty, it was endorsed by former Secretary of Defense Harold Brown, one of the world's brightest authorities on modern armaments; by General David Jones, head of the joint chiefs of staff; and countless others. Thermonuclear McCarthyism is a slander against the wisdom of many great Americans.

Against all these illusions, what is the reality? The reality is that thermonuclear war in any form is suicide.

Our imperative is to change our course — to take the only road which offers a viable hope for the future: not a road to unilateral action of any kind, but a road toward the joint continuation of the SALT process; a road to a long series of mutually verifiable treaties.

I know from experience how maddening protracted negotiations with the Russians can be. I know what these negotiations will demand of us: in the words of St. Francis of Sales, "A cup of science, a barrel of wisdom, and an ocean of patience." But we have no choice. The longer we drift on without firmly capping the arms race, the graver the dangers we create:

● the danger that a suspected violation, some unforeseen new technology or a sudden quantitative surge will trigger a desperate response;

● the danger that we may further split ourselves from Western allies who fear we lack seriousness about negotiation, whether on SALT or on European Theater Nuclear Forces;

● the danger that each new warhead we or the Russians build inevitably increases the possibility of a thermonuclear accident;

● the danger that a growing dependence on nuclear weapons to defend our interests major and minor all over the globe will someday trap us in a choice between Armageddon and surrender;

● the danger that if we don't act now, we shall lose forever the chance to limit future new devices of unimaginable complexity.

The time for action is at hand. That action must begin in Washington, D.C. — begin with the same urgency and effectiveness the Administration has shown in confronting our serious economic difficulties; the same urgency and courage the President has shown in already beginning a major build-up in our conventional forces.

President Reagan has pledged to "negotiate as long as necessary to reduce the numbers of nuclear weapons to a point where neither side threatens the survival of the other." Those negotiations have not yet started, and dangers escalate. Each week's delay makes the problem greater.

In response to George Kennan's recent drastic yet creative disarmament proposal, the designated head of the Administration's Arms Control Agency, Eugene Rostow, said not only that the Administration was "taking a serious look" at this proposal but added that "the whole miserable business is mad. We must find a way out."

President Reagan is riding a deserved high tide of popularity. I urge that he seize the moment to find that way out. The time has come for all of us, under his leadership, to listen to the honored Americans — beginning with Truman, Baruch, Eisenhower, and Bradley — who have called for an end to the insanity of the arms race. The time has come for all of us to reject the scenarios of the theoreticians mesmerized by computer projections into thinking that the leaders of the Soviet Union would bet their homeland on a lottery chance at victory. The time has come to realize that our nuclear deterrent is robust under any possible contingency. Let our politicians and arms technicians stop poor-mouthing it. Above all, the time has come for a new effort to cap the strategic arms race — cap it through a verifiable treaty which gives both sides the security they require.

SALT II offers a good framework. Minor changes could be made at the negotiating table if necessary. But there is little time before technology and pressures on both sides push us into a new and unmanageable spiral. We cannot wait for improved Soviet behavior around the world, or for better U.S.-Soviet relations. Control of strategic arms is not a concession to the Soviets. It must not be linked to irrelevant issues. Those who urge delay take an awesome responsibility on their shoulders.

Twenty-eight years ago in Sanders Theater, in Cambridge, a great American journalist, Elmer Davis, delivered the annual Phi Beta Kappa oration. It was a time of darkness and witch hunts and false accusations. In calling upon friends of freedom to stand up and fight, he quoted the first book of Samuel, which tells of the fear of the Philistines as they face a formidable foe.

"Woe unto us!" they said. "Who shall deliver us out of the hands of these mighty gods?" But when they looked around and saw that no one else was going to deliver them, they said to one another: "Be strong, and quit yourselves like men; and fight." And they did, and they saved themselves.

The title of that Phi Beta Kappa oration was: "Are We Worth Saving? And If So Why?" The title of my remarks today might be: "Can We Be Saved? And If So How?"

I have tried to suggest some answers. And despite the somberness of my theme, I remain an optimist. I regard the first atomic explosion in 1945 as an arrival — a culmination of mankind's long advance in ever greater mastery over the forces of nature. I regard that explosion also as a watershed; because it signaled man's capability for the first time to destroy himself and the earth he lives on. But I do not regard that explosion of 1945 as a beginning of the end.

The time has come for all human beings to realize that we must live together or die together. I believe we have the reason and the realism and the common sense to choose life.

Cease This Madness!

GEORGE F. KENNAN

I. A MODEST PROPOSAL

Adequate words are lacking to express the full seriousness of our present situation. It is not just that our government and the Soviet government are for the moment on a collision course politically; it is not just that the process of direct communication between them seems to have broken down entirely; it is not just that complications in other parts of the world could easily throw them into insoluble conflicts at any moment; it is also — and even more importantly — the fact that the ultimate sanction behind the policies of both these governments is a type and volume of weaponry that could not possibly be used without utter disaster for everyone concerned.

For over thirty years wise and far-seeing people have been warning us about the futility of any war fought with these weapons and about the dangers involved in their very cultivation. Some of the first of these voices were those of great scientists, including outstandingly Albert Einstein himself. But there has been no lack of others. Every president of this country, from Dwight Eisenhower to Jimmy Carter, has tried to remind us that there could be no such thing as victory in a war fought with such weapons. So have a great many other eminent persons.

When one looks back today over the history of these warnings, one has the impression that something has now been lost of the sense of urgency, the hopes, and the excitement that initially inspired them. One senses, even on the part of those who today most acutely perceive the problem and are inwardly most exercised about it, a certain discouragement, resignation, perhaps even despair, when it comes to the question of raising the subject publicly again. What's to be gained by it? people ask. The danger is obvious. So much has already been said. What does it do to continue to beat this drum? Look, after all, at the record. Over all these years the competition in the development of nuclear weaponry has proceeded steadily, relentlessly, without the faintest regard for all these warning voices. We have gone on piling weapon upon weapon, missile upon missile, new levels of destructiveness upon old ones. We have done this helplessly, almost involuntarily: like the victims of some sort of hypnotism, like men in a dream, like lemmings heading for the sea, like the children of Hamelin marching blindly behind their Pied Piper. And the result is that today we have achieved, we and the Russians together, in the numbers of these devices, in their means of delivery, and above all in their destructiveness, levels of redundancy of such grotesque dimensions as to defy rational understanding.

I say redundancy. I know of no better way to describe it. But actually the word is too mild. It implies that there could be levels of these weapons that would not be redundant. Personally, I doubt that there could. I question whether these devices are really weapons at all. A true weapon is at best something with which you endeavor to affect the behavior of another society by influencing usefully the minds, the calculations, the intentions, of the men who control it; it is not something with which you destroy indiscriminately the lives, the substance, the culture, the civilization, the hopes, of entire peoples. What a confession of intellectual poverty it would be — what a bankruptcy of intelligent statesmanship — if we had to admit that such blind, senseless, and irreparable destruction was the best use we could make of what we have come to view as the leading element of our military strength! To my mind, the nuclear bomb is the most useless weapon ever invented. It can be employed to no constructive purpose. It is not even an effective defense against itself. It is only something with which, in a moment of petulance or panic, you perpetrate upon the helpless people of another country such fearful acts of destruction as no sane person would ever wish to have upon his conscience.

There are those who will agree, with a sigh, to much of what I have just said, but will point to the need for something called deterrence. Deterrence is, of course, a concept which by implication attributes to others — to others who, like ourselves, were born of women, walk on two legs, and love their children, to human beings, in short — the most fiendish and inhuman of tendencies. But all right: accepting for the sake of argument the incredible iniquity of these adversaries, no one could deny, I think, that the present Soviet and American arsenals, presenting over a million times the destructive power of the Hiroshima bomb, are simply fantastically redundant to the purpose in question. If the same relative proportions were to be preserved, something well less than 20 percent of these stocks would surely suffice for the most sanguine concepts of deterrence, whether as between the two nuclear superpowers or with relation to any of those other governments that have been so ill-advised as to enter upon the nuclear path. Whatever their suspicions of each other, there can be no excuse on the part of these two governments for holding, poised against each other and poised in a sense against the whole Northern Hemisphere, quantities of these weapons so vastly in excess of any demonstrable requirements.

How have we got ourselves into this dangerous mess?

Let us not confuse the question by blaming it all on our Soviet adversaries. They have, of course, their share of the blame, and not least in their cavalier dismissal of the Baruch Plan so many years ago. They too have made their mistakes; and I should be the last to deny it. But we must remember that it has been we Americans who, at almost every step of the road, have taken the lead in the development of this sort of weaponry. It was we who first produced and tested such a device; we who were the first to raise its destructiveness to a new level with the hydrogen bomb; we who introduced the multiple warhead; we who have declined every proposal for the renunciation of the principle of "first use"; and we alone, so help us God, who have used the weapon in anger against others, and against tens of thousands of helpless noncombatants at that.

I know that reasons were offered for some of these things. I know that others might have taken this sort of lead had we not done so. But let us not, in the face of this record, so lose ourselves in self-righteousness and hypocrisy as to forget the measure of our own complicity in creating the situation we face today.

What is it, then, if not our own will, and not the supposed wickedness of our opponents that has brought us to this pass?

The answer, I think, is clear. It is primarily the inner momentum, the independent momentum, of the weapons race itself — the compulsions that arise and take charge of great powers when they enter upon a competition with each other in the building up of major armaments of any sort.

This is nothing new. I am a diplomatic historian. I see this same phenomenon playing its fateful part in the relations among the great European powers as much as a century ago. I see this competitive build-up of armaments conceived initially as a means to an end, soon becoming the end in itself. I see it taking possession of men's imagination and behavior, becoming a force in its own right, detaching itself from the political differences that initially inspired it, and then leading both parties, invariably and inexorably, to the war they no longer know how to avoid.

This compulsion is a species of fixation, brewed out of many components. There are fears, resentments, national pride, personal pride. There are misreadings of the adversary's intentions — sometimes even the refusal to consider them at all. There is the tendency of national communities to idealize themselves and to dehumanize the opponent. There is the blinkered, narrow vision of the professional military planner, and his tendency to make war inevitable by assuming its inevitability. Tossed together, these components form a powerful brew. They guide the fears and the ambitions of men. They seize the policies of governments and whip them around like trees before the tempest.

Is it possible to break out of this charmed and vicious circle? It is sobering to recognize that no country, at least to my knowledge, has yet done so. But no country, for that matter, has ever been faced with such great catastrophe, such plain and inalterable catastrophe, at the end of the line. Others in earlier decades, could befuddle themselves with dreams of something called "victory." We, perhaps fortunately, are denied this seductive prospect. We have to break out of the circle. We have no other choice.

How are we to do it?

I must confess that I see no possibility of doing this by means of discussions along the lines of the negotiations that have been in progress, off and on, over this past decade, under the acronym of SALT. I regret, to be sure, that the most recent SALT agreement has not been ratified. I regret it, because if the benefits to be expected from it were slight, the disadvantages were even slighter; and it had a symbolic value which should not have been so lightly sacrificed. But I have, I repeat, no illusion that negotiations on the SALT pattern — negotiations, that is, in which each side is obsessed with the chimera of relative advantage and strives only to retain a maximum of the weaponry for itself while putting its opponent to the maximum disadvantage — I have no illusion that such negotiations could ever be adequate to get us out of this hole. They are not a way of escape from the weapons race; they are an integral part of it. The weapon of mass destruction is not just a weapon like other weapons; there is a point where difference of degree becomes difference of essence.

Whoever does not understand that when it comes to nuclear weapons the whole concept of relative advantage is illusory — whoever does not understand that when you are talking about preposterous quantities of overkill the relative sizes of arsenals have no serious meaning — whoever does not understand that the danger lies not in the possibility that someone else might have more missiles and warheads than you do, but in the very existence of these unconscionable quantities of highly poisonous explosives, and their existence, above all, in hands as weak and shaky and undependable as those of ourselves or our adversaries or any other mere human beings; whoever does not understand these things is never going to guide us out of this increasingly dark and menacing forest of bewilderments into which we have all wandered.

I can see no way out of this dilemma other than by a bold and sweeping departure — a departure that would cut surgically through all the exaggerated anxieties, the self-engendered nightmares, and the sophisticated mathematics of destruction in which we have all been entangled over these recent years, and would permit us to move smartly, with courage and decision, to the heart of the problem.

President Reagan recently said, and I think very wisely, that he would "negotiate as long as necessary to reduce the numbers of nuclear weapons to a point where neither side threatens the survival of the other." Now that is, of course, precisely the thought to which these present observations of mine are addressed. And I wonder whether the negotiations would really have to be at such great length. What I would like to see the President do, after proper consultation with the Congress, would be to propose to the Soviet government an immediate across-the-boards reduction by 50 percent of the nuclear arsenals now being maintained by the two super-powers — a reduction affecting in equal measure all forms of the weapon, strategic, medium-range, and tactical, as well as all means of their delivery — all this to be implemented at once and without further wrangling among the experts, and to be subject to such national means of verification as now lie at the disposal of the two powers.

Whether the balance of reduction would be precisely even — whether it could be construed to favor statistically one side or the other — would not be the question. Once we start thinking that way, we would be back on the same old fateful track that has brought us where we are today. Whatever the precise results of such a reduction, there would still be plenty of overkill left — so much so that if this first operation were success-ful, I would then like to see a second one put in hand to rid us of at least two thirds of what would be left.

Now I have, of course, no idea of the scientific aspects of such an oper-ation; but I can imagine that serious problems might be presented by the task of removing, and disposing safely of, the radioactive contents of the many thousands of warheads that would have to be dismantled. Should this be the case, I would like to see the president couple his appeal for a 50 percent reduction with the proposal that there be established a joint Soviet-American scientific committee, under the chairmanship of a distinguished neutral figure, to study jointly and in all humility the problem not only of the safe disposal of these wastes but also the question of how they could be utilized in such a way as to make a positive contribution to human life, either in the two countries themselves or — perhaps preferably — elsewhere. In such a joint scientific venture we might both atone for some of our past follies and lay the foundation for a more constructive future relationship.

It will be said: this proposal, whatever its merits, deals with only a part of the problem. This is perfectly true. Behind it, even if it were to be im-plemented, there would still lurk the serious political differences that now divide us from the Soviet government. Behind it would still lie the problems recently treated, and still to be treated, in the SALT forum. Behind it would still lie the great question of the acceptability of war itself, any war, even a conventional one, as a means of solving problems among great in-dustrial powers in this age of high technology. What has been suggested here would not prejudice the continued treatment of these questions just as they might be treated today, in whatever forums and under whatever safeguards the two powers find necessary. The conflicts and arguments over these questions could all still proceed to the heart's content of all those who view them with such passionate commitment. The stakes would simply be smaller; and that would be a great relief to all of us.

What I have suggested is, of course, only a beginning. But a beginning has to be made somewhere; and if it has to be made, is it not best that it should be made where the dangers are the greatest, and their necessity the least? If a step of this nature could be successfully taken, people might find heart to tackle with greater confidence and determination the many problems that would still remain.

It will also be argued that there would be risks involved. Possibly so. I do not see them. I do not deny the possibility. But if there are, so what? Is it possible to conceive of any dangers greater than those that lie at the end of the collision course on which we are now embarked? And if not, why choose the greater — why choose, in fact, the greatest — of all risks, in the hopes of avoiding the lesser ones?

We are confronted here with two courses. At the end of the one lies hope — faint hope, if you will — uncertain hope, hope surrounded with dangers, if you insist — but hope nevertheless. At the end of the other lies, so far as I am able to see, no hope at all. Can there be — in the light of our duty not just to ourselves (for we are all going to die sooner or later) but of our duty to our own kind, our duty to the continuity of the generations, our duty to the great experiment of civilized life on this rare and rich and marvelous planet — can there really be, in the light of these claims on our loyalty, any question as to which course we should adopt?

In the final week of his life, Albert Einstein signed the last of the collective appeals against the development of nuclear weapons that he was ever to sign. He was dead before it could see publication. It was an appeal drafted, I gather, by Bertrand Russell. I had my differences with Russell at the time, as I do now in retrospect. But I would like to quote one sentence from the final paragraph of that statement, not just because it was the last one Einstein ever signed, but because it sums up, I think, all that I have been trying to say on the subject. It reads as follows:

> We appeal, as human beings to human beings: Remember your humanity, and forget the rest.

II. SCHOLARSHIP, POLITICS, AND THE EAST-WEST RELATIONSHIP

The professional concerns that unite all of us here in this room tonight are of course scholarly ones — cognitive, not political. They are concerns springing from the cultivation and dissemination of knowledge about a part of the world, the immense importance of which for both the past and the future of our civilization is obvious to all of us.

Nevertheless, we are all equally aware, I think, that the study of this part of the world has been extensively affected, and for the most part unfavorably affected, over these many years, by political conditions. This is my first excuse, if one be needed, for departing tonight from the strict terrain of scholarship and for presenting to you a few thoughts about the historical development and present state of the great tensions between the Western world, which so many of us here represent, and the political authority — namely, the Soviet regime — which has confronted us for more than 60 years on the other side of the ideological barrier. Beyond that, in a gathering of scholars whose professional interests are bound to continue to be affected by what takes place on the political scene, and possibly even more sharply affected than in the past, it does not seem to me that we can avoid entirely a glance at what is now taking place on the political scene.

Let me begin by saying that when I glance back over these past 50 years, it seems evident to me that the East-West relationship has been burdened at all times by certain factors which lie in the very nature of the respective societies — factors, that is, that reflect not just the policies of any given government at any given moment but rather deeply rooted, habitual, in part subconscious, but in any case more or less permanent features of the behavior of the respective political establishments.

When it comes to describing these factors, permit me, so far as the Western side is concerned, to confine myself primarily to my own American society, and, when it comes to the Communist part of the world, primarily to the Soviet Union. Comparable things might be said, I am sure, with relation to the associated powers on both sides, but to attempt to include them specifically in this discussion would surely take us too far.

I have no doubt that there are a number of habits, customs, and uniformities of behavior, all deeply ingrained in the American tradition, which complicate, for others, the conduct of relations with the American government. There is, for example, the extensive fragmentation of authority throughout our governmental system — a fragmentation which often makes it hard for the foreign representative to know who speaks for the American government as a whole and with whom it might be useful for him to speak. There is the absence of any collective cabinet responsibility, or indeed of any system of mutual responsibility between the executive and legislative branches of government. There are the large powers exercised, even in matters that affect foreign relations, by state, local, or even private authorities with which the foreign representative cannot normally deal. There is the susceptibility of the political establishment to the emotional moods and vagaries of public opinion, particularly in this day of confusing interaction between the public and the various commercialized mass media. There is the inordinate influence exercised over American foreign policy by individual lobbies and other organized minorities. And there is the extraordinary difficulty which a democratic society such as ours experiences in taking a balanced view of any other country which has acquired the image of a military and political opponent or enemy — the tendency, that is, to dehumanize that image, to oversimplify it, to ignore its complexities. Democratic societies do very poorly in coping, philosophically, with the phenomenon of serious challenge and hostility to their values.

In the light of these conditions, and others that might be mentioned, I can well understand that to have to deal with our government can be a frustrating experience at times for the foreign statesman — even for the Communist statesman. I regret these circumstances, as do some other Americans. They constitute one of the reasons why I personally advocate a more modest, less ambitious American foreign policy than do many of my compatriots. But these are, I reiterate, conditions that flow from the very nature of our society, and they are not likely to be significantly changed at any early date.

And if I mention them here I do so primarily because when I go on to mention similar permanent angularities on the Soviet side, I would not like to create the impression that I view these latter as the only such impediments to a better relationship. I recognize that we Americans present a few such impediments ourselves.

But the fact is that when we look at the Soviet regime, we also encounter a whole series of customs and habits, equally deeply rooted historically, which also weigh heavily — in my opinion, even more heavily — on the external relationships of that regime. These, strangely enough, seem to have been inherited much less from the models of the recent Petersburg epoch than from those of the earlier Grand Duchy of Muscovy. And they have found a remarkable reinforcement in some of the established traditions of Leninist Marxism itself: in its high sense of orthodoxy, its intolerance for contrary opinion, its tendency to identify ideological dissent with moral perversity, its ingrained distrust of the heretical outsider.

I might mention, as one example, the extraordinary passion for secrecy in all governmental affairs — a passion that prevents the Soviet authorities from revealing to outsiders even those aspects of their own motivation which, if revealed, would be reassuring to others and would redound to their own credit. Excessive secrecy tends, after all, to invite excessive curiosity, and thus serves to provoke the very impulses against which it professes to guard.

Along with this passion for secrecy there goes a certain conspiratorial style and tradition of decision-taking, particularly within the Party — a practice which may have its internal uses but often leaves others in uncertainty and inspires one degree or another of distrust. And then, too, there is the extraordinary espionomania — the preoccupation with the phenomenon of espionage — which appears to pervade so much of Soviet official thinking. Espionage is a minor nuisance, I suppose, to most governments. But nowhere, unless it be in Albania, is the preoccupation with it so intense as it appears to be in the Soviet Union. For parallels to it, one has to turn to the Middle Ages. And this surprises; because if one expected to encounter it anywhere in the modern world, it would be in a weak and precariously situated state, not in one of the world's greatest and most secure military powers.

However that may be, this state of mind expresses itself, of course, in an extreme suspiciousness with relation to the individual foreigner and in the maintenance of an unusually elaborate system of supervision and control over his contacts with Soviet citizens. The Soviet leaders, I am sure, regard this as purely an internal matter; but it is difficult for others of us to see it entirely this way; because relationships among individuals across international frontiers make up a large portion of the significant relations among states; and it seems to us that this elaborate system of controls affects Soviet external relations, and affects them unfortunately, in a host of ways.

These extreme tendencies, so little in accord with general international practice, are particularly puzzling and disconcerting for the outsider, because they contrast so sharply with the correct and disarming facade of official Soviet conduct which one often encounters when questions of internal security do not come into play. The foreigner who has to deal with the Soviet government often has the impression of being confronted, in rapid succession, with two quite disparate, and not easily reconcilable, Soviet political personalities: one—a correct and reasonably friendly personality which would like to see the relationship assume a normal, relaxed, and agreeable form; the other—a personality marked by a suspiciousness so dark and morbid, so sinister in its implications, as to constitute in itself a form of hostility, or at least to be explicable in no other way.

Finally, there is the habit of polemic exaggeration and distortion in political discourse—a habit carried often to the point of the denial of the obvious and the solemn assertion of the absurd—a habit which has offended a host of foreign observers over the course of the years.

I sometimes wonder whether the Soviet leaders ever realize how much they damage their own interests by the indulgence of these proclivities, how heavily they weigh upon the whole structure of Soviet foreign relations, how extensively they play into the hands of people who would like to portray the Soviet Union as a crafty, untrustworthy, and menacing giant. This, I suspect, has much to do with the extraordinary fact that whereas Soviet military power has never been stronger, never has that country been more severely isolated, morally and politically, than it is today among the members of the international community.

These then, are what I might call some of the permanent complications of the East-West relationship. They would exist, and would play their unfortunate role, in any circumstances. They place limitations on the type of coexistence that can prevail between the two worlds. On the other hand, they would not alone preclude any coexistence at all. If they were the only major complications to which the relationship were subject, one could still struggle along and muddle through as one has been doing for so many years—and this, without disaster. But they are, unfortunately, not the only complications. There are, and have been, others, less permanent in some instances, but even more serious. And it is to these that we must now turn.

The first of these, and the one that marked the relationship throughout much of the 1920s and 1930s, was the world-revolutionary commitment of the early Leninist regime, with its accompanying expressions in rhetoric and activity. It is true, of course, that the period of the intensive pursuit of world-revolutionary undertakings was brief. As early as 1921, aims of this nature were already ceasing to enjoy the highest priority in the policies of the Kremlin. Their place was being taken by considerations of self-preservation of the regime and the development of its economic and military strength. But the world-revolutionary rhetoric remained substantially unchanged down throughout the remaining years of the twenties and much of the thirties. Moscow continued throughout that period to maintain in the various Western countries small factions of local Communist followers over whom it exerted the strictest discipline, whom it endeavored to use as instruments for the explication and pursuit of its own policies, and whose unquestioning loyalty it demanded even when this conflicted with any conceivable loyalty of these people to their own governments. So unusual were these practices, so unprecedented in modern usage, and so disturbing to Western governments and publics, that they formed in those years, as I then saw it and still see it in retrospect, the main cause for the high degree of tension and uncertainty prevailing in the relations between Russia and the West.

With the triumph of Hitler in Germany, however, an important change occurred. It could not be said that the original political and ideological antagonism between Soviet Russia and the West or the offensive undertakings of the Comintern were wholly forgotten in Western circles; but beginning with about 1935 the menace of Hitler began to loom larger in Western eyes than did the ideological differences with Soviet Communism or the resentment of world-revolutionary activities. The result was that the Soviet Union came to be viewed in the West no longer primarily from the standpoint of its hostility to Western capitalism but rather from the standpoint of its relationship to Nazi Germany.

And this had several confusing consequences. For one thing, it tended to obscure from the attention of the Western public the full savagery and horror of the Stalinist purges of the late 1930s. But then, too, after 1941 the common association of the Western powers with the Soviet Union in the war against Germany gave rise to sentimental enthusiams of one sort or another in the West and to unreal hopes of a happy and constructive collaboration with Soviet Russia in the coming postwar period. It was this factor which brought the various Western statesmen, now wholly preoccupied with the struggle against Nazi Germany, to accept without serious remonstrance, as the war came to an end, not only the recovery by the Soviet Union of those border areas of the former Russian Empire that had been lost at the time of the Revolution but also the establishment of a virtual Soviet military-political hegemony over the entire remainder of the eastern half of the European continent — in other words, a geopolitical change of historic dimensions, bound to complicate the restoration in the postwar years of anything resembling a really stable balance of power.

It was not surprising, in these circumstances, that when the war came to an end, and when people in the West turned to the problems of the construction of a new world order, a reaction — indeed, an overreaction — set in. There was a sudden realization that the destruction of Germany's armed power and the effective cession to the Soviet Union of a vast area of military deployment in the very heart of the continent had left Western Europe highly vulnerable to a Soviet military attack, or at least to heavy military-political pressures from the Soviet side. Added to this was the growing realization that with the establishment of Communist regimes, subservient to Moscow, in the various Eastern European countries, the relations of those countries with the West had become subject to the same complicating and limiting factors that already operated in relations with the Soviet Union. Then came the Korean War — a conflict which, though Soviet forces were not actually involved, people in the West soon came to see as a manifestation of Soviet aggressiveness. And it was just at this time, of course, that the nuclear weapon began to cast its baleful shadow over the entire world scene, stirring up all those reactions of fear, confusion, and defensive panic, which were bound to surround a weapon of such apocalyptic, and indeed suicidal, implications.

The death of Stalin, the establishment of the dominant position of Khrushchev, and the accompanying relaxations in Soviet policy gave rise, of course, to new hopes for the peaceful accommodation of East-West differences. Although Khrushchev was a crude man, he was one who wanted, after all, no war; and he did believe in human communication. But he overplayed his hand. And such favorable prospects as his influence presented went largely without response in the West. The compulsions of military competition and military thinking were already too powerful.

For over this entire period the Soviet leaders persisted in the traditional Russian tendency to overdo in the cultivation of military strength, particularly conventional strength. They continued to maintain along their western borders, as their Tsarist predecessors had done before them, forces numerically greater than anyone else could see the need for. For a European public already conditioned by unhappy historical experience to see the threat of military invasion behind any serious conflict with a neighboring power, this was enough to arouse the most lively apprehensions. And the situation was not made better by the tendency of Western strategists and military leaders to exaggerate the strength of these Soviet forces and to emphasize the weaknesses of their own, with a view to wheedling larger military appropriations out of their own reluctant parliaments. And it was not made better by the tendency of the Western press and other media to dramatize these exaggerations as a means of capturing public attention.

The Americans, meanwhile, unable to accommodate themselves to the recognition that the long-range nuclear missile had rendered their great country no longer defensible, threw themselves headlong into the nuclear arms race, followed at every turn by the Russians. In the U-2 episode and the Cuban missile crisis the two great nuclear powers traded fateful mistakes, further confirming each other in the conviction that armed force, and armed force alone, would eventually determine the outcome of their differences. And out of all these ingredients, including some of more recent origin, there was brewed that immensely disturbing and tragic situation in which we find ourselves today: this anxious competition in the development of new armaments; this blind dehumanization of the prospective adversary; this systematic distortion of that adversary's motivation and intentions; this steady displacement of political considerations by military ones in the calculations of statesmanship; in short, this dreadful militarization of the entire East-West relationship in concept, in rhetoric, and in assumption, which is the commanding feature — endlessly dangerous, endlessly discouraging — of this present unhappy day.

My friends; there are certain specific features of this moral and political cul de sac I have just described which warrant, I think, our attention on this occasion.

First: it represents a basic change, as compared with the first two decades of Soviet power, in the source of East-West tension. Gone, or largely gone, is the world-revolutionary fervor that marked the early stages of Soviet power. Gone, too, are the anxieties that fervor provoked in the West. The Soviet Union is still seen as a menace, yes — but primarily as an aggressive military menace. It is not the capacity of the Kremlin for promoting social revolution in other countries that is feared and resented. Even the Soviet efforts to gain influence in the Third World are viewed primarily not from the standpoint of their possible stimulus to social revolution as such but from the standpoint of their effects on the world balance of military power. Were the various military anxieties that command us all to be suddenly abstracted tomorrow from the contemporary scene, the Soviet Union would still stand out on the horizons of Western statesmanship as a problem. There would still, of course, be great differences and conflicts of interest. The permanent complicating factors I mentioned earlier on would still be there. There would still remain the serious geopolitical problems presented by the abnormal Soviet positions in Eastern Europe, in Cuba, and in Afghanistan. But the Soviet Union would present a wholly different sort of a problem than it presented in the 1920s. Moscow would no longer figure as the greatest inspirational source, and particularly not as the only source, of social revolution. For that, its moral and intellectual authority is too deeply shattered, its version of Marxism — too seriously outdated.

Secondly, I would point out that this whole great militarization of concept about the Cold War is largely unnecessary. There is no rational reason for it. Neither side wants a third world war. Neither side sees in such a war a promising means of advancing its interests. The West has no intention of attacking the Soviet Union. The Soviet leadership, I am satisfied, has no intention, and has never had any intention, of attacking Western Europe. The interests of the two sides conflict, to be sure, at a number of more distant points. Experience has proven, most unfortunately, that in smaller and more remote conflicts, where the stakes are less than total, armed force on a limited scale continues to have its part to play, whether we like it or not. The use of it for limited purposes cannot, in any case, be excluded. The United States has used its armed forces in this manner four times since World War II: in Korea, in Lebanon, in Santo Domingo, in Vietnam. The Soviet Union now does likewise in Afghanistan. I am not entertaining, by these remarks, the chimera of a total world disarmament. But for the maintenance of armed force on a scale so vast and destructive as to envisage the total destruction of an entire people, not to mention the immense attendant danger to the attacking power itself and to millions of innocent by-standers: for this, there is no rational justification. Such a practice can flow only from fear — sheer fear — and irrational fear at that. It can reflect no positive aspirations. And this irrationality expresses itself in the very fantastic excessiveness of the respective nuclear arsenals. It is sobering to reflect (and this is not an exaggeration) that both of the great nuclear powers could afford today to reduce their nuclear arsenals by 90 percent, and what would remain would still be more than enough for the most sanguine concepts of deterrence. The rest is pure overkill — a menace to us all by its very existence.

Thirdly, while this militarization of concept and behavior is thus devoid of rational basis, it is a phenomenon of the greatest conceivable seriousness and dangerousness. It is dangerous precisely because it *needs* no rational basis — because it feeds upon itself and provides its own momentum. In fact, it commands the actions and reactions of governments to a degree greater, I fear, than any positive purpose could ever achieve.

No one will understand the danger we are all in today unless he recognizes that governments in this modern world have not yet learned to cope with the compulsions that arise for them not just from an adversary's cultivation of armed force on a major scale but from their own as well. I repeat: peoples and governments of this present age have not yet learned how to create and cultivate great military establishments, and particularly those that include the weapons of mass destruction, without becoming the servants rather than the masters of that which they have created, and without resigning themselves helplessly to the compulsive forces they have thus unleashed.

The historical research with which I have recently been occupied has carried me back to the diplomacy of the European powers of a century ago; and I find these truths clearly evidenced in the record of those times, even though the terribleness of the weapons then at the disposal of governments did not approach what we know today. I find instances there of great powers which had no seriously conflicting interests at all — no conflicts of interest, that is, which could remotely have justified the sacrifices and miseries of a war. Yet they, too, were carried helplessly along into the catastrophe of the first world war; and the force that carried them in that direction was simply the momentum of the weapons race in which they were then involved.

Now, this not only *can* happen again. It *is* happening. We are all being carried along at this very moment towards a new military conflict

—a conflict which could not conceivably end, for any of the parties, in anything less than disaster. It is sobering to remember that modern history offers no example of the cultivation by rival powers of armed force on a massive scale which did not in the end lead to an outbreak of hostilities. And there is no reason to believe that our measure of control over this fateful process is any larger than that of the powers that have been caught up in it in the past. We are not greater, or wiser, than our ancestors. It would take a measure of insight — of understanding, of restraint, of willingness to accept the minor risks in order to avoid the supreme ones — it would take a measure of these qualities greater than anything yet visible on either side to permit us to release ourselves from this terrible convulsion and to save ourselves, and others, from the catastrophe to which it is leading. One is obliged to doubt that there could be any voice from within the societies of the two super-powers strong enough to bring about this act of self-emancipation, on which the future of civilization itself may depend. It would take a very strong voice, indeed a powerful chorus of voices, from the outside, to say to the Russian and American decision-makers what should be said to them:

> For the love of God, for the love of your children, and of the civilization to which you belong, cease this madness. You are mortal men. You are capable of error. You have no right to hold in your hands — there is no one wise enough and strong enough to hold in his hands — destructive powers sufficient to put an end to civilized life on a great portion of our planet. You have a duty not just to the generation of the present — you have a duty to civilization's past, which you threaten to render meaningless, and to its future, which you threaten to render non-existent. No one should wish to have in his hands such powers. Thrust them from you. The risks you might thereby assume are not greater — could not be greater — than those which you are now incurring for us all.

This, I repeat, is what should be said to those who pursue the nuclear weapons race. But where is the voice powerful enough to say it?

There is a very special tragedy in this present military competition. It is tragic because it creates the illusion of a total conflict of interest between the two societies; and it does this at a time when their problems are in large measure really common ones. It tends to conceal the fact that both of these societies are today confronted with new internal problems which were never envisaged in either of the ideologies that originally divided them — new problems that supercede the essentially nineteenth-century conditions to which both of these ideologies, and Leninist Marxism in particular, were addressed.

In part, I am referring to the environmental problems with which we are now all familiar: the question as to whether great industrial societies can learn to exist without polluting, exhausting, and thus destroying, the natural resources essential to their very existence. These are not only problems common to the two ideological worlds; they are ones, for the solution of which these two worlds require each other's collaboration, not each other's enmity.

But beyond that, there are deeper problems — social and even moral and spiritual — which are coming increasingly to affect all the highly industrialized, urbanized, and technologically advanced societies of this modern age. What is involved here is essentially the question as to how life is to be given an adequate meaning, how the quality of life and experience is to be assured, for the individual citizen in the highly artificial and overcomplicated social environment that modern technology has created. Neither of us — neither we in the West nor they in the East — is doing too well in the solution of these problems. Neither of us has much to be proud about. We are both failing — each in his own way. If you want an example of this, look only at our respective failures in our approach to teenage youth. The Russians demoralize their young people by giving them too little freedom. We demoralize ours by giving them too much. Neither system finds itself able to give to them what they need in the way of leadership and inspiration and guidance if they are to realize their own potentialities as individuals and to meet the responsibilities which the future is inevitably going to place upon them.

And this is only one of the points at which we are failing. Neither here nor there is the direction society is taking really under control. We are all being swept along, in our fatuous pride, by currents which we do not understand and over which we have no command. And we will not protect ourselves from the resulting dangers by continuing to pour great portions of our substance, year after year, into the instruments of military destruction. On the contrary, we will only be depriving ourselves, by this prodigality, of the resources essential for any hopeful attack on these profound emerging problems.

The present moment is, my friends, as I said at the outset of these remarks, a crucial one. Not for thirty years back has the political tension reached so high and dangerous a point as it has attained today. Not in all this time has there been so high a degree of misunderstanding, of suspicion, of bewilderment, of sheer military fear.

We must expect that in both the Soviet Union and the United States the coming months will see extensive changes in governmental leadership. Will the new leaders be able to reverse these trends?

It will not be too late for them to make the effort to do so. There are limits, of course, to what they could hope to achieve. The permanent impediments to a happier relationship, which I outlined at the outset of this address, would still be there and would not be rapidly overcome, even in the best of circumstances. But they would not preclude the attainment of a real turning point in international life — a turning point beyond which anxiety and pessimism would begin to be replaced by hope and confidence for people everywhere.

What is necessary is only the overcoming of the military fixations that now command in so high degree the reactions on both sides, and the mustering of great courage by the statesmen in facing up to the task of relating military affairs to the other needs of the modern society. What is needed is that statesmen on both sides of the line should take their military establishments in hand and insist that these establishments should become the servants, not the masters and determinants, of political action. Both sides must learn to accept the fact that there is no security to be found in the quest for military superiority – that only in the reduction, not the multiplication, of the existing monstrous arsenals can the true security of any nation be found.

But beyond this, we must learn to recognize the gravity of the social, environmental, and even spiritual problems that assail us all in this unreal world of the machine, the television screen, and the computer. And we must also recognize the community of interest we all have – we and our Marxist friends alike – in finding hopeful responses to these obscure and subtle but insidious and, over the long run, highly dangerous problems.

If we, the scholars, with our patient and unsensational labors, can help the statesmen to understand these basic truths – if we can help them to understand not only the dangers we face and the responsibility they bear for overcoming these dangers but also the constructive and hopeful possibilities that lie there to be opened up by wiser, more restrained, and more realistic policies – if we can do these things, then we will be richly repaid for our dedication and our persistence; because we will then have the satisfaction of knowing that scholarship, the highest work of the mind, has served, as it should, the highest interests of civilization.

RELIGION

Give me that old-time religion
It's good enough for me.

Many of the Christians who now join the "old-time religion" chorus are actually practicing what, for evangelicals, is a new political religion of getting out the vote for specific New Right candidates. Also, ironically, the "Old-Time Gospel Hour" has been one of the pioneering programs of the electronic church, which adopts sophisticated new television technologies and innovative mass-oriented fund-raising through telecommunications. All might be well if only new times needed nothing more than old-time answers.

With reason, however, Diana Eck of the Center for the Study of World Religions asks: "What are we to think of an Old-Time Religion which has reeled off 'Ninety-five Theses for the 1980s' not one of which has to do with the struggle for economic justice and racial harmony, the shrinking natural resources of the world, and the very real dangers of nuclear confrontation?"

One way right-wing political gatherings are newly relating to traditional religion is to sing nontraditional words to traditional hymn tunes. For example, Young Americans for Freedom gleefully sing these lines to the tune of "The Battle Hymn of the Republic":

> Mine eyes have seen the horrors of the militant extreme.
> I have heard about their tennis shoes and eyes that madly gleam.
> They are armed and more fanatical than you would ever dream.
> I'll track down every one.

They also sing the following words to a Christmas carol, "Deck the Halls with Boughs of Holly," inverting the traditional spirit as they sing:

> Deck the halls with Commie corpses,
> Fa la la la la la la la la,
> 'Tis the time to be remorseless,
> Fa la la la la la la la la,
> Wield we now our sharp stiletti,
> Fa la la la la la la la la,
> Carve the pinks into confetti,
> Fa la la la la la la la la.

Right-wing songs against the Commies fuse with their fight against Big Government to create the frenzy of a holy crusade for freedom. Nonetheless, the reality of the New Right goal is to realize government coercion to:

Deny women the right to choose.

Crush the women's movement.

Censor the media.

Bypass action of the Supreme Court of the United States.

Jail homosexuals.

Suppress dissent against our military-industrial complex.

In addition to these negative counsels, this political religion expresses a series of positive New Right religious imperatives of power:

Bring America back to God's infallible Book.

Take children out of public schools; put them in Christian schools.

Help fund Christian schools through government vouchers.

Vote for candidates who support prayer in public schools.

Thank God daily for America since, she — above all nations — has honored the principles of the Bible.

To reckon with these religious dimensions of the New Right, Speak Out *first presents the viewpoint of Robert McAfee Brown. Not one readily to relinquish the resources of our biblical heritage to the true believers who act as if the Book dropped from the sky, Dr. Brown represents continuing engagement in Protestant-Catholic dialogue on current issues. He has been Professor of Religion at Stanford University and Professor of Ecumenics and World Christianity at Union Theological Seminary in New York and is now Professor of Theology and Ethics at the Pacific School of Religion at Berkeley, California. He brings to* Speak Out *a background of prophetic involvement with the Civil Rights movement, the anti–Vietnam war movement, and continuing action to create a local-national-international liberal coalition relating religion and politics.*

Our second critique of the New Religious Right is by Jack Mendelsohn, a minister and author who brings to Speak Out *his service as a lively interpreter of the public role of liberal religion in urban America and world affairs. His ministry in Bedford, Massachusetts, was preceded by others in Rockford and Chicago, Illinois; Indianapolis, Indiana; and the Arlington Street Church in Boston. His books include* Why I am a Unitarian Universalist *and* Channing: The Reluctant Liberal.

The Need for a Moral Minority

ROBERT McAFEE BROWN

Some of you may have misread the title "The Need for a Moral Minority," and assumed that I was going to address the Moral Majority. I am going to make some references to the Moral Majority in the course of these remarks, but I do not want to concentrate exclusively on that movement. I particularly do not want to have the Moral Majority setting my agenda, or our agendas, for the eighties. I think that agenda is somewhat politically naive and theologically un-Biblical; I will try to footnote that in a little while.

My overall concern is much more how we can relate religion and politics positively. If along the way we can learn some things from the Moral Majority, about how not to do it, I am willing to call that a gain.

This whole problem of a religious presence on the political scene which has been highlighted for us in this rather recent emergence of the theological right wing, the problem of religion of the political scene is illustrated for me by a comment from an anonymous 17th century writer, one of my favorite anonymous comments. This writer wrote: "I had rather see coming toward me a whole regiment with drawn swords, than one lone Calvinist convinced that he is doing the will of God." Now that statement illustrates both the glory and demonry of Calvinism, and by a not very difficult extension, the potential glory and potential demonry of all political involvement on the part of religiously minded persons. On the one hand, there is something immensely freeing and energizing about the feeling that one is doing God's will, and that the outcome of one's activity is therefore safe in God's hands. Such an attitude can liberate one to new kinds of courage, to immense risk taking, even to the point of death. Archbishop Romero of El Salvador is surely an example of this. He became convinced that the junta in his country, the one we are currently supporting, was an instrument of injustice and repression against the poor, and he said so, boldly and loudly, knowing the risks; and soon after he began speaking out he was gunned down in the very act of saying mass for his people. There have been glorious chapters in the history of faith that have been written and enacted by those who felt that in commitment to God's will, they had to oppose the will of other human leaders.

But there can be a demonry as well in the invoking of God's support which we find exhibited when individuals or groups decide what they want to impose on others, and then claim divine sanction for it. This gives them carte blanche to do whatever they feel is necessary to stop their opponents since their opponents, being opposed to them, are clearly opposed to God as well, and do not finally deserve the right to speak or act or persuade, and Christians have often been guilty of this. The Crusades were an example, Christian anti-Semitism is another, and sometimes the Christian willingness to kill, whether in support of a Nazi ideology, or extreme nationalism, whether of the Russian or American variety, these are other instances that come to mind. And as I look at the current American religious scene, it is this tendency that seems to me in danger of characterizing this recently emerged religious right of which Moral Majority is at least one very clear-cut example.

Mr. Falwell, Jerry Falwell, the leader of that movement, states that he knows just what is wrong with our country, and tells us: "God has called me to action. I have a divine mandate to go into the halls of Congress and fight for laws that will save America." As this position develops, it turns out that those who disagree with him are really by definition disagreeing with God, since he, and not they, have access to God's will. Liberals, for example, who Mr. Falwell abominates, are not just political liberals or theological liberals, they are godless liberals. They are the ones who must be removed from public office, since they are not only wrong, but evil. What we must have in office are God-fearing, Bible-believing Christians, which is bad news to Jews and secularists.

I do not for a moment challenge Mr. Falwell's right or anybody's right to get into the American political process, to work for change, to support candidates, urge people to vote and all the rest. That is the way the American system works, and the more people that are doing that, the better for the health of the system. And it would be a very perverse logic to claim that only people with whom I agree ought to be engaging in political activity and I want no part of such an argument. I have taken my own political stands in the past; I intend to keep doing so in the present and in the future, so can and should everyone, whether named Billy Graham or Bill Coffin, whether named Jerry Falwell or Robert Drinan.

Furthermore, this emergence of the Radical Right on the political scene, means that there is one ancient battle we are not going to have to fight for a while. For the most of my adult life, at any rate, people on the theological right have been saying religion and politics do not mix. The rest of us have been saying, "They do too mix." And now, for better or for worse, that message has been heard.

The question is no longer, "Do religion and politics mix?" The question is simply, "What is the nature of the mix?" And it is the nature of the mix, as far as groups like Moral Majority are concerned, that is increasingly concerning me, and even on some levels beginning to frighten me. Now let me say just enough about that kind of mix so that I can then set the stage in the latter part of these comments, for what seems to me a more appropriate alternative.

In Christian terms, and I think in terms with which all Jews could also agree, my real complaint about the Moral Majority's intrusion of the Bible into American politics, is that they are not biblical enough. I do not for a moment concede that they have the Bible on their side and that the rest of us are nothing but godless liberals or secular humanists which, in Mr. Falwell's lexicon, is very close to being either a Socialist or a Communist.

So let me illustrate that in two ways. First of all, it seems to me that the Moral Majority's biblically inspired political agenda involves a very selective, very partial, and therefore very distorted use of the Bible. They have isolated a set of concerns that they say get to the heart of what is wrong with America — homosexuality, abortion, and pornography. These are the things that are wrong and that are destroying our nation. What we need to do, what we need to be for, basically for prayer in public schools, and for more bombs. Jesus wants our kids to pray and he wants the Pentagon to be able to kill more people if necessary. I know that sounds a little crude, but I believe it is. I am not denying that there are moral dimensions involved in all those issues and that people can take different moral positions in response to them, but the notion that they represent what the Hebrew and Christian scriptures offer us as the key for understanding what is wrong with the world today, is one that strikes me as grotesque.

Take the issue of homosexuality. If one turns to the scriptures as a whole, to try to come up with their central concerns, homosexuality is going to be very low on such a list even if indeed it makes the list at all. There are perhaps seven very ambiguous verses in the whole biblical canon that even allude to it and I will any day subordinate the minuscule import of those seven verses, isolated verses, to hundreds and hundreds of places where the scriptures are dealing over and over again with questions of social justice, the tendency of the rich to exploit the poor, the need for all of us to have a commitment to the hungry, the need for nations not to put their major trust in armaments, the concern for the sick, the recognition that all people are children of God, even if they are Russians or Cubans or Salvadoreans. The Moral Majority creates an agenda and then proceeds to impose that agenda on scripture by developing little strings of unrelated verses to give divine sanction to the position. As those who work with the Bible know, one can prove absolutely anything that way. You can make a biblical case for militarism or pacifism, nationalism or internationalism, for male dominance or for women's rights, though it is a bit more difficult with women's rights. One can make a case for capital punishment or for letting the prisoners go free. One can make a case for socialism or for capitalism, simply by selecting a few verses very carefully and ignoring all the others.

It seems clear to me that there are great and central overriding themes and concerns in the scriptures. You and I might have slightly different lists of what these themes would be, but there would be certain ones that simply could not be ignored if we were going to respond honestly to the text. There are huge sections, for example, on the dangers of national idolatry, that is to say, making the nation into God, accepting uncritically whatever we have to do as a nation against other nations.

Those major emphases stand in very sharp contrast to Mr. Falwell's assessment that we should have done whatever we needed to win in Vietnam because our national honor was at stake. That was the criterion and I submit that national honor is a criterion that the Bible unremittingly attacks. There are long sections in scripture dealing with the need to be concerned about the poor and the destitute. There are treatments of the "virus" of racism. There are many recognitions that those with wealth will always be tempted to act repressively against the poor and so on and so on. It is breathtaking that when one looks over the agendas of the Moral Majority there is absolutely no mention of such things, there is a total silence. We seem to be living in two different worlds, reading two different books.

I will summarize that difference in this way: There seem to me to be some biblical passages that help to pull together many others, that help to encapsulate much of that message. I suggest that one such passage is Jesus' famous picture or parable of the Last Judgment. That represents his indictment of what is wrong in our society and how it should be changed. I remembered Mr. Falwell's indictment: pornography, abortion, homosexuality, no prayers in public schools, too little money for defense spending. How does this biblical indictment go? In Jesus' assessment, the nation, not just individuals. (We need to remember that story of the Last Judgment is addressed to the nations.) The nations are called to account and judged on the following basis: whether or not as a nation we gave food to the hungry, whether or not as a nation we gave drink to the thirsty, whether or not as a nation we took in strangers, whether or not as a nation we clothed the naked, whether or not as a nation we visited the sick, whether or not as a nation we went to those in prison and whether or not as a nation we did these things not just for folks like us, but to the very least of our sisters and brothers. So I say, "Yes, let the Moral Majority take an agenda to the American people. Let them call it a message based on special concern for the middle class. Let them appeal, if they wish, more to fears than to hopes. Let them make a patriotic pitch to keep America number one in the arms race at all costs; but let them not, I say, call that biblical. Let them not say, "That is a platform toward which the Jewish and Christian scriptures are pushing us."

Well, where do we go when that's been said? I am convinced first of all, that it is important to have said it to clear the air of it, but then we need to begin to look in different directions. I would like to start that looking by rejecting attempts to juxtapose the words moral and majority; they do not belong together. The Jewish and Christian scriptures talk about moral majorities. They talk about remnants, about minorities. Christians have a lot to learn from Jews about this. The Hebrew prophets were invariably on the side of the minority. They were taking on the status quo; they were getting into trouble. They never played the numbers game. Otherwise, Amos would never have gotten even third prize in the Bethel Chamber of Commerce competition for promising young dressers of sycamore trees, and you can be sure he never would have maintained a TV rating beyond the first week of a broadcast. There is a professor at Fuller Seminary, Bill Funnell, who says the book of Amos is full of quotations and none of them make good bumper stickers.

Now in the Jewish-Christian perspective, the truth is not likely to be found with the majority, but with the minorities, the remnants. In the Bible, truth comes in small packages. It was when the early Christians became the moral majority in the Roman Empire around the fourth century that things started going to pieces. Once Constantine recognized Christianity as the official religion, this little repressed minority began acting like an oppressing majority. The Pope raised armies, conversions were forced, there were pogroms, rights of those who disagreed were surpressed, unbelievers were tortured and killed, and this is a set of policies that as long as they could our own Protestant forbears carried on in their day. No, I think the human family has had enough of a taste of what one could call this "Christendom in Power League" in which Christians decide to try to run the show for everyone else. I don't think we want it back under Constantine, Jerry Falwell, or anyone else. The trouble with moral majorities is that they tend to see themselves as moral monopolies. So I suggest that the need is to build moral minorities, to create groups that will try to be a leaven in our national lump, that will say some of the things most people do not want to hear, that will try to avoid simplistic answers, that will acknowledge complexities, that will seek arenas for debate rather than a fundamentalistic fulmination, and that will try to enlarge our vision beyond national boundaries to global perspectives.

So let me now, to conclude, suggest very briefly five characteristics that I think would be appropriate to the moral minority, and I say that since Jews have had a long history of being a moral minority, we Christians have some things to learn from them, and I hope that they will begin to share long years of wisdom with us. I will not now try to speak for Jews, which would be condescending, but suggest some things that we, as Christians, out of our own heritage could begin to do to become a moral minority.

First, I said a moment ago that the Bible does not talk about minorities as much as about remnants. Since the demise of what we call this Constantinian Christianity, where Christians were running the show and that demise took place several hundred years ago, only a lot of Christians have not heard that word yet. Since that time this remnant posture has become both appropriate and descriptive for Christians. We are a small percentage, a remnant, of the whole human family, particularly when we look at ourselves globally. Let me suggest even a further refinement of that image. A moral minority might be called a remnant within the remnant. By and large, institutional Christianity is going to reflect the culture around it more than it will challenge it, but there could be a remnant within that remnant to define some ways to offer a different model. There is an exciting set of experiences out of the church in Latin America that offers a way of thinking about that model. For centuries, as you know, the Catholic Church in Latin America was at the beck and call of a little group of the wealthy who had all the power, who had all the money, all the prestige and who had enough military hardware to keep everyone else in line. But in recent years, the churches have been getting away from that uncritical alliance with those in power, and there have grown up literally tens of thousands of what they call "communitatas da basa," base communities or grassroots communities. These people do not wait for the word to come through an ecclesiastical chain of command. They tackle a local problem, oppression by a local large land holder, or inadequate wages to live on, or the disappearance of someone who is speaking out politically, and they look for ways to act, perhaps fifteen or twenty of them together. They put all this in the context of their ongoing liturgical life, in the midst of prayer, Bible study, the eucharist, they try to combine what they call reflection and action. They become a leaven in the life of the larger church, and hope gradually that thereby the larger church can become a leaven in the even larger community. I think that we could create models in our own community which would take that kind of experiment seriously. Is there a local problem here in Minneapolis that nobody is tackling that needs attention? A small group could begin to deal with it, maybe from within one church, maybe across denominational lines, or by concerned folk who are Christians and Jews and whoever, whatever the nature of the mix calls for. The point is, one does not need to be a loner, one also does not have to have a huge structure behind one in order to begin to act.

Secondly, what would be the resources such a group could employ? Here I think we have a couple of very good things going for us. One of them is the Bible. If we could break out of the kind of "culturally-conditioned" ways we have read the Bible, we would find it an explosive arsenal of materials for creative change. In the last two years I have had to begin rereading the Bible in the light of what I have learned from Christians in such places as Latin America, trying to see it through their eyes, hear it with their ears, and I am amazed at what is in this book. We tend to spiritualize away all the rough edges. When the Bible talks about good news for the poor we immediately interpret that to mean the spiritually poor, the spiritually impoverished, and we are all part of that, so there is no rough edge left. Now, I am sure that is part of what was meant, but it seems to me very clear what is also meant, that when Jesus is talking about the poor, he also meant the materially poor, the really impoverished, who did not have enough to eat, who did not have enough food, who did not have enough power. When he said the poor have the good news preached to them, that is part of what he meant, those people down on the bottom of the pile. Jesus' message of liberty to the oppressed is addressed to those not only under the oppression of neurosis and other middle-class ailments, but to those who were oppressed as victims of economic, political and military oppression. We have a phrase, that is in Jesus' sermon at Nazareth, which talks about proclaiming what our translations call "the acceptable year of the Lord." That washes right over us. What was that referring to? That was the jubilee year, which is about as political as you can get. Debts were to be forgiven, slaves were to be freed, land was to revert to its former owners.

There is plenty of stuff within this old black book for a minority posture to emerge. We could also realize that we have dealt with our own past Christian history in very selective ways. We have known all about the church that emerged triumphantly in the 4th century and a lot of people wish it were still around. But before that, Christians were this little minority, a tiny handful, quite analogous to what we, in our world today, are becoming. Maybe those first centuries are a clue to what we should be about, welcoming the down and outers, challenging Caesar, cutting across lines that divide people off from one another, being a time were those whom the world calls worthless are treated as having infinite worth. We look at the Reformation, we Protestants, and we trot out Luther and Calvin and maybe Thomas Hooker or some other Anglican, and we forget that there were other people involved in the Reformation — Quakers, Mennonites, Anabaptists, Diggers, revelers, the crazies, we like to think — who were doing such things as challenging the right and the fitness of Christians going to war, who were challenging the right of governments to be the definers of conscience, who were casting their lot with the poor. There is a whole lot in that heritage which we have buried that maybe we need to recover. So there is a biblical and historical resource we could bring to bear.

The third thing the moral majority could stress, perhaps the most important thing in the time in which we live, would be the necessity of a global perspective. This world is now just too small to allow for anything else. And to look at the world simply in terms of what is good for the United States, is ultimately going to be self-defeating. To put the main stress and priority on more weapons, as the national debate is now suggesting, is truly likely to increase the likelihood that we will use them. A perspective can no longer be national or regional, it has to be global. In terms of the remnant within the remnant, the great thing, it seems to me, that we have going for us, is that we do not have to start out and create that global community from scratch. It already exists. There is a small network of courageous people all over the world, some of whose courage might even begin to rub off on us. I have been fortunate, in the last few years, to have visited some parts of the world I never expected to visit — Chile, Argentina, Cambodia, Laos, Kenya, South Africa, Russia, India. What impresses me is that in places where it is not expedient to do so and involves great risks, little groups of people speak and act in defiance of what repressive governments demand of them. They refuse a sheerly nationalistic perspective. They insist on seeing who they are in relation to everyone else — Dom Helder Camara in Brazil, Alan Bosack and Desmond Tutu in South Africa — many courageous folk in repressive regimes in Chile and Argentina which our administration is about to reward with more shipments of arms; ministers in South Korea; whoever or wherever there is the moral minority, where people are taking their lives, putting their lives on the line, every time they speak. This brotherhood, this sisterhood of the remnant within the remnant of the moral minority already exists and we can be empowered by them. If they can risk their lives, we might at least risk a little bit of our reputations.

That suggests a fourth thing the moral minority might become; it could become that group in our society which is genuinely committed to the powerless and the voiceless. The World Council of Churches and Pope John Paul II have recently been describing the task of the church as being, as they state, the voice of the voiceless, insisting that the church must speak on behalf of those who cannot speak, act on behalf of those who cannot act. I believe we must improve on that. Rather than just trying to be the voice of the voiceless, the church, it seems to me, or at least the moral minority in the church, must be that place where the voiceless are empowered to speak on their own behalf, and are guaranteed a hearing. Instead of the church speaking through a microphone to the world on behalf of the voiceless, the church must be the place where the microphone is offered to those who have not been able to gain access to it. Now you have to decide what this might mean in Minnesota, who are the powerless here, Indians, members of other minority groups, women? A moral minority would try to see to it that the ones without representation, the ones denied a hearing, the ones written off by the rest of the society, could be heard and taken seriously and empowered.

Fifth, and finally, a moral minority must, as I have been implying, set its own agendas. You may not like the ones that I have been suggesting so far. Certainly there can be others. That would be one thing to deal with among members of a moral minority. Our agendas must not be set by the Moral Majority movement. We must not fall into a trap of single-issue politics, or politics narrowly conceived on a tiny set of issues. I find it kind of morally oppressive to be told, again and again, some kind of obsession about other people's sex life is the burning issue of the day, when the majority of the human family went to bed hungry every night or to be told to rally around getting prayers back into schools when millions of people are unable to find jobs, or get minimal help if they are unemployed and disadvantaged. So I hope we can find ways to begin to rally around the problems, for the whole human family is hurting from the mad escalation of the arms race, the need for more equitable distribution of food, coming to terms with denials, both abroad and at home, of basic human rights, such as education and medical care and jobs and all the rest.

I think we need to rally around these problems in a context which provides a forum for seeking the good of all, not just small segments of the population. We must try to present issues without demagoguery cheating. We must acknowledge that problems are complex and that simplistic solutions will be misleading and wrong, and acknowledge also that ambiguities abound not only within the positions of those with whom we disagree, but within our own positions as well. With some such way of engaging in political life, we might be able to create a moral minority that could propose convictions without arrogance but insight without absolutism, with commitment but without coercion and with democracy but without demagoguery.

A Heimlich Maneuver
for America

JACK MENDELSOHN

"Honk if you love Jesus, then honk again if you hate the big-spending, bra-burning, sex-crazed, homosexual, lesbian, abortionist, commie, secular humanists who gave away the Panama Canal."

–author's lampoon of Moral Majority, Inc.

The country is choking on a scam: the manipulation of politics by religious absolutists, and the manipulation of spiritual malaise by reactionary politicians. What is needed is a Heimlich Maneuver, an intervention in behalf of life. In the Heimlich Maneuver, someone with concern and skill extends prompt aid. Thought was required to learn how to do it. Will is required to do it. The aim is rescue. It is not just a mechanical procedure. It is a liberating act.

The Heimlich Maneuver is a metaphor of what religious liberals, in coalition with other caring religious bodies, must undertake. It is a metaphor of self-transcending energy, and of the respect all progressive and compassionate spiritual communities hold for the disciplines required to practice life-serving skills, and to exercise redemptive powers.

The immediate task is a realistic assessment of the threats religious chauvinists pose to the democratic process and to the struggle for social justice and peace. We must expose and oppose, but without making scapegoats of them for the miasmas on which they fasten and flourish. They prosper because they attack vulnerabilities in our political and religious perceptions. The need of the 1980s is for new creations of American political thought and theologies of politics. A cooperative, broadly ecumenical agenda is required. Many lively contributors are welcome.

The New Religious Right has brought multitudes of formerly apolitical, born-again Christians into the political arena. While we have reason for restrained joy, it is still true that democracy stands to gain when more citizens are involved. Whether religious convictions and politics should "mix" has never been the question. The nature of the mix is the issue: what use of religious convictions resulting in what kind of politics?

In the mid–1960s, I preached a sermon at Arlington Street Church: "Christians Who Believe That God Is Dead." My theme was the latest excitement in religious circles generated by a group of earnest Christian theologians — William Hamilton, Thomas Altizer, and the rest — who proclaimed that the God of traditional Biblical religion can neither help nor hinder, because that God's reality and believability were forever destroyed by the holocaust of Nazi Europe and Hiroshima, by Vietnam, by racial injustice, by the stench of poverty and misery in our own cities, and in the world around. In April 1966, they made the cover of *Time*. Think of that.

Their inspiration was not an earlier announcer of God's demise, Friedrich Nietzsche, but the Bible itself, and particularly the Jesus of the Bible, for whom they held fervent mystical and moral feelings. Understandably, there were those who described their message as: "There is no God, and Jesus is His only begotten son."

They found in Jesus, with the supernaturalism peeled off, a person "for others" — the great exemplar of total commitment to love and service of one's fellow beings. Jesus is not a savior or icon, they said. Jesus is "the place to be." And the place of this Christ is in the midst of the struggle for justice, equality and peace, in the emerging forms of technological society, and in the arts, sciences and humanities of the secular world. In this time of the death of God, they declared, we, too, have a place to be. It is in the world, in the midst of human sin, suffering and degradation, with the needy and oppressed, with the neighbor, and, yes, with the enemy.

It is amazing what less than two decades can do to where the center of spiritual gravity might be.

Death of God theology was a radical protest against American Christianity's affluent self-satisfaction, media hype and edifice complex; against congregations that make worship an exercise in nostalgia; against preachers who pray in leaded-glass voices, and exploit the gullible.

Where have they gone, these death of God theologians? Into obscurity. And we know who replaced them on the cover of *Time:* Moral Majority's Jerry Falwell. For him and for the 2,500 other Christian Right leaders who assembled in Washington in January 1981 to celebrate Ronald Reagan's victory, the Bible and Christ are still "the place to be." But what an extraordinarily different place.

God, they exulted, is alive and rejoicing in an awakened Christian America about to smite, hip and thigh, abortion, liberalism, welfare, food stamps, affirmative action, sex education, the United Nations, aid to the third world, disarmament, and the Soviet Union. They even managed to round up a black clergyman who applauded the slave trade. "The greatest thing God ever did for blacks in this country," he cried, "was to send some white men in ships to Africa and bring us back to this country so that we could know Jesus Christ." The overwhelmingly white audience gave him a standing ovation.

How can we take this seriously, while still retaining our sense of humor and purpose? We'd better. In one hundred and ninety days — from Inauguration to passage of the Reagan budget and tax cut — a new national administration and its Christian Right allies created a whopping reversal of direction for this country, threatening visions of America as an embodiment of a just and humane society.

There are rougher seas ahead. For religious liberals it is a time to remember that we are not alone. If resisting the scriptural irrationality that eggs on the nation's rush into reaction was solely the task of Unitarian Universalists, we would do well either to become an underground remnant, or to convert, practice singing "The Old Rugged Cross" for real, and pray for the best. We need friends and allies. We need coalitions. And they are out there, as this volume testifies. They are out there among evangelicals and fundamentalists, as appalled as we are by their noisier, better financed co-religionists. Their faith expresses compassion, respect for religious differences, and commitments to social justice, as Biblical imperatives. Who would know, reading the press, watching television, that there are movements like Sojourners, and publications like *Christianity Today*, whose rigorous orthodoxy prompts them to pray for a reconciliation of the U.S. and the U.S.S.R., to work for disarmament, to uphold church-state separation, and to undertake a radical discipleship on social issues? These fundamentalists and evangelicals, multitudes of them, are our natural allies as the onslaught of the Religious Right quickens.

Equally stricken is the leadership of mainline member bodies of the National Council of Churches, and broad segments of Roman Catholicism and Judaism. Whether it is prevention of nuclear war, constitutional protection of thought, expression and association, or governmental jurisdiction over the uterus, we need one another. The help we can give to one another is real.

On a day Thoreau walked from Walden into Concord to exchange beans for rice, he was arrested for refusing to pay his poll tax. The government supported slavery and was backing the Mexican War; well, he would not support the government. He spent a fruitful night in jail. It inspired his essay on Civil Disobedience. Emerson reportedly turned up the next morning. "Henry, what are you doing in there?" asked the great sage. "Waldo, what are you doing out there?" Thoreau replied.

If those who call themselves the Moral Majority are indeed that, then the only place for believers in religious liberty, political democracy and social justice to be is in the Immoral Minority. Right? Wrong! Labels are not the issue. There's a history that is. In the Boston of the 1720s, two youthful brothers, James and Benjamin Franklin, published an irreverent weekly newspaper, the *New England Courant*, which was dedicated to puncturing the pomposities of Puritan preachers and politicians. The Franklin brothers created a fictional staff of droll correspondents, among them Tabitha Talkative, Ichabod Henroost, Fanny Mournful and Silence Dogood, whose letters ravaged the hypocrisies of a ruling order in which religion and politics exploited one another, to the disgrace of each's integrity.

We are well launched into another era of intolerant religiosity engaged in manipulating the electorate with regressive politics. Exposure as biting and skillful as that of the *New England Courant* of 260 years ago is indicated. And the heat and humor will no more be welcomed by the New Religious Right than it was by old Cotton Mather, who bitterly denounced the young Franklins: "This practice of supporting and publishing each week a libel on purpose to burlesque the virtuous ministers of religion and render the services of their ministry despicable, even detestable, is a wickedness that was never known before in any country, Christian, Turkish, or pagan on the face of the earth!"

The Franklins were charmed at first by the outburst: delicious confirmation of their case. But James was clapt in prison for three weeks for "contempt." Their weekly was clapt in chains of heavy censorship. Benjamin, seventeen at the time, fled to the freer climate of Philadelphia. The lesson they taught is renewable: self-righteousness is the undoing of democracy; claiming God as absolute enforcer of particular opinions of policies is dangerous to a society's health. As Alan Geyer, of the Center for Theology and Public Policy, expresses it: "There is this dark side of the Puritan tradition, especially its addiction to the kind of moral indignation which generates hostility in all directions, forsakes social justice for self-aggrandizement and victimizes so many persons whose intolerable sin is that they have an honest difference of opinion on some political issue."

Sustained by a pluralistic and frequently effective religious tradition, it is crucial that we neither panic nor forsake reason and humor. If democracy be true, reason and humor are ultimate persuaders, along with faith, courage, and empowering alliances.

Valuing the integrity of both religion and politics these days means helping the American mind to understand how it is being led backwards. When the Senate in its wisdom voted to bar the victim of rape from being assisted by federal funds in obtaining an abortion, Senator Lowell Weicker, a Republican, pled with the leader of the move to prohibit assistance, fellow-Republican Jesse Helms, by pointing out that the harshness was not only unconscionable but had no sanction in our moral tradition. Such an interdiction, said Senator Weicker, can hardly be said to come down to us from Mount Sinai. On the contrary, replied Senator Helms, Mount Sinai is precisely where it does come down from; and if this smacks of Cotton Mather, so be it.

The chairman of Moral Majority in Illinois, the Reverend George A. Zarris, encourages his members to conduct library search-and-destroy missions. "I would think," he said, "moral-minded people might object to books that are philosophically alien to what they believe. If they have the books, and feel like burning them, fine." According to Art Buchwald, in a column reminiscent of *New England Courant*, if burning the books isn't enough to restore "the old moral values that made this country great . . . then, we must burn the people." The Reverend Dwight Wymer, pastor of Immanuel Baptist Church, Grand Rapids, Michigan, has undertaken a tentative first step. He uses a home-made "electric stool" and a 12-volt battery to shock his young Bible students into "hearing God's word."

Our devout Secretary of State, Alexander M. Haig, Jr., justifies our present indulgence toward the Government of Argentina, despite the terror it practices against many of its citizens, on the ground that Argentina and the United States are theological kinfolk: "We both believe in God."

Granted we've been through a devastating decade of political disillusionment in America, how can we account for the sheer power of the current Regressive Revolution in piety and government? Is it significantly different from similar forays we have experienced, even in this century?

"Keeping cool with Cal" in the 1920s included, along with political conservatism and rampant materialism, Ku Klux Klan terror, militant, book-burning, anti-evolution fundamentalism, Prohibition, and languor in the main line and liberal churches.

Roosevelt's pragmatic progressivism in the 1930s was assaulted weekly by the nation's most popular radio personality, a fascistically inclined priest named Charles Coughlin, and by a clamorous, aggressive America First movement.

Shaken by the cold war and Mao's China triumph, great segments of the nation turned in the 1950s to a messiah named Senator Joseph McCarthy, whose allies, the Christian anti-Communist crusade, thumped noisily for repression, while Billy Graham rose like a meteor, preaching a privatized, politically conservative revivalism.

By the early 1960s, the Republican Party presented a presidential candidate, Senator Barry Goldwater, who proudly celebrated "extremism" as the answer to our ills, while the John Birch Society, Carl McIntyre, and phalanxes of White Citizens Councils rallied the country against equal voting rights, fair employment practices, foreign aid and other heinous heresies.

What is different? Again, Alan Geyer offers a valuable clue. The current cadres of the religious and political right, he says, "show an intellectual (or at least pseudo-intellectual) sophistication largely absent in those earlier rounds. There are think tanks which buy up the expertise, even hire house theologians, generate dogmas, flood the political and academic markets with their publications, increasingly dominate the op-ed pages and television, provide platoons of consultants to politicans and do much of the dirty work for single-issue and special interest lobbies."

The religious platoons of the Regressive Revolution, via the electronic church, have made, in the 1980s, a quantum leap beyond the past, both in reaching mass markets and in hugely successful fund-raising. A significant difference.

Someone has measured the total audience to which Jesus preached as no more than twenty or thirty thousand persons. Today's electronic preachers speak regularly to millions. Pat Robertson's dazzling Christian Broadcasting Network beams its "700 Club" daily to more viewers than the Johnny Carson Show. Robertson, Falwell, Oral Roberts, et al., are paragons of up-to-the-minute communications technique.

Dr. Roberts reported a while back: (1) that Jesus had appeared to him in a vision at 7:00 P.M. on May 25, 1980, (2) that the vision was "about 900 feet tall," (3) that Jesus lifted the unfinished Tulsa hospital Dr. Roberts is building high in the air, and (4) that Jesus simultaneously promised that funds would be forthcoming to finish the structure.

Item 4 proved to be a remarkable winner. After sharing his vision with his followers by direct mail, Dr. Roberts received almost $5 million in donations, which works out to approximately $5,555 per Jesus-foot.

Some of this money comes from corporate and individual angels, even from repressive foreign governments, like South Africa's, but more impressive are the amounts that come from persons and families of modest means.

Gone are the nickel and dime days of the early broadcast evangelists. Now, computers at lightning speed churn out differentiated mailing lists, containing all kinds of pre-programmed information. They extrude mountains of "individualized" letters, prayers, political action alerts, and financial appeals, sorted by topic, personalized by individual problem, clued by that trail of interests, values, socioeconomic levels and lifestyles we all leave behind by credit cards, subscriptions, installment accounts, and charitable or political contributions.

Why is so much of this effort politically right-wing? It is only fair to credit whatever heartfelt political convictions the electronic evangelists may have. It is also crucial to reckon with this country's "free enterprise" syndrome. The airwaves are open to those who can pay. Who can pay? Those who know how to appeal to a paying audience. The electronic evangelists have learned who is able and willing to supply cash!

For nearly twenty years, Jerry Falwell's "Old Time Gospel Hour" was an unremarkable feature of Sunday morning, Bible-belt television. Its familiar fundamentalism was heavy on personal sin, revivalism and rebirth, light on social concern, empty of politics.

Then revelation struck. Christians, it was disclosed to Falwell, should band together under a Biblical banner, register, and vote for (or against) candidates on the basis of how they stand on issues ranging from prayer in the public schools to vast increases in military spending. Falwell's cup, ever since, runneth over.

Never mind that Falwell and his peers use hard-sell tactics, and that the aged, frightened, bereft and afflicted are often exploited. It's all for the glory of the Gospel and the Lord, for an America armed to the teeth, and for an end to pornography, food stamps and "forced bussin'." The reactionary evangelicals go for the gut. Get right with God. Get right with your loved ones. Get right with your country. Above all, know and punish thine enemies! It's all very emotional and satisfying. It's also heady, which inevitably means the overdoing that becomes undoing. Billy Graham, confessing past sins, now distances himself from the Religious Right. Barry Goldwater, galled by Moral Majority vituperation against the nomination of his friend Sandra O'Connor to the Supreme Court, tells Falwell caustically to "back off."

But the costs will continue to mount. The religio-political predicament we confront in the 1980s is deep and real. Regressive revivalism rides on a technological wave, its passions unspent, promoting paranoia, and reducing complex problematical elements of our common life to simplistic strictures of abomination.

As we plan our own revivals of ecumenical social action, of struggles for justice and peace, of "promoting the general welfare," of securing the blessings of liberty for all, it is crucial to recognize that the Religious Right is more a symptom of our problems than their cause. It nurtures and manipulates primitive elements in our ethos, from sexual obsessions to wounded national pride. The social context that empowers its success is rooted in profound disenchantments, dating roughly from the assassination of John F. Kennedy. While we of the mainline and liberal spiritual bodies enjoyed status as religious newsmakers, a war on poverty in America was lost to a shooting war in Vietnam which tore us apart at home. Confidence in business, labor unions, public education and government plummeted. A president admired by millions left office in disgrace. Inflation soared. Energy became a jarring problem. Hostages were seized in Iran. International tensions mounted one upon another. Divorce soared. Pornography flourished. And for many who were over thirty in the 1960s, the radical changes in young people's values and lifestyles underscored the overthrow of a taken-for-granted American morality.

The marvelous box with the magic tube left our innocence largely in place through the 1950s when the ratings champs were Milton Berle and Red Skeleton. But in succeeding decades, as the gore and hate of war and civil strife poured ever more vividly into our homes, our malaise deepened. Now the tube brings as well the electronic church, and its message is comforting to many. It offers hope and certainty. It offers targets of wrath. It is the counterculture of the 1980s. It mirrors a stampede toward conservatism. Culturally, large segments of our population are ready for change, backwards. Conservative political and economic views have a greater credibility than at any time since before the Great Depression. The electronic evangelists offer something that appeals, something to believe in. But that does not make them political geniuses, as time will tell, and as complex realities press their stubborn demands.

Progressive and compassionate religious forces, like a silhouette painting, will begin to take new shape by what the rampant right in religion and politics is seemingly driven to do. There's nothing wrong with religious communities committed to a just and humane society that repeated assaults on the First Amendment and incessant banging into what people can see, write, read and hear won't cure. There's nothing wrong with them that

20 percent inflation spurred by wild military spending won't cure. There's nothing wrong with them that preempting "religious" in such a way that nobody else can claim the name won't cure. There's nothing wrong with them that tests for political office and responsible citizenship which exclude as minions of Satan all who disagree won't cure.

The American piety that fuels a Moral Majority and dumps on the poor also prompted Goodwill Industries and Alcoholics Anonymous. The American piety that oozes the unguents of Charles Colson and the poisons of Pat Robertson also inspired the social gospels of Walter Rauschenbush and Martin Luther King, Jr.

Selective-issue, sex-obsessed politics is not "the Gospel." Briefs for the Pentagon, the oil industry and male-dominated society are not "the message of Jesus." A profoundly religious country, which ours is, will stand for only so much of this brokerage of ideology against reality.

The inspirations of a revitalized, progressive ecumenism are clearly these:

• The resources, divine and human, are available for the achievement of a more just and loving human community.

• There is a moral obligation to direct our efforts toward the establishment of such a community.

• The decisive forms of goodness in society are institutional. Faith cannot properly be placed in merely individual virtue, even though it is a prerequisite for societal virtues.

• Revelation is continuous. Meaning has not been finally captured. Relations between persons rest ideally not on coercion but on mutual, free consent.

It is critical, as we construct an activist inter-faith agenda, that we will sanctify no self-serving pieties, no coarse manifestations of greed and privilege, no social amnesia in the name of personal salvation; that we will be defined by a sense of the holy that is genuinely liberating as well as commanding. There will be no play-acting, no mumbling by rote, no posturing. We will commit ourselves to what transcends ourselves, to what makes the whole world, not just our private corners of it, more fit for living. We will cleave to history's higher rather than its meaner meanings. We will act for the freedom and dignity of those to whom freedom and dignity are now a farce. Our disciplines will be humility and hope. Our faith will exalt love, justice and moral power, a marvelous mixture of openness and conviction.

SEX

Sex is at the center of America's new battle of faiths. New Right impera-tives of power concerning female-male relations include the following:

> *Oppose sex education, contraceptives, and abortion.*
>
> *Reverse the Supreme Court decision on abortion; pass a Human Life Amendment.*
>
> *Rejoice that ERA is dead.*
>
> *Establish a Family Protection Agency to restore parental power.*
>
> *Limit homosexuals' rights; don't let them teach school.*
>
> *Remember what God says concerning homosexuals: "They shall surely be put to death" (Lev. 20:13).*
>
> *Fight legalizing prostitution.*
>
> *End sexual anarchy at our universities.*
>
> *Don't have day care; mothering is a full-time task.*
>
> *Avoid federal intervention in husband-wife relations, for then women could sue their husbands for rape.*

These single imperatives concerning issues of sex and the family may be seen in wider context if we consider what the religious New Right re-gards as the five major problems moral Americans need to face. Does the list include strengthening the chances for human survival through reversing nuclear arms build-up? In no way. Rather, we are told that the five major problems that plague us and call for moral leadership are the following:

> *1. So-called Christian America has murdered more unborn in-nocents than the six million Jews murdered in Nazi atrocities.*
>
> *2. The National Civil Rights Act of 1979 legalizes homosex-uals as a legitimate minority entitled to their sexual preference.*
>
> *3. The four billion dollar per year pornographic industry is the number one enemy of the family.*
>
> *4. Humanism is the philosophy that underlies secular educa-tion and which has forced prayer and Bible reading out of public schools.*
>
> *5. Divorce is skyrocketing, so the American family may well approach extinction in the next twenty years.*

For our Speak Out *on these issues, we turn first to a co-founder and editor of* MS. *magazine, Gloria Steinem, whose notes on "The Nazi Connection" are based on research on international feminism that she did at the Woodrow Wilson International Center of the Smithsonian Institution.*

With respect to abortion, Charles Hartshorne argues: "That persons have rights is a universal belief in our society, but that a fetus is already an actual person — about that there is and there can be no consensus. Coercion in such matters is tyranny." Hartshorne is a philosopher of life whom persons of diverse religious traditions honor for his vision of God, sometimes known as process theology or panentheism. The philosopher of freedom affirms that each act of every creature is a deathless contribution to the divine cosmic Life which evermore lives in ever new ways forever and ever. Quincy Wright, in his monumental lifework, A Study of War, *re*commended Hartshorne's religious philosophy as a workable foundation of world peace.

As we confront the New Right in America's battle of faiths today, the antiabortion position is being yoked with a proposed Human Life Amendment (HLA) to the Constitution of the United States. HLA in fact provides for classification of abortion as murder.

The Nazi Connection

GLORIA STEINEM

I. IF HITLER WERE ALIVE, WHOSE SIDE WOULD HE BE ON?

> Six million . . . is the number generally assigned not only to
> Jews who died under Hitler but to babies who have died under
> the Supreme Court.
>
> > —Patrick Riley
> > *National Catholic Register,*
> > May 13, 1979

> Auschwitz, Dachau, and Margaret Sanger: Three of a Kind
> > —sign at the 1979 Right-to-Life Convention

> Just as the Jews were depicted as "untermenschen," so the un-
> born are depicted as nonhuman.
>
> > —Raymond J. Adamek
> > *Human Life Review,* Fall/1977

Using the same analogy to Nazi Germany made by many of
the speakers, [Congressman Robert K.] Drinan said, "We
know in this country what is going on. Some of the Germans
had the excuse they weren't sure.
> —The Washington *Post,* January 23, 1977

This is not the time to "cool the rhetoric" . . . We are not
"sliding toward Auschwitz." We are not "headed for a Holocaust." We are living in the very midst of one. . . . The American Abolitionist League calls on the conscience of the pro-life
community to . . . padlock the slaughterhouses. Stage sit-ins.
Let this nation know that the laws of the Supreme Being take
precedence over the laws of the Supreme Court.
> —*The Abolitionist,* an antiabortion newsletter
> published in Pittsburgh

[At the National Right-to-Life Convention] Professor William
C. Brennan . . . said [the company] which manufactures devices and medicines used in abortion [is] in the same position
as I. G. Farben, the German firm that made chemicals used in
the mass execution of Jews.
> —*The Catholic News,* July 5, 1979

If you haven't been at an antiabortion rally lately, or stumbled on the right-wing effort on behalf of the 1980 Republican Platform and its support for a Constitutional ban aganist abortion, then the quotes you've just read may seem bizarre and exceptional.

Certainly, the groups that use these and other inflammatory arguments don't trust the major media. (The same Professor Brennan quoted above, for instance, went on to compare the American press with that in Nazi Germany, and to condemn it for "concealing the facts.") That's why they have created their own media world of right-wing newsletters, pamphlets, and books distributed through churches and local organizations, or through computerized mailing lists for which they claim 10 million names, plus television shows that reach into 14 million homes weekly.

But feminists who have been working on the issues of reproductive freedom especially — and those few reporters who cover the ultraright wing — have been sending back warnings of this increasingly vicious campaign ever since the 1973 Supreme Court decisions on abortion. By 1974, for instance, Marion K. Sanders, distinguished reporter for *Harper's* magazine, reported that "the analogy with Hitler's extermination program . . . has proved potent propaganda. The implication is that legal abortion is only a first step toward compulsory abortion for 'undesirables,' raising the specter of genocide for black people."

As it turned out, most of the black community rejected the genocide argument made by these overwhelmingly white, right-wing groups. If black women were having a disproportionate number of abortions, as the antiabortion groups often cited as proof of "genocide," it was because they had less access to good health care and contraception. In fact, the white birthrate declined just as much after contraception and abortion became legal, and it remains lower than that for black Americans. More important, a very disproportionate number of the women whose health and lives were saved by safe, legal abortion were black. (In Harlem Hospital alone, for instance, in the first year following the 1971 liberalization of New York State's abortion law, there were about 750 fewer admissions of women suffering from self-induced or illegal abortions.) Moreover, legally available or Medicaid-funded abortions as a matter of right meant that black and other minority women were less vulnerable to racist "bargaining": a safe abortion in return for agreeing to be sterilized.

Altogether, many of the antiabortion groups seemed more motivated by concern with the decline of the white birthrate to a low unprecedented in American history — even producing too few "adoptable" white infants to meet the demand — than with the need to protect the reproductive rights of poor or minority Americans. (In some states, antiabortion legislators had advocated withholding of welfare from women with three or more children until those women agreed to be sterilized.) The self-description of "abolitionist" by groups working to abolish legal abortion still tries for an emotional connection to the movement against slavery. So does their odd equating of the Dred Scott and the 1973 Supreme Court decisions, as if denying legal personhood to a slave and to a fetus were exactly the same thing. But right-wing literature now focuses on those who fear change most: the white middle class, the elderly, religious fundamentalists, and others who may feel that they or their lifestyles are endangered.

Abortion is constantly presented to them as the symbolic beginning of some horrifying future. It will destroy marriage and morality by removing the inevitability of childbearing as the only goal of sex and as God's will; it will endanger the birth of future people like them; it will endanger old or handicapped people by paving the way for euthanasia; it will masculinize women by allowing them to choose an identity other than the vessels for other people's lives; and finally it will be the same as legalizing murder.

The fear may vary, but the metaphor for terror is often the same: Hitler's philosophy and concentration camps; the closest modern memory can come to an earthly version of hell.

"Is there much difference between the concept of a 'Master Race' (quality race)," Dr. and Mr. J. C. Willke ask rhetorically in their *Handbook on Abortion,* "and the 'quality of life' of our modern proabortionist social planners?" According to this obscurely published, widely distributed paperback (with a photograph of a white teenage girl listening attentively to a white male doctor on the cover), the answer is no. "Although never legalized, abortion had become in fact the accepted answer for the mother's social problem in the 1920s and '30s in Germany," the Willkes allege. "The above physicians, accustomed to accepting the killing of one group of humans who were socially burdensome (the unborn), were apparently able to move logically to killing other classes of humans."

By ignoring the rights of the patient and focusing only on the doctor, these authors equate two opposite acts: performing an abortion for a woman who has freely chosen it (and who has a logical right to decide a pregnancy that cannot go forward without the use of her body and all its life-support systems), and the death of an autonomous person who has requested no such thing (not even, presumably, the right to suicide or a planned and peaceful death). The crucial question of *who decides* and *where the authority lies* is never discussed in these emotional comparisons between abortion and death camps; between a belief in reproductive choice as an individual right *against* the dictates of government, and a Nazi authoritarianism that declared the very idea of individual rights to be dangerous.

"True idealism," as Hitler wrote in *Mein Kampf,* "is nothing but the subordination of the interests and life of the individual to the community . . .[5] The sacrifice of personal existence is necessary to secure the preservation of the species."

Does this begin to sound familiar? It should — because the second flaw in the fervent condemnations of pro-choice advocates as Nazis is that Hitler himself, and the Nazi doctrine he created, were unequivocally opposed to any individual right to abortion. In fact, Hitler's National

Socialist Movement preached against and punished contraception, homo-sexuality, women whose main purpose was not motherhood, men who did not prove their manhood by fathering many children — and anything else that failed to serve the need of preserving and expanding the German state.

In *Mein Kampf,* Hitler wrote that "We must also do away with the conception that the treatment of the body is the affair of every indi-vidual." It was a direct slap at the feminist movement of Germany in the late 19th and early 20th century, an influential force for, among other things, divorce, contraception, and abortion; in short, for a woman's right to control her own body.

German feminists not only shared the goals of their sisters in other countries, but they had won a few earlier and greater successes: they achieved the vote in 1918 as part of the Weimar Constitution that fol-lowed World War I, for instance, and by 1926, women deputies to the Reichstag, the national parliamentary body that symbolized this brief flowering of democracy, just as the great German novelists and the Bauhaus came to symbolize the between-the-wars flowering of literature and art. (In the same era, there were only 15 women members of the British Parliament, and women in the United States Congress had reached the total of three.) Radical German feminists had also begun to organize against the protective legislation that kept women out of many jobs, and to work toward such international goals as pacifism. German families had become much smaller, and married women had gained the right to their own salaries.

Precisely because such changes were both obvious in daily lifestyles and profound, they were often resented by those who longed for the hierarchical, "undefeated" days before the war. As unemployment and inflation grew worse, women in the work force were scapegoated along with Marxists and Jews; any group that stood for a challenge to power based on the Aryan idea of power based on race, sex, and class. The Weimar Republic began to ban married women from competing with men for government jobs, and to restrict access to contraception out of alarm at the declining birthrate and its impact on Germany's future. But the Nazi Party promised much more.

"The right of personal freedom," Hitler explained in *Mein Kampf,* "recedes before the duty to preserve the race." The Nazi leaders would not deprive women of the vote, they said, but they ridiculed feminists, liberals, and socialists who were "masculinizing" women by treating them *the same as* men. Their own answer to women was *"gleichwertig aber nicht gleichartig":* equivalent but not the same.

A return to a strong family life, women's primary identity as mothers, tax penalties for remaining single, loans for young married couples and subsidies for childbearing, prohibition of prostitution and homosexuality, contraception, and abortion: all these were issues that the Roman Catholic Church, the Catholic Center Party, and the Nazi Party could agree on, even while they disagreed bitterly on which patriarchy should prevail, the church or the state.

As British historian Tim Mason wrote: "This type of partial or apparent consensus on a basic issue among different sectional interests and elite groups was one of the most important foundations of Nazi rule . . . Anti-feminism was not a minor or opportunistic component of National Socialism, but a central part of it."

And once Hitler came to power, popularly elected in part by the patriarchal backlash against feminist successes, he delivered on his promise to restore male supremacy.

Whether moderate or radical, feminist organizations were disbanded and feminist publications were closed down or censored, but traditional women's organizations — like the Evangelical Women's Association or the National Association of German Housewives — were welcomed into *Frauenfront*, the Nazi women's association. In 1933, feminists were removed from teaching and other public posts by the same law that removed "non-Aryans" from such jobs. All women were banned from the Reichstag, from judgeships, and from other decision-making posts. To the extent that labor needs allowed, married women were persuaded or forced to stay at home and leave paid jobs to men. Propaganda portrayed the ideal woman as healthy, blond, no makeup; a chaste and energetic worker while single, a devoted wife and mother as soon as possible. The magazine advertisements for contraception that had been commonplace were outlawed as pornographic. Birth-control clinics were padlocked — much as some antiabortion groups are demanding today.

Under Hitler, choosing abortion became sabotage; a crime punishable by hard labor for the woman and a possible death penalty for the abortionist. It was an act of the individual against the state; an exaggeration in degree, but not kind, of current arguments that women must have children "for Jesus and the church" or, as the Supreme Court ruled in allowing poor women to be deprived of Medicaid funds for abortion, "legitimate government interest." In Hitler's words, "It must be considered as reprehensible conduct to refrain from giving healthy children to the nation."

The key word was, of course, "healthy." Since non-Aryans were "racially impure" and thus unhealthy, Jews, Gypsies, Poles, and victims of serious handicaps and diseases (Hitler was, for instance, obsessed with syphilis) were all discouraged or prevented from reproducing by methods that varied from segregation, threats, labor camps, abortion, and sterilization to imprisonment or death in a concentration camp. The choice of method depended largely on whether they were needed as workers, though the inconvenience of a pregnant worker was often harder to handle by abortion than by the gas chamber.

The horrors of concentration camps appear over and over again in current right-wing literature as the analogue of abortion clinics; extremist arguments that may well incite, consciously or not, such extremist acts as the fire-bombing of abortion clinics in Minnesota or the picketing and actual invasion of clinics in many other states.

There are antiabortion activists who also fear such results. Dr. Bernard Nathanson, a physician who once performed abortions and who now has cowritten a militantly antiabortion book called *Aborting America*, explains: "As a Jew, I cannot remain silent at this facile use of the Nazi analogy, though I realize that some antiabortion Jews use it. If this argument is so compelling, why do Jews remain generally favorable toward abortion?"

Liberal Catholic publications, like most individual Catholics, are alarmed by these false comparisons coming from a Right-to-Life movement that is often identified with the Catholic hierarchy. "There is something wrong in a movement," the *National Catholic Reporter* editorialized, "which in spite of its current clever adaptation of abolitionist sloganeering, can value life in just one stage of human development."

But even such objectors may use words like "exaggeration," as if abortion were lesser in degree, similar in kind.

We still need to draw the clear line of difference based on *where the power lies* if we're to identify authoritarianism in all its forms. Though Hitler stated the crucial difference between the individual's right to choose and the state's right to impose — whether it was abortion or anything else — today's religious ultrarightists may obscure that difference with rhetoric.

"If you are pro-life and then support capital punishment or the arms race," a student was reported as arguing at a Right-to-Life Convention in St. Louis, "you're inconsistent."

"But," the report continued, "a common rebuke to that argument among Right-to-Life members was that unborn life is 'perfect' life, born life 'imperfect.' "

The same reservation appears in more secular form in "The Phyllis Schlafly Report" (publication of the Eagle Forum), which carefully advocates only "the right to life of all *innocent* persons from conception to natural death." That proviso allows support for the killing of the "guilty," as decided by the state, whether in capital punishment or wars.

Hitler also supported capital punishment "because of its deterrent effect."

Perhaps the only argument among authoritarians is over what level of patriarchal power will be supreme: family, country, or religion. What all agree on, however, is the patriarchal family as the bottom line and basis for any further authoritarianism. It was the basic cell (*Keimzelle*) of the state for Germany's National Socialism. In the more mixed philosophy of the Eagle Forum, it is just "the basic unit of society." For more religious groups like the American Life Lobby, it's a three-step progression: "the family, the nation, the very laws of God."

But at that first and basic level of the family and the resistance to any self-determination for women within it, authoritarian preachings sound alike.

Current antiabortion argument includes a description of a family with poor health, many members, and great hardship. When the audience agrees that the mother should have the right to an abortion under those circumstances, the lecturer says, "Congratulations. You have just killed Bach."

In fact, the argument sounds like this: "Supposing Bach's mother, after her fifth or sixth or even twelfth child, had said 'that'll do, enough is enough' — the works of Bach would never have been written."

That last quote comes from Heinrich Himmler, founder of the SS, head of all concentration camps, and founder of the Lebensborn homes where Aryan pregnant women who were unwed, deserted, or having children by lovers other than their husbands could go to have the children that Himmler feared they might otherwise have aborted. They could choose to keep the child and be supported by the state, or give it up for adoption to a good German family of carefully matched social background. What they could not do was choose *not* to have the child — and thus control the means of reproduction in defiance of the patriarchal state.

There are many echoes here: a hopeful burst of individual rights, both racial and sexual, followed by an ultra-right-wing backlash. Perhaps those who accuse feminists of being "Nazis" have done us an inadvertent favor by sending us back to read history in self-defense.

As it turns out, there are many, many more parallels to learn from.

II. AUTHORITARIANISM BEGINS AT HOME

Politicians and the press were gradually becoming more sympathetic to the goals of feminism. Women in industry, offices, and the professions weren't oddities any more. Unlike feminist movements in most other Western countries, this one was giving organizational support to radical feminist demands for contraception, abortion, the same rights for "illegitimate" children as for those of married parents, government aid for single mothers, an end to the idea that childbearing was the only purpose of marriage or of women, and a "new morality" that required equal rights for women and men, in or outside marriage.

The place was Germany. The time was the first decade of the 1900s. Most activist women were focused on issues that seemed more immediate than the vote: parliamentary democracy was a new and limited possibility in Germany before World War I. But feminists had won popular support for an unprecedented campaign to decriminalize prostitution (its illegality created the familiar result of brothels protected or run by the police), and they almost succeeded in their careful lobbying effort to delete abortion from the criminal code by arguing that "the competence of the modern State . . . is limited by the necessity of preserving the freedom of the individual over his [or her] own body."

This challenging of the sexual caste system met great resistance from agricultural, religious, and military parts of German society, plus reservations from some reformist or religious women who worked to replace radical feminist leaders of national organizations with those who cited motherhood and "superior morality" as reasons that women should be given more (but not equal) rights. The national obsession with a declining birthrate, combined with new Darwinian theories on who should or should not be encouraged to reproduce, encouraged these nonfeminist reformers to cite healthy German motherhood as their justification of educational and other rights.

Nonetheless, feminists were changing minds and eroding public hostility at the end of half a century or so of women's activism. They were, that is, until 1912 when a small group of military officers, conservative politicians, racist geneticists, and academics resentful of female competition (all of whom, as the press noted, shared the distinction of being unknown or so out-of-date as to be "among the living dead") formed the League for the Prevention of the Emancipation of Women.

For the first time, there was organized antifeminist propaganda. As evidence of both German conservatism and feminist successes, the "Anti-League" felt compelled to issue an antifeminist manifesto. At its first congress, an ultra-right-wing aristocrat explained: "The German Empire was created with blood and iron. That was man's work! If women helped, [they] stood behind their men in battle and fired them on to kill as many enemies as possible. (Fervent applause.)"

By 1913, the Anti-League had gained support from a white-collar union of male clerks convinced that Jews, the lower classes, and "the invasion of female elements into the profession" were taking their jobs away. Union leaders condemned feminists as "men-women," "degenerate," and "perverse."

In 1914, the Anti-League imported Lady Griselda Cheape, an English antisuffrage leader, perhaps the Phyllis Schlafly of her day, to give lectures in Berlin.

Though feminists were divided on whether to take this challenge seriously or ignore it (some thought it ridiculous enough to be inadvertently helpful), its theme of woman-hating struck a deep chord in patriarchal society. Groups such as the Anti-League never had many members, but they did publicly scapegoat feminists in particular and active women in general for all that was changing or difficult in modern life — something that the military, the church, and other traditionalists could agree on, even when they could agree on nothing else.

As Richard Evans, one of the few male scholars to take women's history seriously, explained in *The Feminist Movement in Germany: 1894–1933*, antifeminist arguments "were based on the belief that Germany was subject to growing hostility and danger from forces inside the country and without. . . . The women's movement was creating fresh divisions by rousing women against men. It was destroying the family . . . by encouraging married women to take jobs, by supporting unmarried mothers, and by urging women in general to be more independent. It was endangering Germany's military potential by discouraging marriage [encouraging family planning and thus lowering the birthrate]. It was outraging nature by campaigning for the systematic equalization of the sexes and by inciting women to do things they were unsuited for. It was international in spirit and unpatriotic."

In other words, the Nazi campaign against feminism as anti-German, subversive—and therefore an obvious product of a Communist/Jewish conspiracy—was not invented by Hitler or by the philosophy of National Socialism. His promise to return women to "Children, Cooking, Church" *("Kinder, Küche, Kirche")*, and thus to restore the male-dominant family as the model of authoritarianism, was just a practical solution of religious and other ultra-right-wing demands that had been around since the early twentieth century. True, they were intensified by Germany's humiliation during and after World War I, but the atavistic elements of this obsession with male supremacy and restoration of "the Fatherland" were already there. It just took a national leader willing to pander to such desires; to add the force and respectability of a party platform in which they were key emotional planks.

In 1972, a group of modern American historians became concerned enough about apparent parallels between modern political tensions in the United States and in Germany of the Weimar Republic, the period that preceded Hitler's popular election, to hold a special conference on the subject.[1] Given such similar developments as race- and sex-based challenges to traditional power, reduced influence in the world, pressures of inflation and unemployment at home, and an increasing impatience with elected leadership, could Americans go down the same authoritarian path?

Their conclusion was no. The United States had a much longer tradition of democratic government and acceptance of diversity than did the Germans. Even developments that seemed alarmingly similar in kind were still very different in degree.

In the eight years since then, America has suffered its first humiliating defeat in war. The loss of 55,000 soldiers in faraway Vietnam is hardly comparable to Germany's homeland devastation and loss of 2 million in World War I. Furthermore, many fewer Americans perceived our government's defeat as due to weakness or cowardice: years before it happened, polls showed 70 percent support for United States withdrawal. Nonetheless, justifications of our military presence in Vietnam continue to get big emotional responses from some powerful constituencies. The Veterans of Foreign Wars, for instance, gave Ronald Reagan an ovation for describing Vietnam as "in truth, a noble cause" and "a war our government" was "afraid" to win. They broke 80 years of nonendorsement to support his candidacy.

There is now the additional national pressure of an energy crisis that has made us intimately dependent on "foreigners" for the first time; on non-Westerners and non-Christians at that. U.S. industrial and trade supremacy has also leveled off; inflation and unemployment are up; the challenge from racial minorities and women of every description continues; confidence in our elected leadership is at a historic low; and the daily drama of the Iranian hostage crisis has pointed up national impotence to some and a wrongheaded foreign policy to others.

In a 1976 Gallup poll, Americans were asked if they thought the country needed "really strong leadership that would try to solve problems directly without worrying about how Congress or the Supreme Court might feel." Forty-nine percent agreed. By 1979, 66 percent of those questioned in a New York *Times*/CBS poll said they would vote for "someone who would step on some toes and bend some rules to get things done."

This impatience with recent or current leadership does not mean, as right-wing wishful thinkers often insist, that "the whole country has moved to the right." On almost every issue of social justice — from more equitable distribution of income to a new equality based on race and sex; even a willingness to cut back on material living standards if it makes environmental sense to do so — there is a majority and still-growing support in national polls. More right-wing candidates are winning mainly because large segments of this majority are either too complacent or turned off to vote.

A lust for strong "top-down" leadership was also a hallmark of the Weimar Republic in which National Socialism grew — and not all such longing came from the traditional right wing.

After all, Hitler presented himself as a champion of the lower classes against inherited wealth and power (hence his "Socialism"), as well as against the "international conspiracy" of powerful Jews. From a poor working-class family himself, he replaced upper-class superiority with racial superiority, thus justifying his own right to rise to the top. Basic texts like *The Nazi Primer* emphasized hard work and talent as the ways any German/Aryan could succeed (hence, "*National* Socialism").

A repressed would-be architecture student shocked by the sinfulness of Munich; a vegetarian who didn't smoke or drink and who was obsessed by supposed sexual attacks on nice German girls (though only by "the black-haired Jewish youth [who] lurks in wait," as Hitler wrote in *Mein Kampf*); an obscure and angry worker who felt exploited by the rich and powerful, Hitler entered the city's beer halls and workingmen's clubs and discovered a gift for emotional speeches that unlocked dreams of revenge.

For those of us who believe evil is obvious, it's important to remember that he often seemed both selfless and charming. "The Führer comes to greet me with outstretched hand," a woman journalist for *Paris-Soir* wrote in 1936. "I am surprised and astonished by the blue of his eyes, which look brown in photographs, and I prefer the reality — the face that brims with intelligence and energy and lights up when he speaks. At this moment, I comprehend the magical influence . . . and his power over the masses."

The message of the interviewer's own second-class status as a female was sugarcoated; a parallel to the National Socialist description of non-Aryans: "No real differences in quality, but rather differences in kind."

"I grant women the same right as men, but I don't think they're identical," Hitler explained jovially. "Woman is man's companion in life. She shouldn't be burdened with the tasks for which man was created. I don't envisage any women's battalions . . . women are better suited to social work."

But even very different forms of authoritarianism must start out with a belief in some group's greater right to power, whether it's based on sex, race, class, religion — or all four. However far it may expand, the progression inevitably begins with unequal power and airtight roles within the family.

ITEMS

● "If the man's world is said to be the State . . . her world is her husband, her family, her children and her home . . . Every child that a woman brings into the world is a battle, a battle waged for the existence of her people. . . . It is not true . . . that respect depends on the overlapping of the spheres of activity of the sexes; this respect demands that neither sex should try to do that which belongs to the sphere of the other." —*Hitler's speech to the National Socialist Women's Organization, September, 1934.*

● ". . . the attack on the family is an attack on civilization itself . . . men are by nature mobile and aggressive, whereas women are by nature committed to stability, permanence, and futurity . . . welfare, day-care centers, and affirmative action or preferential hiring of women diminish the role of the male as a provider. . . . They thus promote the dissolution of society . . ." — *Communism, the Family, and the Equal Rights Amendment," Christian Anti-Communist Crusade, California, March 1975.*

● "Perhaps the three points most stressed in family theory," U.S. sociologist Clifford Kirkpatrick wrote in 1937 about Nazi Germany, "are reproduction, sex differences, and strengthened homelife."

● "Ninety percent of our problems with children," explained a booklet distributed by members of the Pro-Family Caucus at a recent White House Conference on Families, "are probably the result of a mother who has (1) failed to learn how to really love her man and submit to him, (2) tried to escape staying at home, or (3) hindered her husband in the discipline of the children."

● "A Child's Declaration of Rights," published by Phyllis Schlafly's Eagle Forum, includes the right: "To be taught from textbooks that honor the traditional family as a basic unit of society, women's role as wife and mother, and man's role as provider and protector . . ."

● "No funds [will be] authorized . . . under federal law [for] purchase or preparation of any educational materials or studies relating to the preparation of educational materials, if such materials would tend to denigrate, diminish, or deny the role differences between the sexes . . ." — *The Family Protection Act, an omnibus federal bill introduced in 1979 by Senator Paul Laxalt (R.-Nev.), which would also deny federally funded legal services for abortion rights, school desegregation, gay rights, and so on.*

Once we grow callous in our earliest, most intimate worlds to a power difference among our own family members, how much easier is it to accept other hierarchies? If men do not maintain control over women's bodies and thus the means of reproduction, how can they keep those other hierarchies of race and class "pure"?

ITEMS:

● "The slogan 'Emancipation of Women' was invented by Jewish intellectuals . . . our National Socialist women's movement has in reality but one single point," Hitler told women in his 1934 speech, "and that point is the child . . ." In *Mein Kampf*, a copy of which was presented to every newly married Aryan couple in Germany, he wrote, "Just as [the Jew] himself systematically ruins women and girls . . . it was and is Jews who bring Negroes into the Rhineland . . . ruining the hated white race by the necessarily resulting bastardization . . . rising [himself] to be its master."

● "Russia has an ERA and their birthrate has fallen below population zero," reported *The Thunderbolt,* a publication of the American, avowedly white-supremacist National States Rights Party. "The time is *now* to act to protect the family and *motherhood* itself . . . Laws requiring men and women to be separated in prison would be invalidated. A negro judge has already used these equality laws in Chattanooga to lock a White woman in the same cell with a black man. She was then raped . . ."

● Father Paul Marx, director of the Human Life Center, an anti-abortion "think tank" in Minnesota, has traveled to more than 30 countries as part of his campaign. In an interview this year (characterized by the Minneapolis *Star* as centering on his fear that "the white Western world is committing suicide through abortion and contraception"), Marx's explanation was reported: "I guess we have 250,000 Vietnamese here already, and they are going to have large families — the Orientals always do. There are Koreans, and Filipinos . . . God knows how many Mexicans come across the border every night . . . And if we ever have to fight the Russians, I wonder if these people will be willing to stake their lives."

Extreme beliefs? Maybe. But the belief that the male-headed family or church or state owns women's bodies is the root injustice from which these ideas flow and on which they are built. In pleading for reproductive freedom 70 years ago, one German feminist said, "Woman has often been reduced — callously, if unconsciously — to the level of a childbearing machine, her children regarded as the property of the State while still in the womb." Another said angrily, "If we women do not take a stand for our own responsibility for ourselves here, in the most female of all tasks in life, that of 'giving life,' if we do not take a stand against our being regarded merely as the involuntary producers of cannon fodder — then in my opinion, we do not deserve to be regarded as anything else!"

Many women in Hitler's Germany did take a public stand against his sexual caste system, as well as against the anti-Semitism that, being a punishment from which men could also suffer, was a more accepted and international cause. ("National Socialism has grown big in its fight against Jews and women," said a leader of Germany's largest feminist organization. "Today, I am for struggle.") Many demonstrated against Hitler's closing of contraception clinics and banning of any individual right to abortion. A German feminist, long resident of this country, remembers that as "the first thing Hitler did." Even women who miscarried had to prove they had not tried to abort.

Still others tried unsuccessfully to save their organizations by becoming less "political"; by fighting the Nazi diatribe against them with dry "factual corrections"; or even by using Hitler's own racist arguments to try vainly to get Aryan women into positions of influence where they might reform from within.

Jewish women in Germany were not only purged from any important jobs, but progressively endangered and abandoned, often by their own non-Jewish husbands and friends. First discouraged from marriage or having children, then forced out of both, they were eventually used as forced labor or sent to concentration camps. (Ravensbrüch, the one camp exclusively for women, was also the one where most Nazi "medical experiments" were performed; perhaps more easily inflicted on bodies seen as twice different from their Aryan masters.)

Meanwhile, Hitler assumed that women were attracted to his military image, and stayed single partly to inspire women followers. Some National Socialists claimed that "it was the women's vote that brought Hitler to triumph," but that was no more true than the current argument that it's mainly or only women who are preventing state legislatures from ratifying the ERA. (Hindenberg, president of Germany from 1925 to 1934, got more women's votes in 1932 than did Hitler, both in absolute numbers and percentage.) But some women did vote for National Socialism. They were largely the very young who knew little or nothing about the feminist struggles of their foremothers. Many were excited by the romance of Hitler's heroine/goddess images; or wanted to be only housewives instead of poorly paid workers as well; or believed Hitler's promise of a bridegroom for every young woman in a country where World War I had left many more women than men.

Ironically, women's traditional workload and their skepticism about help from any men, including National Socialists, saved many from Nazi involvement. "The mass of German women did not want to be organized," explained American historian Jill Stephenson, "and their passive resistance to attempts to involve the housebound housewife, above all in the 'women's work of the nation,' ensured that the Nazi women's organization remained a minority concern."

There can be no doubt that feminists would have been more effective in opposing Hitler if they had possessed local centers as did the churches, or work communities as did the unions, or an international network as did both.

As it was, their major organizations were easily outlawed or taken over. And their diverse, multi-issue approach was no match for the simple emotionalism of the opposition. "Whereas the cause of women's emancipation," explained historian Tim Mason, "[was] promoted by a very wide range of small and normally uncoordinated groups with different partial goals and political outlooks, the cause of the restoration of men's preeminence could be made to appear a relatively simple single issue and could be preempted by a single political movement of incomparably greater power."

And that was tragic for men as well as women, not only in Germany but in all the areas decimated by German expansionism. Feminists had been virtually alone in challenging the patriarchal family as the basic unit of society; in trying to replace the primacy of this hierarchical group with the primacy of individual rights. Many religious groups supported Hitler's view of the family and of women, and disagreed only with the primacy of the state instead of the church — but by then it was too late. Liberal political groups talked and worked for human rights, including women's rights in the marketplace or in the voting booth, but also stopped at the family door.

According to our own traditional right wing or "New Right," the goal is also to protect the traditional family, plus the power of the church, from any intrusion of "big government." Since the family, like the church, is clearly defined by them as male-led and hierarchical, that means *eliminating any direct relationship between women and federal law or children and federal law.* This is the theme of the Family Protection Act and other "profamily" documents that oppose everything from the ERA to federal laws against child abuse, from a teacher's right to choose textbooks without parental consent to the individual's right to choose any form of sexual expression outside the patriarchal family.

Purposefully or not, this leaves the group superior to the individual, and limits the government's basic function of protecting human rights. It keeps a birth-determined caste system intact, and thus preserves the model for other authoritarianisms of race and class.

There are many other parallels between past and present, though each is importantly different in degree. Could the current spate of right-wing efforts to censor school libraries (including censorship of many books by feminists, family-planning educators, and black authors) grow into Nazi-style book burnings (which also included feminist, family-planning, and Jewish authors)? Could the effort of some current politicians to defeat the right wing by imitating it become as disastrous a mistake as the Weimar Republic's concessions to anti-Semitism and resentment of women in the paid labor force?

Certainly, there are big differences in style as well as content. Our nationalism doesn't use anti-Semitism as the internal and external danger, but it sometimes makes anti-Communism into an obsession that borders on paranoia. Here, resistance to human rights for women and minorities takes the subtle form of condemning as "selfish" — or as "the Me Generation" — all nonestablishment groups who are now demanding their fair share.

Feminists, however, still seem to be the only group fighting for human rights for everyone, from the bottom up. Antifeminist forces may see this more clearly than our liberal allies do. "Orthodox feminism is an especially militant manifestation," *The Human Life Review*, an antiabortion quarterly, warned last year, "of a larger, increasingly prevalent social philosophy which holds that the 'needs' of the individual are self-validating and that no person or institution may restrict those needs."

Meanwhile, our supposed supporters often remain unwilling or unable to take the "profamily" or "emotional" issues of the ultraright wing seriously. Some even pave the way for further authoritarianism by agreeing with the right wing on women in the family. Having accepted this basic inequity, and the violence that is required to perpetuate it, they are then surprised when the need for superiority grows into dominance toward more groups, a militaristic foreign policy, or some other area that they consider worthy enough, and dangerous enough to them personally, to oppose.

It all sounds a little too familiar. But at least we now know that feminism has a history — and that it is the keystone of any organic or lasting democracy.

NOTES

1.   Proceedings published in *Social Research*, summer 1972.

Concerning Abortion:
An Attempt at a Rational View

CHARLES HARTSHORNE

My onetime colleague T. V. Smith once wrote a book called *Beyond Conscience*, in which he waxed eloquent in showing "the harm that good men do." To live according to one's conscience may be a fine thing, but what if A's conscience leads A to try to compel B and C to live, not according to B's or C's conscience, but according to A's? That is what many opponents of abortion are trying to do. To propose a constitutional amendment to this effect is one of the most outrageous attempts to tyrannize over others that I can recall in my long lifetime as an American citizen. Proponents of the antiabortion amendment make their case, if possible, even worse when they defend themselves with the contention "It isn't my conscience only — it is a commandment of religion." For now one particular form of religion (certainly not the only form) is being used in an attempt to tyrannize over other forms of religious or philosophical belief. The separation of church and state evidently means little to such people.

IN WHAT SENSE 'HUMAN'?

Ours is a country that has many diverse religious groups, and many people who cannot find truth in any organized religious body. It is a country that has great difficulty in effectively opposing forms of killing that *everyone* admits to be wrong. Those who would saddle the legal system with matters about which consciences sincerely and strongly differ show a disregard of the country's primary needs. (The same is to be said about crusades to make things difficult for homosexuals.) There can be little freedom if we lose sight of the vital distinction between moral questions and legal ones. The law compels and coerces, with the implicit threat of violence; morals seek to persuade. It is a poor society that forgets this difference.

What is the *moral* question regarding abortion? We are told that the fetus is alive and that therefore killing it is wrong. Since mosquitoes, bacteria, apes and whales are also alive, the argument is less than clear.

Even plants are alive. I am not impressed by the rebuttal "But plants, mosquitoes, bacteria and whales are not human, and the fetus is." For the issue now becomes, *in what sense* is the fetus human? No one denies that its origin is human, as is its *possible* destiny. But the same is true of every unfertilized egg in the body of a nun. Is it wrong that some such eggs are not made or allowed to become human individuals?

Granted that a fetus is human in origin and possible destiny, in what further sense is it human? The entire problem lies here. If there are pro-life activists who have thrown much light on this question, I do not know their names.

One theologian who writes on the subject — Paul Ramsey — thinks that a human egg cell becomes a human individual with a moral claim to survive if it has been fertilized. Yet this egg cell has none of the qualities that we have in mind when we proclaim our superior worth to the chimpanzees or dolphins. It cannot speak, reason or judge between right and wrong. It cannot have personal relations, without which a person is not functionally a person at all, until months — and not, except minimally, until years — have passed. And even then, it will not be a person in the normal sense unless some who are already fully persons have taken pains to help it become a human being in the full value sense, functioning as such. The antiabortionist is commanding some person or persons to undertake this effort. For without it, the fetus will *never* be human in the relevant sense. It will be human only in origin, but otherwise a subhuman animal.

The fertilized egg is an individual egg, but not an individual human being. For such a being is, in its body, a multicellular organism, a *metazoan* — to use the scientific Greek — and the egg is a single cell. The first thing the egg cell does is to begin dividing into many cells. For some weeks the fetus is not a single individual at all, but a colony of cells. During its first weeks there seems to be no ground for regarding the fetus as comparable to an individual animal. Only in possible or probable destiny is it an individual. Otherwise it is an organized society of single-celled individuals.

A possible individual person is one thing; an actual person is another. If this difference is not important, what is? There is in the long run no room in the solar system, or even in the known universe, for all human eggs — even all fertilized eggs, as things now stand — to become human persons. Indeed, it is mathematically demonstrable that the present rate of population growth must be lowered somehow. It is not a moral imperative that all possibilities of human persons become actual persons.

Of course, some may say that the fertilized egg already has a human soul, but on what evidence? The evidence of soul in the relevant sense is the capacity to reason, judge right and wrong, and the like.

GENETIC AND OTHER INFLUENCES

One may also say that since the fertilized egg has a combination of genes (the units of physical inheritance) from both parents, in this sense it is already a human individual. There are two objections, either one in my opinion conclusive but only one of which is taken into account by Ramsey. The one he does mention is that identical twins have the same gene combination. The theologian does not see this as decisive, but I do.

The other objection is that it amounts to a very crude form of materialism to identify individuality with the gene-combination. Genes are the chemical bearers of inherited traits. This chemical basis of inheritance presumably influences everything about the development of the individual —*influences,* but does not fully determine. To say that the entire life of the person is determined by heredity is a theory of unfreedom that my religious conviction can only regard as monstrous. And there are biophysicists and neurophysiologists who agree with me.

From the gene-determined chemistry to a human person is a long, long step. As soon as the nervous system forming in the embryo begins to function as a whole — and not before — the cell colony begins to turn into a genuinely individual animal. One may reasonably suppose that this change is accompanied by some extremely primitive individual animal feelings. They cannot be recognizably human feelings, much less human thoughts, and cannot compare with the feelings of a porpoise or chimpanzee in level of consciousness. That much seems as certain as anything about the fetus except its origin and possible destiny. The nervous system of a very premature baby has been compared by an expert to that of a pig. And we know, if we know anything about this matter, that it is the nervous system that counts where individuality is concerned.

Identical twins are different individuals, each unique in consciousness. Though having the same genetic makeup, they will have been differently situated in the womb and hence will have received different stimuli. For that reason, if for no other, they will have developed differently, especially in their brains and nervous systems.

But there are additional reasons for the difference in development. One is the role of chance, which takes many forms. We are passing through a great cultural change in which the idea, long dominant in science, that chance is "only a word for our ignorance of causes" is being replaced by the view that the real laws of nature are probabilistic and allow for aspects of genuine chance.

Another reason is that it is reasonable to admit a reverse influence of the developing life of feelings in the fetus on the nervous system, as well as of the system upon the feelings. And since I, along with some famous philosophers and scientists, believe in freedom (not solely of mature human beings but — in some slight degree — of all individuals in nature, down to the atoms and farther), I hold that even in the fetus the incipient individual is unconsciously making what on higher levels we call "decisions." These decisions influence the developing nervous system. Thus to a certain extent we *make our own bodies* by our feelings and thoughts. An English poet with Platonic ideas expressed this concept as follows:

> The body from the soul its form doth take,
> For soul is form and doth the body make.

The word soul is, for me, incidental. The point is that feelings, thoughts experiences react on the body and partly mold its development.

THE RIGHTS OF PERSONS

Paul Ramsey argues (as does William Buckley in a letter to me) that if a fetus is not fully human, then neither is an infant. Of course an infant is not fully human. No one thinks it can, while an infant, be taught to speak, reason or judge right and wrong. But it is much closer to that stage than is a three-month fetus. It is beginning to have primitive social relations not open to a fetus; and since there is no sharp line anywhere between an infant and a child able to speak a few words, or between the latter and a child able to speak very many words, we have to regard the infant as significantly different from a three-month or four-month fetus. Nevertheless, I have little sympathy with the idea that infanticide is just another form of murder. Persons who are already functionally persons in the full sense have more important rights even than infants. Infanticide can be wrong without being fully comparable to the killing of persons in the full sense.

Does this distinction apply to the killing of a hopelessly senile person (or one in a permanent coma)? For me it does. I hope that no one will think that if, God forbid, I ever reach that stage, it must be for my sake that I should be treated with the respect due to normal human beings. Rather, it is for the sake of others that such respect may be imperative. Symbolically, one who has been a person may have to be treated as a person. There are difficulties and hazards in not so treating such individuals.

Religious people (I would so describe myself) may argue that once a fetus starts to develop, it is for God, not human beings, to decide whether the fetus survives and how long it lives. This argument assumes, against all evidence, that human life-spans are independent of human decisions. Our medical hygiene has radically altered the original "balance of nature." Hence the population explosion. Our technology makes pregnancy more and more a matter of human decision; more and more our choices are influencing the weal and woe of the animals on this earth. It is an awesome responsibility, but one that we cannot avoid. And, after all, the book of Genesis essentially predicted our dominion over terrestrial life. In addition, no one is proposing to make abortion compulsory for those morally opposed to it. I add that everyone who smokes is taking a hand in deciding how long he or she will live. Also everyone who, by failing to exercise reasonably, allows his or her heart to lose its vigor. Our destinies are not simply "acts of God."

I may be told that if I value my life I must be glad that I was not aborted in the fetus state. Yes, I am glad, but this expression does not constitute a claim to having already had a "right," against which no other right could prevail, to the life I have enjoyed. I feel no indignation or horror at contemplating the idea the world might have had to do without me. The world could have managed, and as for what I would have missed, there would have been no such "I" to miss it.

POTENTIAL, NOT ACTUAL

With almost everything they say, the fanatics against abortion show that they will not, or cannot, face the known facts of this matter. The inability of a fetus to say "I" is not merely a lack of skill; there is nothing there to which the pronoun could properly refer. A fetus is not a person but a *potential* person. The "life" to which "pro-life" refers is nonpersonal, by any criterion that makes sense to some of us. It is subpersonal animal life only. The mother, however, *is* a person.

I resent strongly the way many males tend to dictate to females their behavior, even though many females encourage them in this. Of course, the male parent of a fetus also has certain rights, but it remains true that the female parent is the one most directly and vitally concerned.

I shall not forget talking about this whole matter to a wonderful woman, the widow of a philosopher known for his idealism. She was doing social work with young women and had come to the conclusion that abortion is, in some cases, the lesser evil. She told me that her late husband had said, when she broached the subject to him, "But you can't do that." "My darling," she replied, "we *are* doing it." I see no reason to rate the consciences of the pro-lifers higher than this woman's conscience. She knew what the problem was for certain mothers. In a society that flaunts sex (its pleasures more than its serious hazards, problems and spiritual values) in all the media, makes it difficult for the young to avoid unwanted pregnancy, and does little to help them with the most difficult of all problems of self-discipline, we tell young persons that they are murderers if they resort to abortion. And so we should not be surprised that Margaret Mead, that clear-sighted observer of our society (and of other societies), should say, "Abortion is a nasty thing, but our society deserves it." Alas, it is too true.

I share something of the disgust of hard-core opponents of abortion that contraceptives, combined with the availability of abortion, may deprive sexual intercourse of spiritual meaning. For me the sacramental view of marriage has always had appeal, and my life has been lived accordingly. Abortion is indeed a nasty thing, but unfortunately there are in our society many even nastier things, like the fact that some children are growing up unwanted. This for my conscience is a great deal nastier, and truly horrible. An overcrowded world is also nasty, and could in a few decades become truly catastrophic.

The argument against abortion (used, I am sorry to say, by Pearl Buck) that the fetus may be a potential genius has to be balanced against the much more probable chance of its being a mediocrity, or a destructive enemy of society. Every egg cell is a possible genius and also a possible monster in human form. Where do we stop in calculating such possibilities?

If some who object to abortion work to diminish the number of unwanted, inappropriate pregnancies, or to make bearing a child for adoption by persons able to be its loving foster parents more attractive than it now is, and do this with a minimum of coercion, all honor to them. In view of the population problem, the first of these remedies should have high priority.

Above all, the coercive power of our legal system, already stretched thin, must be used with caution and chiefly against evils about which there is something like universal consensus. That persons have rights is a universal belief in our society, but that a fetus is already an actual person — about that there is and there can be no consensus. Coercion in such matters is tyranny. Alas for our dangerously fragmented and alienated society if we persist in such tyranny.

SCIENCE

Half a century ago three historic events occurred in natural science which deserve to command our continuing attention. First, in 1926 American physicist Robert S. Goddard launched the world's first liquid-fueled rocket and thereby opened the space age for war and peace. Second, the 1925 Scopes trial in Tennessee was an open battle of faiths: between verifiable trust in natural evolution and traditional trust in the biblical story of creation. The third event was the unraveling of the secrets of nuclear structure, particularly from 1932 to 1938 when the center of the atom was revealed and the processes of fission, fusion, and radioactivity were discovered. We shall consider, in this section of Speak Out, how these three events relate to America's new battle of faiths.

Indeed, our opening selection of "Science and Survival" by Carl Sagan reckons sharply with all three aspects of the battle before us. He is Professor of Astronomy and Space Sciences and Director, Laboratory for Planetary Studies, at Cornell University. Dr. Sagan's involvement with the U.S. space program includes a leading role in the Mariner, Viking and Voyager missions to the planets, for which he received the NASA Medal for Exceptional Scientific Achievement and (twice) the NASA Medal for Distinguished Public Service, as well as the Joseph Priestley Award "for distinguished contributions to the welfare of Mankind." His most recent book, Cosmos, published in conjunction with his popular public television series of the same name, has so far been on The New York Times bestseller list every week for more than a year. At the moment of this writing, 930,000 copies are in print and more than a dozen foreign countries are already publishing this explanation of the first thirteen billion years of the universe's evolution.

Our second selection focuses on "The 'Threat' of Creationism." Isaac Asimov, the Boston University School of Medicine biochemist known for his many science fiction and non-fiction books, presents a critique of the arguments of the New Right to creationists who have been surprisingly successful in their campaign to legalize the biblical story of how life and the universe began. Dr. Asimov describes the frightening force of what he calls the new army of the night — tens of millions of marching Americans armed with Bibles — and he dares to suggest that this Counterrevolution of the Right just might succeed in reversing the Scientific Revolution of the modern age.

Next, the Harvard paleontologist, Stephen Jay Gould, who has received exceptional acclaim for his books on natural history — Ever Since Darwin and The Panda's Thumb — presents arguments from the scientific side in order to affirm evolution both as a theory and as fact. In Discover magazine, James Gorman states that the arguments advanced by Dr. Gould — one of creationism's chief antagonists — may well represent the case of the scientific community in the trial to come. Indeed, the nature of the coming campaign to put evolution on trial is already visible on the battle-ground of the school. A California decision affirms that the schools must avoid "dogmatism" about human origins. A new law in Arkansas requiring public schools to give equal time to evolution and creationism was over-turned in January 1982 by federal district Judge William Ray Overton, who sharply declared that " 'Creation Science' has no scientific merit or educa-tional value." Nevertheless, the now overturned Arkansas law did not stand alone. Missouri, Wisconsin and parts of Florida make the same require-ments. In fully a dozen other states similar action is pending.

Consider the New Right imperatives of power which are guiding this new battle against science:

> Write creationism into science textbooks.
>
> Don't teach value-neutral science, as if the Holy Bible might be wrong.
>
> Screen no social-science film that could make children ashamed of America.
>
> Cut or discontinue federal funding for social science.

Fear of science has long been associated with the destructive potential which ever flows from new knowledge. Never has that power been more manifest than in the past half century since nuclear physics has existed. Victor F. Weisskopf, the author of the concluding selection in Speak Out, has calculated that the fission chain-reaction that brought nuclear energy within reach is 20 million times more powerful than the most potent ordinary chemical reaction. When before has humanity increased its power 20 million times in a single generation?

Born in Vienna, Austria in 1908, Dr. Weisskopf came to the United States 29 years later to join the faculty of the University of Rochester. In 1943 he joined the Manhattan Project at Los Alamos, New Mexico, where he worked on the exploitation of nuclear energy. In 1945 he was appointed professor of physics at M.I.T. After serving from 1961 to 1966 as Director General of the European Center of Nuclear Research, which operated the world's most powerful particle accelerator, he returned to M.I.T. with the rare distinction of being named an Institute Professor. He now holds that position emeritus.

In 1944 Weisskopf participated in the founding of the Federation of Atomic Scientists, whose aims were to warn the public of the dangers of atomic war and to support the peaceful uses of atomic energy. In 1949 he became a member of the emergency committee of scientists whose president was Albert Einstein, fighting for control of atomic weapons and for understanding between East and West. An action-intellectual much admired by his peers, Victor Weisskopf recently served with high distinction as President of the American Academy of Arts and Sciences. Speak Out concludes with his prophetic selection, "On Avoiding Nuclear Holocaust."

Science and Survival

A Commencement Address to the Senior Class,
Yale College, May 23, 1981

CARL SAGAN

In East Africa, in the records of the rocks dating back to about a million years ago, you can find a sequence of worked tools that our ancestors designed and executed. Their lives depended on making and using these tools well. This was, of course, Stone Age technology. Stones were used for all sorts of activities — chipping, flaking, cutting, carving. Although there are many ways of making stone tools, what is remarkable is that in a given site for enormous periods of time the tools are prepared in the same way — which means that there must have been educational institutions hundreds of thousands of years ago. There must have been professors and students, examinations and failing grades, laboratory courses, graduating ceremonies and post-graduate education.

The education that you are receiving is part of a long and distinguished human tradition. There is a reason for it. Our ability to learn from experience and to incorporate what previous generations have uncovered for themselves is the secret of our success as a species. Unaided, we are not stronger, or faster, or better camouflaged, or better swimmers or flyers than other animals. The only things we are better at are thinking and building. For that reason we have a long childhood in which many facts and attitudes are learned, different from generation to generation. We continue our education into adulthood and, indeed, for all our lives. That sequence of learning experiences has produced the most remarkable transformation of ourselves and our planet. If you drive through Manhattan, there are vistas in which nothing of the natural landscape is left, nothing that our ancestors of a hundred thousand years ago would recognize as familiar — except the people. We're dressed and coiffed differently, some of us are clean-shaven, but we ourselves would be entirely recognizable to our forebears. However, we have changed the environment profoundly.

Our enormous powers have, as everybody recognizes, not always been used for human benefit. In the four years since you have entered Yale College, more than a thousand strategic nuclear warheads have been deployed in ballistic missiles by the United States and the Soviet Union. These, in turn, were responses to other warheads introduced in previous years. Many of these warheads have yields of one or two megatons. A megaton is the equivalent of a million tons of TNT going off all at once. If you add up the

160

yields of all the bombs dropped by all the combatants in the Second World War, you find that it comes to two million tons of TNT, the yield of one modern nuclear weapon. A thousand World War II's have been stockpiled and targeted while you have been here at Yale College. That is something that distinguishes this class from other classes. You are not responsible for it, but you will have an opportunity to do something about it.

In the same four years, 20 new worlds have been examined close-up for the first time by the human species by means of two remarkable spacecraft called Voyager 1 and Voyager 2. They have flown by the planet Jupiter, discovered its ring system, and examined its remarkably diverse array of moons. Then they were accelerated by the gravity of that massive planet to approach Saturn where they examined that planet and its elegant system of rings and moons. Voyager 2 will then continue on and in five years (if it survives that long) will examine the planet Uranus. Both spacecraft will eventually find themselves expelled from the solar system as the human species' third and fourth interstellar spacecraft.

Until this four-year period, 1977–1981, Jupiter, its rings and its moons, and Saturn, its rings and its moons, could be seen indistinctly at best. No surface details on these moons were detectable at all from the Earth. But now we have a vast library — approaching 100,000 detailed photographs of these worlds, and their diversity is astonishing. There is a world with an underground ocean of liquid sulfur. There is one that looks like a sphere of cracked crystal. There is a moon with an atmosphere denser than that of the Earth, and an unbroken cloud layer made of organic molecules. There are worlds made of ice. There are ring systems of billions of individual orbiting snowballs. There are many worlds we have never seen before. Only one generation in the history of the human species is privileged to live during the time those great discoveries are first made; that generation is ours.

It is remarkable that these two sets of events use very much the same physics, that of Isaac Newton, which is equally good at propelling devastating warheads to Moscow and to Washington, and at sending vehicles engaged in the peaceful and benign exploration of the solar system to Jupiter and Saturn.

We have instruments of mythic power at our command. The question clearly is: Are we wise enough to use them properly? Science and technology are ancient tools, the distinction of our species. They are also a kind of seed-corn. They are the means for our future survival. They provide solutions to many problems, some of which we are not yet wise enough even to identify. Eating the seed-corn can get you through one more winter. But the following winter you are in desperate trouble.

At the same time that these and hundreds of other remarkable scientific accomplishments have been happening, there have been some interesting pushes and pulls: conflicting trends in opposite directions. One trend is illustrated by the recent request by the Reagan administration in the United States to cut essentially to zero all of the budget of the National Science Foundation devoted to science education, particularly in keeping science teachers up-to-date. That is clearly eating the seed-corn. The budgetary savings are trivial, the potential damage enormous.

In many areas of science the great accomplishments are made by young people, people in their twenties and early thirties. I think it likely that a number of science graduates in this class will make such significant contributions. But because this tends to happen at early ages the generation time for scientific progress is short. Abandoning scientific education for a decade turns out to be something not easily repaired. It can produce an enormous gap in our scientific expertise, one extremely difficult to remedy later on, when we come to our senses.

You can see it, for example, in the Soviet Union where Trofim Lysenko, strongly supported by Stalin and later by Khrushchev, decided that Mendelian genetics was heretical, ideologically distasteful, and so it was not taught. Well into the early development of molecular biology in the West, the best Soviet scientists were steered away from this dubious research area. Today, almost 50 years later, there is still almost no world-class fundamental molecular biology in the Soviet Union. The United States can also, if we are sufficiently short-sighted, bring fundamental scientific research to an abrupt halt — at least here.

On the other hand, there are clear signs of the enormous popularity of science. Among the most popular motion pictures of recent times are several which, on some level, are concerned with science. There are about half a dozen new magazines devoted to science. They are doing extremely well and every time a new one comes on the market, the others increase rather than decrease their circulation. There have been some successful science programs on television as well.

Many years ago, I was engaged in writing a book for a major corporate conglomerate in the United States. I would write, "Here are the data. Some people think *this* is the explanation; some people think *that* is the explanation." My editor would say, "Don't confuse the readers with alternatives; just tell them what's right." I protested: "But I don't know what's right; that's why I give alternatives." And he replied, "Well, just pick one; they'll never know the difference."

This sort of contempt for the ability of the average person to understand elementary ideas is part of the problem that we face. I think that there is no evidence that such an incapacity actually exists. One of the most satisfying aspects of our experience with the "Cosmos" television series is the thousands of moving, articulate, closely reasoned letters coming from all over the United States, including places not generally thought to be bastions of intellectuality and learning. Many people say, "I'm so happy to find that I can understand something about science. I'd always been taught that I was too dumb to understand. Now I'm going back to school."

I believe that the intelligence of the American people has been systematically shortchanged and downgraded and misevaluated by those who make the decisions about what fare shall be on television, in magazines and in books. Why? Why is there a sense that "Science is not for me"? There are a number of answers. One of them falls squarely on the shoulders of the scientific community. Some scientists have had a disdain for the popularization of science. There has been a tradition — it has been a minority tradition, but it goes back at least to Pythagoras — that the real stuff should be kept for a small scientific elite and not contaminated by exposure to the rank and file. I believe that it is certainly to the benefit of the scientists whose research is dependent on public support to explain what they are about; but it is also essential, in a civilization that runs off science and technology, for people to understand something about science and technology.

The concern and unease about science you can easily see by the way science is presented in the cartoons on Saturday morning television for children. For example, the scientist decides that a good way to solve the "population problem" and the "energy problem" simultaneously is to shrink every human being to one inch high. Then they will eat less, use less energy, and everything will be fine. The superhero has to explain to the scientist that one must first ask permission. Perhaps people will not enjoy being shrunk to one inch high. The scientists are often portrayed as ethical cretins — a grave injustice, considering the many scientists (Linus Pauling, Andrei Sakharov, and dozens of others leap instantly to mind) who, at considerable personal risk, have spoken out on the misapplications of science and technology, and more general ethical problems.

There is no question that such misapplications have produced an unease, a justifiable unease. We are faced, in a very serious way, with problems that no previous generation ever had to worry about. All of the exponentials are beginning to saturate in this particular generation, exponentials about mineral resources, about fossil fuels, about environmental pollution, about the compatibility between population and resources, and about the capacity for human self-destruction. Whatever the source of these problems, I think it is entirely clear that there is no conceivable solution to them that is independent of science and technology. If we wish to make it into the next century or two, we have to understand science and technology and be sure that they are used benignly and creatively for human betterment.

Any attempt to back away from understanding the world, any attempt to obscure what science is about is dangerous. One of the reasons that there is unease about science in certain quarters is because it challenges the prevailing wisdom. It sometimes is counterintuitive. It requires a certain intellectual effort. It occasionally leads us along a road that jars our predispositions.

We can understand the world because there has been a match made by natural selection between how our brains work and how the world works. For example, how is it that the laws of falling bodies are so simple? Why is the distance that an object falls proportional to the square of the time? Why is the velocity linearly proportional to the time? Why such a simple relationship? Why not the Chebyshev polynomial of the time? Why not a full spherical harmonic expansion of the time? Why just proportional to the time?

Let us imagine some of our ancestors of five or ten million years ago brachiating from branch to branch. Those who had to compute the Chebyshev polynomials of the trajectory never made it to the next branch; they left few descendants. The guys who could figure it out left descendants. We come from them. We spring from the creatures who could figure it out. And that figuring out is what we must continue to do.

In Newtonian physics, in relativity, in quantum mechanics, there are many results which seem counterintuitive, which we are not prepared for. Even the idea that an object in motion tends to stay in motion does not conform in a ready way to everyday experience because there is so much friction and atmospheric resistance down here on Earth. The prediction of special relativity that time slows down as you go close to the speed of light does not correspond to everyday experience. That's because we are not in the habit of traveling close to the speed of light. The prediction from quantum mechanics that a particle can ooze through a barrier and find itself on the other side of a wall without having made a hole, sounds absurd. But, in fact, natural radioactivity depends exactly on that process. The idea in evolutionary biology that creatures change slowly from one species to another is not in perfect conformity with everyday experience because it is rare that we find a creature that has transmogrified before our eyes into another species: we have not stuck around long enough.

In many such areas, but especially in the last, you can find today a kind of resurgent know-nothingism, a reactionary response to the findings of human beings objectively addressing the world around them. There is something called "scientific creationism" which claims that the school system should teach the supposed evidence in favor of the cosmology in the first chapter of Genesis on an equal level with the evolutionary findings that Charles Darwin initiated. I believe that this is exceptionally dangerous.

Let me give just one example of how the argument goes. By adding up all the begats in the Book of Genesis you can get the age of the Earth. It turns out to be about six thousand years old — A begat B, B begat C, C begat D. A's lifetime is stated, B's, C's and so on. Then you get up to historical times. Add it all up: 4004 B.C. according to Archbishop Usher. Now, if that is the case, then an interesting question arises. How is it that there are astronomical objects more than 6000 light-years away? It takes light a year to travel a light-year, so if we see an object that is a million light-years away or two million light-years away, we are seeing it as it was one or two million years ago in the past. If the entire universe is only 6,000 years old, what must we deduce from this? I think the only possible conclusion is that 6000 years ago God made all the photons of light coming to the Earth in a coherent format so as to deceive astronomers into thinking there are such things as galaxies, that the universe is vast and old.

Since most of the matter and energy in the universe is in external galaxies farther away than a million light-years, God must have created most of the matter and energy in the universe to deceive human beings. That is such a malevolent theology as well as such an arrogant pretension that I cannot believe anyone, no matter how devoted to the literal interpretation of this or that religious book, could seriously consider it.

Nevertheless, this sort of doctrine is being urged upon us. Already there are trends essentially to prevent the teaching of Darwinian evolution in schools. Since evolution is one of the major insights in the biological sciences, this restriction can only be understood as a serious and major attack on the teaching of science itself. It reminds me of Lysenkoism in the Soviet Union. Since it is precisely the understanding of science by large numbers of people that is essential for our survival, I see this and various related varieties of know-nothingism as serious threats.

Science is about constantly challenging, correcting, asking questions, not accepting arguments from authority, requiring experimental demonstration of claimed truths. As yet we do not often see these methods applied to political or social or economic problems. I think it is safe to say that there is no nation on the Earth today which is optimized for the middle of the 21st century. We face a wide variety of subtle and complex problems. This implies that we need subtle and complex solutions. That in turn means that we need some education in the complexity and subtlety of the natural and human world. Therefore, the widest possible education of the sort that is taught at this and other major universities seems to me essential. Since it is not possible for most of the people of this nation or others to have the privilege of attending such institutions, I believe that you have a serious responsibility to pass your education on to others.

This is a critical moment. You are alive at a remarkable and memorable time. I think it is not too much to say that the survival of civilization and perhaps even of the human species depends profoundly on what is done in the next 10 or 20 years. You will have a major role to play in the next 10 or 20 years. I wish you well.

The "Threat" of Creationism

ISAAC ASIMOV

Scientists thought it was settled.

The universe, they had decided, is about 20 billion years old, and Earth itself is 4.5 billion years old. Simple forms of life came into being more than three billion years ago, having formed spontaneously from non-living matter. They grew more complex through slow evolutionary processes and the first hominid ancestors of humanity appeared more than four million years ago. Homo sapiens itself — the present human species, people like you and me — has walked the earth for at least 50,000 years.

But apparently it isn't settled. There are Americans who believe that the earth is only about 6,000 years old; that human beings and all other species were brought into existence by a divine Creator as eternally separate varieties of beings, and that there has been no evolutionary process.

They are creationists — they call themselves "scientific" creationists — and they are a growing power in the land, demanding that schools be forced to teach their views. State legislatures, mindful of votes, are beginning to succumb to the pressure. In perhaps 15 states, bills have been introduced, putting forth the creationist point of view, and in others, strong movements are gaining momentum. In Arkansas, a law requiring that the teaching of creationism receive equal time was passed and was scheduled to go into effect in September 1982, though the American Civil Liberties Union successfully filed suit on behalf of a group of clergymen, teachers and parents to overturn it. And a California father named Kelly Segraves, the director of the Creation-Science Research Center, sued to have public-school science classes taught that there are other theories of creation besides evolution, and that one of them was the Biblical version. The suit came to trial in March 1981 and the judge ruled that educators must distribute a policy statement to schools and textbook publishers explaining that the theory of evolution should not be seen as "the ultimate cause of origins." Even in New York, the Board of Education has delayed since January in making a final decision, expected this month, on whether schools will be required to include the teaching of creationism in their curriculums.

The Reverend Jerry Falwell, the head of the Moral Majority, who supports the creationist view from his television pulpit, claims that he has 17 million to 25 million viewers (though Arbitron places the figure at a much more modest 1.6 million). But there are 66 electronic ministries which have a total audience of about 20 million. And in parts of the country where the Fundamentalists predominate – the so-called Bible Belt – creationists are in the majority.

They make up a fervid and dedicated group, convinced beyond argument of both their rightness and righteousness. Faced with an apathetic and falsely secure majority, smaller groups have used intense pressure and forceful campaigning – as the creationists do – and have succeeded in disrupting and taking over whole societies.

Yet, though creationists seem to accept the literal truth of the Biblical story of creation, this does not mean that all religious people are creationists. There are millions of Catholics, Protestants and Jews who think of the Bible as a source of spiritual truth and accept much of it as symbolically rather than literally true. They do not consider the Bible to be a textbook of science, even in intent, and have no problem teaching evolution in their secular institutions.

To those who are trained in science, creationism seems like a bad dream, a sudden reliving of a nightmare, a renewed march of an army of the night risen to challenge free thought and enlightenment.

The scientific evidence for the age of the earth and for the evolutionary development of life seems overwhelming to scientists. How can anyone question it? What are the arguments the creationists use? What is the "science" that makes their views "scientific"? Here are some of them:

• The argument from analogy:

A watch implies a watchmaker, say the creationists. If you were to find a beautifully intricate watch in the desert, far from habitation, you would be sure that it had been fashioned by human hands and somehow left there. It would pass the bounds of credibility that it had simply formed, spontaneously, from the sands of the desert.

By analogy, then, if you consider humanity, life, earth and the universe, all infinitely more intricate than a watch, you can believe far less easily that it "just happened." It, too, like the watch, must have been fashioned, but by more-than-human hands – in short by a divine Creator.

This argument seems unanswerable, and it has been used (even though not often explicitly expressed) ever since the dawn of consciousness. To have explained to prescientific human beings that the wind and the rain and the sun follow the laws of nature and do so blindly and without a guiding hand would have been utterly unconvincing to them. In fact, it might well have gotten you stoned to death as a blasphemer.

There are many aspects of the universe that still cannot be explained satisfactorily by science; but ignorance implies only ignorance that may someday be conquered. To surrender to ignorance and call it God has always been premature, and it remains premature today.

In short, the complexity of the universe – and one's inability to explain it in full – is not in itself an argument for a Creator.

- The argument from general consent.

Some creationists point out that belief in a Creator is general among all peoples and all cultures. Surely this unanimous craving hints at a great truth. There would be no unanimous belief in a lie.

General belief, however, is not really surprising. Nearly every people on earth that considers the existence of the world assumes it to have been created by a god or gods. And each group invents full details for the story. No two creation tales are alike. The Greeks, the Norsemen, the Japanese, the Hindus, the American Indians and so on and so on all have their own creation myths, and all of these are recognized by Americans of Judeo-Christian heritage as "just myths."

The ancient Hebrews also had a creation tale — two of them, in fact. There is a primitive Adam-and-Eve-in-Paradise story, with man created first, then animals, then woman. There is also a poetic tale of God fashioning the universe in six days, with animals preceding man, and man and woman created together.

These Hebrew myths are not inherently more credible than any of the others, but they are our myths. General consent, of course, proves nothing: There can be a unanimous belief in something that isn't so. The universal opinion over thousands of years that the earth was flat never flattened its spherical shape by one inch.

- The argument by belittlement.

Creationists frequently stress the fact that evolution is "only a theory," giving the impression that a theory is an idle guess. A scientist, one gathers, arising one morning with nothing particular to do, decides that perhaps the moon is made of Roquefort cheese and instantly advances the Roquefort-cheese theory.

A theory (as the word is used by scientists) is a detailed description of some facet of the universe's workings that is based on long observation and, where possible, experiment. It is the result of careful reasoning from those observations and experiments and has survived the critical study of scientists generally.

For example, we have the description of the cellular nature of living organisms (the "cell theory"); of objects attracting each other according to a fixed rule (the "theory of gravitation"); of energy behaving in discrete bits (the "quantum theory"); of light traveling through a vacuum at a fixed measurable velocity (the "theory of relativity"), and so on.

All are theories; all are firmly founded; all are accepted as valid descriptions of this or that aspect of the universe. They are neither guesses nor speculations. And no theory is better founded, more closely examined, more critically argued and more thoroughly accepted, than the theory of evolution. If it is "only" a theory, that is all it has to be.

Creationism, on the other hand, is not a theory. There is no evidence, in the scientific sense, that supports it. Creationism, or at least the particular variety accepted by many Americans, is an expression of early Middle Eastern legend. It is fairly described as "only a myth."

- The argument from imperfection.

Creationists, in recent years, have stressed the "scientific" background of their beliefs. They point out that there are scientists who base their creationist beliefs on a careful study of geology, paleontology and biology and produce "textbooks" that embody those beliefs.

Virtually the whole scientific corpus of creationism, however, consists of the pointing out of imperfections in the evolutionary view. The creationists insist, for example, that evolutionists cannot show true transition states between species in the fossil evidence; that age determinations through radioactive breakdown are uncertain; that alternate interpretations of this or that piece of evidence are possible, and so on.

Because the evolutionary view is not perfect and is not agreed upon in every detail by all scientists, creationists argue that evolution is false and that scientists, in supporting evolution, are basing their views on blind faith and dogmatism.

To an extent, the creationists are right here: The details of evolution are not perfectly known. Scientists have been adjusting and modifying Charles Darwin's suggestions since he advanced his theory of the origin of species through natural selection back in 1859. After all, much has been learned about physiology, microbiology, biochemistry, ethology and various other branches of life science in the last 125 years, and it is to be expected that we can improve on Darwin. In fact, we have improved on him.

Nor is the process finished. It can never be, as long as human beings continue to question and to strive for better answers.

The details of evolutionary theory are in dispute precisely because scientists are not devotees of blind faith and dogmatism. They do not accept even as great a thinker as Darwin without question, nor do they accept any idea, new or old, without thorough argument. Even after accepting an idea, they stand ready to overrule it, if appropriate new evidence arrives. If, however, we grant that a theory is imperfect and that details remain in dispute, does that disprove the theory as a whole?

Consider. I drive a car, and you drive a car. I do not know exactly how an engine works. Perhaps you do not either. And it may be that our hazy and approximate ideas of the workings of an automobile are in conflict. Must we then conclude from this disagreement that an automobile does not run, or that it does not exist? Or, if our senses force us to conclude that an automobile does exist and run, does that mean it is pulled by an invisible horse, since our engine theory is imperfect?

However much scientists argue their differing beliefs in details of evolutionary theory, or in the interpretation of the necessarily imperfect fossil record, they firmly accept the evolutionary process itself.

- The argument from distorted science.

Creationists have learned enough scientific terminology to use it in their attempts to disprove evolution. They do this in numerous ways, but the most common example, at least in the mail I receive, is the repeated assertion that the second law of thermodynamics demonstrates the evolutionary process to be impossible.

In kindergarten terms, the second law of thermodynamics says that all spontaneous change is in the direction of increasing disorder — that is, in a "downhill" direction. There can be no spontaneous buildup of the complex from the simple, therefore, because that would be moving "uphill." According to the creationist argument, since, by the evolutionary process, complex forms of life evolve from simple forms, that process defies the second law, so creationism must be true.

Such an argument implies that this clearly visible fallacy is somehow invisible to scientists, who must therefore be flying in the face of the second law through sheer perversity.

Scientists, however, do know about the second law and they are not blind. It's just that an argument based on kindergarten terms is suitable only for kindergartens.

To lift the argument a notch above the kindergarten level, the second law of thermodynamics applies to a "closed system" — that is, to a system that does not gain energy from without, or lose energy to the outside. The only truly closed system we know of is the universe as a whole.

Within a closed system, there are subsystems that can gain complexity spontaneously, provided there is a greater loss of complexity in another interlocking subsystem. The overall change then is a complexity loss in line with the dictates of the second law.

Evolution can proceed and build up the complex from the simple, thus moving uphill, without violating the second law, as long as another interlocking part of the system — the sun, which delivers energy to the earth continually — moves downhill (as it does) at a much faster rate than evolution moves uphill.

If the sun were to cease shining, evolution would stop and so, eventually, would life.

Unfortunately, the second law is a subtle concept which most people are not accustomed to dealing with, and it is not easy to see the fallacy in the creationist distortion.

There are many other "scientific" arguments used by creationists, some taking quite clever advantage of present areas of dispute in evolutionary theory, but every one of them is as disingenuous as the second-law argument.

The "scientific" arguments are organized into special creationist textbooks, which have all the surface appearance of the real thing, and which school systems are being heavily pressured to accept. They are written by people who have not made any mark as scientists, and, while they discuss geology, paleontology and biology with correct scientific terminology, they are devoted almost entirely to raising doubts over the legitimacy of the evidence and reasoning underlying evolutionary thinking on the assumption that this leaves creationism as the only possible alternative.

Evidence actually in favor of creationism is not presented, of course, because none exists other than the word of the Bible, which it is current creationist strategy not to use.

- The argument from irrelevance.

Some creationists put all matters of scientific evidence to one side and consider all such things irrelevant. The Creator, they say, brought life and the earth and the entire universe into being 6,000 years ago or so, complete with all the evidence for an eons-long evolutionary development. The fossil record, the decaying radioactivity, the receding galaxies were all created as they are, and the evidence they present is an illusion.

Of course, this argument is itself irrelevant, for it can neither be proved nor disproved. It is not an argument, actually, but a statement. I can say that the entire universe was created two minutes ago, complete with all its history books describing a nonexistent past in detail, and with every living person equipped with a full memory: you, for instance, in the process of reading this article in midstream with a memory of what you had read in the beginning — which you had not really read.

What kind of a Creator would produce a universe containing so intricate an illusion? It would mean that the Creator formed a universe that contained human beings whom He had endowed with the faculty of curiosity and the ability to reason. He supplied those human beings with an enormous amount of subtle and cleverly consistent evidence designed to mislead them and cause them to be convinced that the universe was created 20 billion years ago and developed by evolutionary processes that included the creation and development of life on Earth.

Why?

Does the Creator take pleasure in fooling us? Does it amuse Him to watch us go wrong? Is it part of a test to see if human beings will deny their senses and their reason in order to cling to myth? Can it be that the Creator is a cruel and malicious prankster, with a vicious and adolescent sense of humor?

- The argument from authority.

The Bible says that God created the world in six days, and the Bible is the inspired word of God. To the average creationist this is all that counts. All other arguments are merely a tedious way of countering the propaganda of all those wicked humanists, agnostics and atheists who are not satisfied with the clear word of the Lord.

The creationist leaders do not actually use that argument because that would make their argument a religious one, and they would not be able to use it in fighting a secular school system. They have to borrow the clothing of science, no matter how badly it fits and call themselves "scientific" creationists. They also speak only of the "Creator," and never mention that this Creator is God of the Bible.

We cannot, however, take this sheep's clothing seriously. However much the creationist leaders might hammer away at their "scientific" and "philosophical" points, they would be helpless and a laughing stock if that were all they had.

It is religion that recruits their squadrons. Tens of millions of Americans, who neither know or understand the actual arguments for — or even against — evolution, march in the army of the night with their Bibles held high. And they are a strong and frightening force, impervious to, and immunized against, the feeble lance of mere reason.

Even if I am right and the evolutionists' case is very strong, have not creationists, whatever the emptiness of their case, a right to be heard?

If their case is empty, isn't it perfectly safe to discuss it since the emptiness would then be apparent?

Why, then, are evolutionists so reluctant to have creationism taught in the public schools on an equal basis with evolutionary theory? Can it be that the evolutionists are not as confident of their case as they pretend. Are they afraid to allow youngsters a clear choice?

First, the creationists are somewhat less than honest in their demand for equal time. It is not their views that are repressed: Schools are by no means the only place in which the dispute between creationism and evolutionary theory is played out.

There are the churches, for instance, which are a much more serious influence on most Americans than the schools are. To be sure, many churches are quite liberal, have made their peace with science and find it easy to live with scientific advance — even with evolution. But many of the less modish and citified churches are bastions of creationism.

The influence of the church is naturally felt in the home, in the newspapers and in all of surrounding society. It makes itself felt in the nation as a whole, even in religiously liberal areas, in thousands of subtle ways: in the nature of holiday observance, in expressions of patriotic fervor, even in total irrelevancies. In 1968, for example, a team of astronauts circling the moon were instructed to read the first few verses of Genesis as though NASA felt it had to placate the public lest they rage against the violation of the firmament. At the present time, even the current President of the United States has expressed his creationist sympathies.

It is only in school that American youngsters in general are ever likely to hear any reasoned exposition of the evolutionary viewpoint. They might find such a viewpoint in books, magazines, newspapers or even, on occasion, on television. But church and family can easily censor printed matter or television. Only the school is beyond their control.

But only just barely beyond. Even though schools are now allowed to teach evolution, teachers are beginning to be apologetic about it, knowing full well their jobs are at the mercy of school boards upon which creationists are a stronger and stronger influence.

Then, too, in schools, students are not required to believe what they learn about evolution — merely to parrot it back on tests. If they fail to do so, their punishment is nothing more than the loss of a few points on a test or two.

In the creationist churches, however, the congregation is required to believe. Impressionable youngsters, taught that they will go to hell if they listen to the evolutionary doctrine, are not likely to listen in comfort or to believe if they do.

Therefore, creationists, who control the church and the society they live in and who face the public school as the only place where evolution is even briefly mentioned in a possibly favorable way, find they cannot stand even so minuscule a competition and demand "equal time."

Do you suppose their devotion to "fairness" is such that they will give equal time to evolution in their churches?

Second, the real danger is the manner in which creationists want their "equal time."

In the scientific world, there is free and open competition of ideas, and even a scientist whose suggestions are not accepted is nevertheless free to continue to argue his case.

In this free and open competition of ideas, creationism has clearly lost. It has been losing in fact, since the time of Copernicus four and a half centuries ago. But creationists, placing myth above reason, refuse to accept the decision and are now calling on the Government to force their views on the schools in lieu of the free expression of ideas. Teachers must be forced to present creationism as though it has equal intellectual respectability with evolutionary doctrine.

What a precedent this sets.

If the Government can mobilize its policemen and its prisons to make certain that teachers give creationism equal time, they can next use force to make sure that teachers declare creationism the victor so that evolution will be evicted from the classroom altogether.

We will have established the full groundwork, in other words, for legally enforced ignorance and for totalitarian thought control.

And what if the creationists win? They might, you know, for there are millions who, faced with the choice between science and their interpretation of the Bible, will choose the Bible and reject science, regardless of the evidence.

This is not entirely because of a traditional and unthinking reverence for the literal words of the Bible; there is also a pervasive uneasiness — even an actual fear — of science that will drive even those who care little for Fundamentalism into the arms of the creationists. For one thing, science is uncertain. Theories are subject to revision; observations are open to a variety of interpretations, and scientists quarrel among themselves. This is disillusioning for those untrained in the scientific method, who thus turn to the rigid certainty of the Bible instead. There is something comfortable about a view that allows for no deviation and that spares you the painful necessity of having to think.

Second, science is complex and chilling. The mathematical language of science is understood by very few. The vistas it presents are scary — an enormous universe ruled by chance and impersonal rules, empty and uncaring, ungraspable and vertiginous. How comfortable to turn instead to a small world, only a few thousand years old, and under God's personal and immediate care; a world in which you are His peculiar concern and where He will not consign you to hell if you are careful to follow every word of the Bible as interpreted for you by your television preacher.

Third, science is dangerous. There is no question but that poison gas, genetic engineering and nuclear weapons and power stations are terrifying. It may be that civilization is falling apart and the world we know is coming to an end. In that case, why not turn to religion and look forward to the Day of Judgment, in which you and your fellow believers will be lifted into eternal bliss and have the added joy of watching the scoffers and disbelievers writhe forever in torment.

So why might they not win?

There are numerous cases of societies in which the armies of the night have ridden triumphantly over minorities in order to establish a powerful orthodoxy which dictates official thought. Invariably, the triumphant ride is toward long-range disaster.

Spain dominated Europe and the world in the sixteenth century, but in Spain orthodoxy came first, and all divergence of opinion was ruthlessly suppressed. The result was that Spain settled back into blankness and did not share in the scientific, technological and commercial ferment that bubbled up in other nations of Western Europe. Spain remained an intellectual backwater for centuries.

In the late seventeenth century, France in the name of orthodoxy revoked the Edict of Nantes and drove out many thousands of Huguenots, who added their intellectual vigor to lands of refuge such as Great Britain, the Netherlands and Prussia, while France was permanently weakened.

In more recent times, Germany hounded out the Jewish scientists of Europe. They arrived in the United States and contributed immeasurably to scientific advancement here, while Germany lost so heavily that there is no telling how long it will take it to regain its former scientific eminence. The Soviet Union, in its fascination with Lysenko, destroyed its geneticists, and set back its biological sciences for decades. China, during the Cultural Revolution, turned against Western science and is still laboring to overcome the devastation that resulted.

Are we now, with all these examples before us, to ride backward into the past under the same tattered banner of orthodoxy? With creationism in the saddle, American science will wither. We will raise a generation of ignoramuses ill equipped to run the industry of tomorrow, much less to generate the new advances of the days after tomorrow.

We will inevitably recede into the backwater of civilization and those nations that retain open scientific thought will take over the leadership of the world and the cutting edge of human advancement.

I don't suppose that the creationists really plan the decline of the United States, but their loudly expressed patriotism is as simple-minded as their "science." If they succeed, they will, in their folly, achieve the opposite of what they say they wish.

Evolution as Fact and Theory

STEPHEN JAY GOULD

Kirtley Mather, who died last year at age 89, was a pillar of both science and the Christian religion in America and one of my dearest friends. The difference of half a century in our ages evaporated before our common interests. The most curious thing we shared was a battle we each fought at the same age. For Kirtley had gone to Tennessee with Clarence Darrow to testify for evolution at the Scopes trial of 1925. When I think that we are enmeshed again in the same struggle for one of the best documented, most compelling and exciting concepts in all of science, I don't know whether to laugh or cry.

According to idealized principles of scientific discourse, the arousal of dormant issues should reflect fresh data that give renewed life to abandoned notions. Those outside the current debate may therefore be excused for suspecting that creationists have come up with something new, or that evolutionists have generated some serious internal trouble. But nothing has changed; the creationists have not a single new fact or argument. Darrow and Bryan were at least more entertaining than we lesser antagonists today. The rise of creationism is politics, pure and simple; it represents one issue (and by no means the major concern) of the resurgent evangelical right. Arguments that seemed kooky just a decade ago have re-entered the mainstream.

CREATIONISM IS NOT SCIENCE

The basic attack of the creationists falls apart on two general counts before we even reach the supposed factual details of their complaints against evolution. First, they play upon a vernacular misunderstanding of the word "theory" to convey the false impression that we evolutionists are covering up the rotten core of our edifice. Second, they misuse a popular philosophy of science to argue that they are behaving scientifically in attacking evolution. Yet the same philosophy demonstrates that their own belief is not science, and that "scientific creationism" is therefore meaningless and self-contradictory, a superb example of what Orwell called "newspeak."

In the American vernacular, "theory" often means "imperfect fact" —part of a hierarchy of confidence running downhill from fact to theory to hypothesis to guess. Thus the power of the creationist argument: evolution is "only" a theory, and intense debate now rages about many aspects of the theory. If evolution is less than a fact, and scientists can't even make up their minds about the theory, then what confidence can we have in it? Indeed, President Reagan echoed this argument before an evangelical group in Dallas when he said (in what I devoutly hope was campaign rhetoric): "Well, it is a theory. It is a scientific theory only, and it has in recent years been challenged in the world of science — that is, not believed in the scientific community to be as infallible as it once was."

Well, evolution *is* a theory. It is also a fact. And facts and theories are different things, not rungs in a hierarchy of increasing certainty. Facts are the world's data. Theories are structures of ideas that explain and interpret facts. Facts do not go away when scientists debate rival theories to explain them. Einstein's theory of gravitation replaced Newton's, but apples did not suspend themselves in mid-air pending the outcome. And human beings evolved from apelike ancestors whether they did so by Darwin's proposed mechanism or by some other, yet to be discovered.

Moreover, "fact" does not mean "absolute certainty." The final proofs of logic and mathematics flow deductively from stated premises and achieve certainty only because they are *not* about the empirical world. Evolutionists make no claim for perpetual truth, though creationists often do (and then attack us for a style of argument that they themselves favor). In science, "fact" can only mean "confirmed to such a degree that it would be perverse to withhold provisional assent." I suppose that apples might start to rise tomorrow, but the possibility does not merit equal time in physics classrooms.

Evolutionists have been clear about this distinction between fact and theory from the very beginning, if only because we have always acknowledged how far we are from completely understanding the mechanisms (theory) by which evolution (fact) occurred. Darwin continually emphasized the difference between his two great and separate accomplishments: establishing the fact of evolution, and proposing a theory — natural selection — to explain the mechanism of evolution. He wrote in *The Descent of Man:* "I had two distinct objects in view; firstly, to show that species had not been separately created, and secondly, that natural selection had been the chief agent of change . . . Hence if I have erred in . . . having exaggerated its [natural selection's] power . . . I have at least, as I hope, done good service in aiding to overthrow the dogma of separate creations."

Thus Darwin acknowledged the provisional nature of natural selection while affirming the fact of evolution. The fruitful theoretical debate that Darwin initiated has never ceased. From the 1940s through the 1960s, Darwin's own theory of natural selection did achieve a temporary hegemony that it never enjoyed in his lifetime. But renewed debate characterizes our decade, and, while no biologist questions the importance of natural selection, many now doubt its ubiquity. In particular, many evolutionists argue that substantial amounts of genetic change may not be subject to natural selection and may spread through populations at random. Others are challenging Darwin's linking of natural selection with gradual, imperceptible change through all intermediary degrees; they are arguing that most evolutionary events may occur far more rapidly than Darwin envisioned.

Scientists regard debates on fundamental issues of theory as a sign of intellectual health and a source of excitement. Science is — and how else can I say it? — most fun when it plays with interesting ideas, examines their implications, and recognizes that old information may be explained in surprisingly new ways. Evolutionary theory is now enjoying this uncommon vigor. Yet amidst all this turmoil no biologist has been led to doubt the fact that evolution occurred; we are debating *how* it happened. We are all trying to explain the same thing: the tree of evolutionary descent linking all organisms by ties of genealogy. Creationists pervert and caricature this debate by conveniently neglecting the common conviction that underlies it, and by falsely suggesting that we now doubt the very phenomenon we are struggling to understand.

Using another invalid argument, creationists claim that "the dogma of separate creations," as Darwin characterized it a century ago, is a scientific theory meriting equal time with evolution in high school biology curricula. But a prevailing viewpoint among philosophers of science belies this creationist argument. Philosopher Karl Popper has argued for decades that the primary criterion of science is the falsifiability of its theories. We can never prove absolutely, but we can falsify. A set of ideas that cannot, in principle, be falsified is not science.

The entire creationist argument involves little more than a rhetorical attempt to falsify evolution by presenting supposed contradictions among its supporters. Their brand of creationism, they claim, is "scientific" because it follows the Popperian model in trying to demolish evolution. Yet Popper's argument must apply in both directions. One does not become a scientist by the simple act of trying to falsify another scientific system; one has to present an alternative system that also meets Popper's criterion — it too must be falsifiable in principle.

"Scientific creationism" is a self-contradictory, nonsense phrase precisely because it cannot be falsified. I can envision observations and experiments that would disprove any evolutionary theory I know, but I cannot imagine what potential data could lead creationists to abandon their beliefs. Unbeatable systems are dogma, not science. Lest I seem harsh or rhetorical, I quote creationism's leading intellectual, Duane Gish, Ph.D., from his recent (1978) book *Evolution? The Fossils Say No!* "By creation we mean the bringing into being by a supernatural Creator of the basic kinds of plants and animals by the process of sudden, or fiat, creation. We do not know how the Creator created, what processes He used, *for He used processes which are not now operating anywhere in the natural universe* [Gish's italics]. This is why we refer to creation as special creation. We cannot discover by scientific investigations anything about the creative processes used by the Creator."

Pray tell, Dr. Gish, in the light of your last sentence, what then is "scientific" creationism?

THE FACT OF EVOLUTION

Our confidence that evolution occurred centers upon three general arguments. First, we have abundant, direct, observational evidence of evolution in action, from both the field and the laboratory. It ranges from countless experiments on change in nearly everything about fruit flies subjected to artificial selection in the laboratory to the famous British moths that turned black when industrial soot darkened the trees upon which they rest. (The moths gain protection from sharp-sighted bird predators by blending into the background.) Creationists do not deny these observations; how could they? Creationists have tightened their act. They now argue that God only created "basic kinds," and allowed for limited evolutionary meandering within them. Thus toy poodles and Great Danes come from the dog kind and moths can change color, but nature cannot convert a dog to a cat or a monkey to a man.

The second and third arguments for evolution — the case for major changes — do not involve direct observation of evolution in action. They rest upon inference, but are no less secure for that reason. Major evolutionary change requires too much time for direct observation on the scale of recorded human history. All historical sciences rest upon inference, and evolution is no different from geology, cosmology, or human history in this respect. In principle, we cannot observe processes that operated in the past. We must infer them from results that still survive: living and fossil organisms for evolution, documents and artifacts for human history, strata and topography for geology.

The second argument — that the imperfection of nature reveals evolution — strikes many people as ironic, for they feel that evolution should be most elegantly displayed in the nearly perfect adaptation expressed by some organisms — the camber of a gull's wing, or butterflies that cannot be seen in ground litter because they mimic leaves so precisely. But perfection could be imposed by a wise creator or evolved by natural selection. Perfection covers the tracks of past history. And past history — the evidence of descent — is our mark of evolution.

Evolution lies exposed in the *imperfections* that record a history of descent. Why should a rat run, a bat fly, a porpoise swim, and I type this essay with structures built of the same bones unless we all inherited them from a common ancestor? An engineer, starting from scratch, could design better limbs in each case. Why should all the large native mammals of Australia be marsupials, unless they descended from a common ancestor isolated on this island continent? Marsupials are not "better," or ideally suited for Australia; many have been wiped out by placental mammals imported by man from other continents. This principle of imperfection extends to all historical sciences. When we recognize the etymology of September, October, November, and December (seventh, eighth, ninth, and tenth, from the Latin), we know that two additional items (January and February) must have been added to an original calendar of ten months.

The third argument is more direct: transitions are often found in the fossil record. Preserved transitions are not common — and should not be, according to our understanding of evolution (see next section) — but they are not entirely wanting, as creationists often claim. The lower jaw of reptiles contains several bones, that of mammals only one. The non-mammalian jawbones are reduced, step by step, in mammalian ancestors until they become tiny nubbins located at the back of the jaw. The "hammer" and "anvil" bones of the mammalian ear are descendants of these nubbins. How could such a transition be accomplished? the creationists ask. Surely a bone is either entirely in the jaw or in the ear. Yet paleontologists have discovered two transitional lineages of therapsids (the so-called mammal-like reptiles) with a double jaw joint — one composed of the old quadrate and articular bones (soon to become the hammer and anvil), the other of the squamosal and dentary bones (as in modern mammals). For that matter, what better transitional form could we desire than the oldest human, *Australopithecus afarensis*, with its apelike palate, its human upright stance, and a cranial capacity larger than any ape's of the same body size but a full 1,000 cubic centimeters below ours? If God made each of the half dozen human species discovered in ancient rocks, why did he create in an unbroken temporal sequence of progressively more modern features — increasing cranial capacity, reduced face and teeth, larger body size? Did he create to mimic evolution and test our faith thereby?

AN EXAMPLE OF CREATIONIST ARGUMENT

Faced with these facts of evolution and the philosophical bankruptcy of their own position, creationists rely upon distortion and innuendo to buttress their rhetorical claim. If I sound sharp or bitter, indeed I am — for I have become a major target of these practices.

I count myself among the evolutionists who argue for a jerky, or episodic, rather than a smoothly gradual, pace of change. In 1972 my colleague Niles Eldredge and I developed the theory of punctuated equilibrium. We argued that two outstanding facts of the fossil record — geologically "sudden" origin of new species and failure to change thereafter (stasis) — reflect the predictions of evolutionary theory, not the imperfections of the fossil record. In most theories, small isolated populations are the source of new species, and the process of speciation takes thousands or tens of thousands of years. This amount of time, so long when measured against our lives, is a geological microsecond. It represents much less than 1 percent of the average life span for a fossil invertebrate species — more than 10 million years. Large, widespread, and well established species, on the other hand, are not expected to change very much. We believe that the inertia of large populations explains the stasis of most fossil species over millions of years.

We proposed the theory of punctuated equilibrium largely to provide a different explanation for pervasive trends in the fossil record. Trends, we argued, cannot be attributed to gradual transformation within lineages, but must arise from the differential success of certain kinds of species. A trend, we argued, is more like climbing a flight of stairs (punctuations and stasis) than rolling up an inclined plane.

Since we proposed punctuated equilibria to explain trends, it is infuriating to be quoted again and again by creationists — whether through design or stupidity, I do not know — as admitting that the fossil record includes no transitional forms. Transitional forms are generally lacking at the species level, but are abundant between larger groups. The evolution from reptiles to mammals, as mentioned earlier, is well documented. Yet a pamphlet entitled "Harvard Scientists Agree Evolution Is a Hoax" states: "The facts of punctuated equilibrium which Gould and Eldredge . . . are forcing Darwinists to swallow fit the picture that Bryan insisted on, and which God has revealed to us in the Bible."

Continuing the distortion, several creationists have equated the theory of punctuated equilibrium with a caricature of the beliefs of Richard Goldschmidt, a great early geneticist. Goldschmidt argued, in a famous book published in 1940, that new groups can arise all at once through major mutations. He referred to these suddenly transformed creatures as "hopeful monsters." (I am attracted to some aspects of the non-caricatured version, but Goldschmidt's theory still has nothing to do with punctuated equilibrium.) Creationist Luther Sunderland talks of the "punctuated equilibrium hopeful monster theory" and tells his hopeful readers that "it amounts to tacit admission that anti-evolutionists are correct in asserting there is no fossil evidence supporting the theory that all life is connected to a common ancestor." Duane Gish writes, "According to Goldschmidt, and now apparently according to Gould, a reptile laid an egg from which the first bird, feathers and all, was produced." Any evolutionist who believed such nonsense would rightly be laughed off the intellectual stage; yet the only theory that could ever envision such a scenario for the evolution of birds is creationism — God acts in the egg.

CONCLUSION

I am both angry at and amused by the creationists; but mostly I am deeply sad. Sad for many reasons. Sad because so many people who respond to creationist appeals are troubled for the right reason, but venting their anger at the wrong target. It is true that scientists have often been dogmatic and elitist. It is true that we have often allowed the white-coated, advertising image to represent us — "Scientists say that Brand X cures bunions ten times faster than . . ." We have not fought it adequately because we derive benefits from appearing as a new priesthood. It is also true that faceless bureaucratic state power intrudes more and more into our lives and removes choices that should belong to individuals and communities. I can understand that requiring that evolution be taught in the schools might be seen as one more insult on all these grounds. But the culprit is not, and cannot be, evolution or any other fact of the natural world. Identify and fight your legitimate enemies by all means, but we are not among them.

I am sad because the practical result of this brouhaha will not be expanded coverage to include creationism (that would also make me sad), but the reduction or excision of evolution from high school curricula. Evolution is one of the half dozen "great ideas" developed by science. It speaks to the profound issues of genealogy that fascinate all of us — the "roots" phenomenon writ large. Where did we come from? Where did life arise? How did it develop? How are organisms related? It forces us to think, ponder, and wonder. Shall we deprive millions of this knowledge and once again teach biology as a set of dull and unconnected facts, without the thread that weaves diverse material into a supple unity?

But most of all I am saddened by a trend I am just beginning to discern among my colleagues. I sense that some now wish to mute the healthy debate about theory that has brought new life to evolutionary biology. It provides grist for creationist mills, they say, even if only by distortion. Perhaps we should lie low and rally round the flag of strict Darwinism, at least for the moment — a kind of old-time religion on our part.

But we should borrow another metaphor and recognize that we too have to tread a straight and narrow path, surrounded by roads to perdition. For if we ever begin to suppress our search to understand nature, to quench our own intellectual excitement in a misguided effort to present a united front where it does not and should not exist, then we are truly lost.

On Avoiding
Nuclear Holocaust

VICTOR F. WEISSKOPF

Since 1930, physicists have penetrated the innermost parts of matter and have found forces and energies that normally are inactive here on Earth. These are "cosmic" forces in the real sense of the word: the energy of the sun is driven by these forces; the explosions of supernovas, and other cataclysmic phenomena, are caused by them.

There are, of course, natural radioactive substances, but these are not a true part of the Earth's contemporary environment. They are the leftovers of a much earlier time, the last embers of a cosmic fire in which our terrestrial matter was created 7 billion years ago. By delving into these inner nuclear energies, we are dealing with an order of magnitude much higher than in any other terrestrial form of energy. A chemical process — even the strongest chemical explosion — releases only a millionth, per atom, of the energy released in nuclear processes such as fission or fusion. So when these energies were first applied by human beings, the strength of technology immediately grew by a factor of a million.

It was only 40 years ago that we began to develop this process, and World War II exerted special pressure on this country to apply these great energies to weapons that would enable us to win the war. Many scientists, including myself, collaborated in this effort because of the danger — a clear and present danger at that time — that people like Hitler and political systems like Nazism would get hold of such weapons before we did. So, from 1940 to 1945, we developed ways to release these cosmic forces suddenly, creating the world's first nuclear bomb. (In some ways, it's easier to release these energies suddenly than continuously, as in a power reactor. But I will not discuss power reactors here, although many people are concerned about them — I want to deal with a much more serious problem.)

I was present on July 16, 1945, when the first atomic bomb was exploded in the desert in southern New Mexico. And while wearing sunglasses, I watched it: the amount of light released was 20 times more intense than midday sunlight. Two days later, I drove a jeep to the place where the bomb was exploded. My passengers were Hans Bethe, Enrico Fermi, Robert Oppenheimer, and General Leslie Groves (the military leader of the project). We found the desert sand molten and glazed over a radius of about 200 yards. And General Groves's remark was, "Is that all?" He probably expected a hole to the center of the earth.

Three weeks later, one plane — the Enola Gay — flew over Hiroshima and dropped another such bomb on that city. Allied planes had been routinely making "fire raids" over the cities of Japan around that time, but the effect of this one bomb was worse than the damage inflicted by a thousand such planes: 100 thousand people were dead immediately, and many died soon afterward of diseases and other effects. That was only an "old-fashioned" bomb, the equivalent of 20 thousand tons of TNT. Now-adays, we have modernized A-bombs and H-bombs, fission and fusion bombs with yields up to many megatons, with effects correspondingly greater.

THINKING THE UNTHINKABLE

Let us suppose that one relatively big bomb — a 20-megaton bomb — fell on the center of Boston. The result would be no more city, but a crater about half a mile in diameter and 200 feet deep. Out to almost two miles, the fireball, which would have stopped growing at that radius, would bathe the surface in an atmosphere of incandescent air. Temperatures at ground level would be a few thousand degrees for the first 15 seconds or so until the fireball started to rise. And within a radius of four miles there would be total destruction: *everything*, even the strongest concrete building, would probably remain standing, but all frame and brick buildings would and from Everett to Dorchester, encompassing most of the city's hospitals and clinics. Farther out, to a radius of six miles, strong concrete buildings would probably remain stainding, but all frame and brick buildings would be destroyed or badly damaged. That would go to Newton, Arlington, and Milton. Up to fifteen miles from the center, including Saugus, Quincy, Weston, and Lexington, frame buildings — most private homes — would be beyond repair.

There would be other destructive effects. Within the first 4 miles, everybody would be dead — about 750,000 people. People within 20 miles of the center could suffer second-degree burns. Flammable materials would instantly catch fire. At distances up to 40 miles, those who looked at the detonation could be blinded forever from the flash. The blast wave would be followed by winds of hundreds of miles per hour, fanning the fires over large distances. Fire storms much worse than those in the Second World War could develop up to 20 miles from the center. Within the fire storm, one could estimate that another 1.5 million people would die, for a total of over 2.2 million people. And the survivors would be badly burned.

These are all short-range, short-term effects; consider also the radia-tion effects. If you are exposed to more than 600 roentgens (R), you die. And the 600–R limit, depending on whether the bomb exploded near the ground or higher up, can extend as far as five or six miles. When the bomb explodes on the ground, materials at ground level are hurled into the air, absorb large amounts of radioactivity, and then fall down after about half an hour, covering the ground with a radioactive blanket. So if you survive the blast — if you are in a "shelter" you must remain inside for several more days. You thus cannot help other people, and the shelter's provisions, if indeed there are any, may not be adequate to sustain you.

The social fabric will break down from the effect of this one bomb: there will be no food supply, no water, no shelter, no power, no medical care. In Boston there are now 6,500 physicians; 5,000 of them would be dead or critically injured within the inner circle. There would be roughly 2,000 patients per doctor, or 10 minutes per patient over 20 days — not a realistic schedule. Add to that no beds, no equipment, and no drugs, and the chaos and suffering become inconceivable. Remember, too, that radiation sickness takes days or weeks to develop, so the sick toll would steadily mount. And imagine the problems posed by inadequate disposal of the dead.

Radioactive material spreads, but its precise pattern depends on the wind. With a bomb like this, deadly levels of radioactivity will cover an area of about 5,000 square miles. We would be "lucky" in Boston if there was a strong west wind and the radioactivity went out to sea, but east winds are common in the region.

This whole scenario is "unthinkable": it is impossible to think rationally about what would happen under such conditions. And that is only one bomb. At present, there are about 40 thousand nuclear bombs, mostly deployed by the United States and the Soviet Union. These are not all 20–megaton bombs, but if only part of the arsenals were used, you could extrapolate this description upward. An all-out war would kill about 100 million people, and that is a conservative estimate. The surviving population would be weakened, to say the least, and the structure of society would be virtually destroyed. Moreover, large parts of the soil would be contaminated, thus becoming unusable for food production, and genetic injuries would haunt us for generations.

OUR PRESENT: TENSE

With all this in mind, let's look at the present nuclear weapons situation. The 40,000 bombs deployed by both sides can be divided into two types: the big "strategic" weapons, of which there are approximately 10,000 (even though 200 would be enough to destroy all cities with a population larger than 100,000 in either country); and the smaller, "tactical" weapons.

The strategic weapons are in intercontinental ballistic missiles (ICBMs) — the first leg of what American policymakers call the "triad"; another third are to be delivered by airplanes; and the remainder are in submarines. Tactical weapons are usually "small," with yields ranging from several thousand to 100 thousand tons of TNT — not in the megaton range, in other words. They are distributed among battlefield weapons (in shells shot from a cannon); short-range missiles ("theater weapons" large enough to hit military facilities, troop gatherings, or maybe nearby cities); and so-called intermediate-range missiles such as the cruise missiles, which fly very near the surface and are hard to detect.

Now let's ask an obvious question: If there are 10,000 strategic weapons, and 200 can destroy all cities with over 100,000 population, don't we have a tremendous oversupply? The number of nuclear weapons seems completely irrational, but these arsenals weren't created overnight — they have resulted from a step-by-step, upwardly spiralling arms race. The large numbers enable one side to destroy many of the other's missile-launching sites in a "first strike." However, I have never understood, and I don't think anybody else quite understands, what the sense of such an action would be. For one thing, if it "succeeded," the nominal winner would not be in much better shape than the loser. But there is a more immediate, strategic impediment: even if the Russians were able to destroy all our land-based missiles in a first strike, we'd still have our submarines and airplanes. Indeed, it is impossible to destroy all these bombers because many are in the air at all times. In other words, a first strike would guarantee retaliation with non-land-based weapons — it would be suicide.

Land-based missiles are unnecessary, and in some ways having them makes us more vulnerable than not having them. Submarine-launched missiles are currently less accurate than land-based missiles yet are accurate enough to destroy cities and factory complexes. The increased accuracy of land-based systems doesn't really buy anything, unless we plan a first strike, but they present a tempting set of targets. Suppose the Russians, succumbing to temptation, pressed the button and hit all our ICBM launching sites with pinpoint accuracy. From 1 to 20 million people in the United States would be killed by the radioactivity from those hits; the wind would transport it east from the launching sites, fumigating the population along the way. (I never have understood why local people protest so much against nuclear power plants while there is so little protest from those who live within 500 miles east of the missile-launching sites.) Submarines, on the other hand, present a poor target: they cannot be found, they cannot be seen, therefore they cannot be attacked. And even if methods were devised to locate them, a hit on a submarine would have much less effect on civilian populations than a hit on a land-based missile.

SALT II was not very restrictive; it did not reduce the number of weapons of any kind. But it did impose limits such that a first-strike capability could not be reached by either side. Now, without the treaty, this may happen. In spite of the completely illogical nature of a first-strike capability, it appears to be the center of strategic thinking both here and in the Soviet Union. The American "response" to Russian first-strike capability, of course, is the famous MX system (although some have observed it could serve admirably in an *American* first strike). The MX is supposed to be relatively invulnerable to enemy attack because it has so many "holes" — only some of which are filled with rockets — that the Russians could not deploy enough rockets to destroy them. As long as there is a restriction on numbers, as the SALT agreement would have given us, this supposition is probabilistically true (as ridiculous as the idea is). But if there is no SALT limit then there is no reason, except financial, that the Russians could not simply increase their number of weapons to hit all silos — the empties as well as the full ones. And it is gruesomely interesting to consider what would happen to this country if they did so: by increasing the target possibilities you increase the number of Russian bombs that would come to our country. The radioactivity developed from hits on MX silos would be sufficient to kill about 50 million people.

Tactical weapons, in contrast to strategic weapons, are not meant to destroy another country — at least in principle. They are not designed for delivery to large population or industrial centers, but are intended for use in direct combat. The idea of the tactical weapons is to use them during a "limited" war, after such a war starts. At first glance, tactical weapons present more of a problem for Europe than for us. An initial confrontation between the United States and Russia would probably be in Europe (although other places, such as the Middle East, are rapidly gaining in likelihood for that honor). But tactical weapons would produce regional damage well beyond the limits of the battlefield, and could trigger levels of combat to even greater scales.

Tactical nuclear weapons can be made to have greater radiation-to-destruction ratios than large, strategic bombs — more radiation per unit of destruction, so to speak. Therefore the use of tactical weapons — against tanks, say — would not only destroy a tank but would poison the neighboring region as well. And Europe is very densely populated.

It is extremely unlikely that a war fought with tactical nuclear weapons will stay limited to tactical nuclear weapons. Larger and larger weapons will be used by those temporarily losing, until, in the last instance, strategic weapons are employed. We have no actual experience in this, of course — we can only rely on the results of computer-assisted "war games" — a strange term, isn't it? — and on common sense (a not-so-common commodity, it seems, among military planners these days). Tactical weapons, in other words, do not really fulfill the purpose for which they were created; on the contrary, they will lead in the end, not with certainty but with great probability, to nuclear holocaust.

WHAT CAN BE DONE?

The worst aspect of the present situation is the almost complete absence of public awareness of the danger. There certainly appears to be public awareness of other issues — nuclear power, for instance. People are very conscious of the dangers that reactors may carry. I won't even tell you whether I'm for or against nuclear power, but one thing is for sure: the probability of anyone reading this article being killed by a reactor in the next 25 years is profoundly smaller than being killed by a nuclear bomb.

Why then is the public so unaware of the problem, or so unwilling to discuss it? One reason, I think, is that people feel it is hopeless. After all, what can one person do? And many accept, quite uncritically, the usual rationalizations: the Russians exist; they are enemies; they are trying to conquer the world; therefore we must possess many more nuclear weapons than they do (no matter that the number may be 200 times more than is necessary to destroy all their cities). I strongly believe that this reasoning is falacious: there are better ways to ensure our survival. If many Americans come to believe this, public opinion can play an enormously powerful role. Public opinion has essentially stopped the construction of nuclear reactors; public opinion stopped the Vietnam War. How then can public opinion reduce the danger of nuclear war?

The first principle to be clearly impressed upon our leaders is that nuclear weapons — including tactical weapons — are no weapons of war. If ever they were used, the holocaust would be highly probable. We simply cannot contemplate using them in any capacity. I am not proposing here a unilateral, bilateral, or global nuclear disarmament. As wonderful as the disappearance of those weapons would be, this is not a realistic aim for the immediate future. But while we possess them, nuclear weapons should function only as deterrents: to prevent the other side from using nuclear weapons. Only an equilibrium reduces the danger of war. This view may seem distasteful and perverse, but it is better than any other policy in a nuclear-armed world.

This equilibrium must include conventional as well as nuclear weapons. We cannot deploy nuclear bombs ("tactical weapons") against tanks, but rather bombs against bombs and tanks against tanks. And this brings us to an interesting point: If we really want an equilibrium of conventional (non-nuclear) weapons — say, in Europe — they must be built. For example, we will need conventional, antitank weapons to replace tactical nuclear weapons, and that means more money. In other words, reducing the danger of nuclear war is not going to save us money, as people often say. It might even increase the military budget. But I can think of no wiser investment in our future.

A second principle involves the elimination of redundant strategic weapons. I would scrap all land-based missiles — just scrap them. They only represent a temptation for the other side. We already have very effective deterrence in submarines and airplanes, so why keep an expensive, unnecessary, dangerous, provocative, and counterproductive target? This step *can* be done unilaterally. I know that such a measure is difficult for many reasons; reducing the number of any weapon is not usually considered a popular act. But there is another sad fact: land-based missiles are controlled by the air force and sea-based missiles are controlled by the navy, and the air force doesn't want its weapons taken away. As politically difficult as such a change might be, we must learn to live without these land-based strategic weapons. And from this it follows that an *increase* — i.e., the MX — is completely senseless.

My third principle concerns proliferation. More and more "small" nations (other than the so-called superpowers) may acquire nuclear weapons. Again I think public opinion in those nations could prevent this. If people come to see that acquisition of nuclear weapons actually reduces their security, they will oppose such a policy. Of course, when you are the only one with a nuclear weapon, you may have a certain military advantage, but it doesn't last. Nuclear weapons are easy and inexpensive for other nations to acquire. If one nation has them, this poses a danger to neighboring nations, who will then acquire their own nuclear weapons in response, and the security of the whole region will be reduced. Control of proliferation cannot be externally imposed, but must involve persuasion. Of course, persuasion by the superpowers must go hand in hand with a reduction of their own strategic weapons, because you cannot tell another country not to have them while you increase your own supply.

The fourth principle is to continue negotiating. SALT has great value: as long as you negotiate, you talk and you do not fight. And there is a lot to negotiate, not only between Russia and the United States. The buildup of the SS-20s by the Russians for European deployment, and the introduction of new weapons (the Pershings and cruise missiles) by the U.S. in Europe, could be negotiated to an equilibrium in conventional and nuclear weapons at a much lower level. The senselessness of these weapons is exactly the same as the senselessness of our land-based missiles — they are tempting targets for nuclear attack.

Finally, there is the moral element. Nuclear weapons are qualitatively different from any other weapons. It is deeply immoral to use such weapons because it will lead to annihilation of much of the human race and other living things. You can always rationalize nuclear strategies with logical arguments and computer simulations, and you might be capable of obtaining any result that you wish, but you must always consider the moral aspect. You must have your heart in the rule that nuclear weapons must not be applied. In the future, nations must formally agree to a global no-first-use policy. There must be a solemn declaration on all sides never to use any atomic bombs — including tactical ones — before others do. This ethical necessity can be realized only if it is forced upon governments by public awareness.

Today the situation looks bleak and the danger of nuclear war increases daily. A miracle may be needed to avoid the holocaust, but this miracle must happen.